Moderate and Radical Islamic Fundamentalism

UNIVERSITY PRESS OF FLORIDA

Florida A&M University, Tallahassee
Florida Atlantic University, Boca Raton
Florida Gulf Coast University, Ft. Myers
Florida International University, Miami
Florida State University, Tallahassee
New College of Florida, Sarasota
University of Central Florida, Orlando
University of Florida, Gainesville
University of North Florida, Jacksonville
University of South Florida, Tampa
University of West Florida, Pensacola

Moderate and Radical Islamic Fundamentalism

The Quest for Modernity, Legitimacy, and the Islamic State

Ahmad S. Moussalli

University Press of Florida

Gainesville · Tallahassee · Tampa · Boca Raton

Pensacola · Orlando · Miami · Jacksonville · Ft. Myers · Sarasota

First cloth printing, 1999
First paperback printing, 2013

Library of Congress Cataloging-in-Publication Data
Mawṣilili, Ahmad.
Moderate and radical Islamic fundamentalism : the quest for modernity,
legitimacy, and the Islamic state / Ahmad S. Moussalli.
p. cm.
Includes bibliographical references and index.
ISBN 978-0-8130-1658-0 (cloth: alk. paper)
ISBN 978-0-8130-4469-9 (pbk.)
1. Islam and politics. 2. Islamic fundamentalism. 3. Islam and state.
4. Islam—20th century. I. Title.
BP173.7.M38   1999
297.2'72 —dc21   98-36151

The University Press of Florida is the scholarly publishing agency for the State
University System of Florida, comprising Florida A&M University, Florida
Atlantic University, Florida Gulf Coast University, Florida International Uni-
versity, Florida State University, New College of Florida, University of Central
Florida, University of Florida, University of North Florida, University of South
Florida, and University of West Florida.

University Press of Florida
15 Northwest 15th Street
Gainesville, FL 32611-2079
http://www.upf.com

Contents

Introduction

More than ever, we live today in an interdependent world. No state, group of people, religion, or civilization can maintain itself in isolation from others. The unprecedented advancement of high technology in all walks of life, the expansion of multinational organizations, the rise of mass social and political movements, increasing state intrusiveness at a time of challenges to the nation-state, new popular quests for empowerment and legitimacy, and the reshaping of a new international order—all of these will remain as challenges of the twenty-first century. As a consequence, we will be forced to rethink our attitudes toward the role of the state and its relationship to technology, science, and religion.

We live in a globalized world, where local events can have an international impact. What happens in India, Egypt, or the United States is a concern not only to the Indians, Egyptians, or Americans but also to the rest of the world. Fundamentalism, as a powerful contemporary and future political and social movement, is neither limited to nor predominant in only one country or region. It is on the rise all over the world. Within the emerging new world order, religion is likely to play a major role in regional and international politics, whether it manifests itself in fundamentalist mass movements or in dynamic features of world civilizations. Hence, constructions of modernization, secularization, and rationalization are giving way to trends of postmodernization, religionization, and spiritualization.

The dawn of the twenty-first century will witness the forceful domination of the world by two powerful domains—concentrated capitalism and invasive technology—both of which are increasingly threatening to the dominant political construct of the nation-state and its nationalist ideology. The spirit and reality of technology and capitalism are, thus, contrary to the spirit and reality of nation-states. In addition, we are already witnessing the growing weakness of the world's nation-states and the rise of constructs based on concepts of religion and civilization inspiring the emergence of regional entities. The threat to the nation-states also emanates from various social forces. While certain of these social forces, like ethnic formations, demand decentralization, autonomy, and independence, those based on religious and civilizational formations demand increased centralization, unity, and interdependence.

The nature of conflict, as well as that of peace, can also be expected to change in the international arena, as such social forces gain ground by becoming either more localized, as in the case of ethnic formations, or more universalized, as in the case of religious and civilizational formations. At the top of both the localized and the universalized agendas stand the quests for new economic, social, and political empowerment, redefining points of reference for legitimacy and reconceptualizing the role of the state.

In this context, Islamic fundamentalism may be seen as an early manifestation of the mass social movements articulating religious and civilizational aspirations and questioning fundamental issues surrounding the morality of technology, the capitalist mode of distribution and upholding popular empowerment, non-state legitimacy, and the non–nation-state paradigms. This is why the study of Islamic fundamentalism requires proper—that is, global—contextualization linked with the study of ideological bases, looking into the underpinnings of Islamic fundamentalist discourses in their various expression—especially the two category types of radical and moderate discourses, which form the essential focus of this study. The dearth of theoretical studies on the frameworks and underpinnings of Islamic fundamentalist political ideologies is obvious and suggests either that there is an assumption that fundamentalism, both radical and moderate, is a shallow phenomenon or that its political thought and ideology are not worthy of in-depth study. Again, while social, economic, and political circumstances help to account for the rise of Islamic fundamentalism, more serious theoretical attempts are needed to further our understanding of this phenomenon within a global context. Islamic fundamentalism is more than just a local movement; it acts toward and reacts to the nation-state and world order. Its complaints and aspirations have local, but also regional and universal, dimensions.

The vast body of literature that examines the activities of Islamic fundamentalist movements and the perceived dangers inherent within them typically fails to grasp these dimensions. Numerous journalistic articles have appeared in the Western press reflecting a fear of fundamentalism. This applies generally to the coverage of events across the Muslim world, especially where the Islamic movements are concerned.[1] Although many questions have been raised, central issues still revolve around the "terrorist" activities of Islamic movements and the incompatibility of the Islamic state with the existing international order.

Of course, more accurate and more extensive articles and studies on the issues of the Islamic state, revolution, and ideology have been published by many academics.[2] However, the doctrine of what constitutes the essentially normative content and form of a modern Islamic state—as well as its connotations, aspirations, and role, according to Islamic fundamentalist discourses—has not yet been fully developed, appreciated, or criticized.

Today scholars disagree on the nature of modern Islamic movements. Some describe them as nondemocratic and aggressive, while others see them as democratic and nonaggressive.[3] Very few see them as a world phenomenon that will have more than just a political impact on the West.[4] Issues of pluralism, tolerance, and world order as related to the Islamic world are discussed under evocative titles such as "From Beirut to Sarajevo," "Against Cultural Terrorism," or "When Galileo Meets Allah."[5] Mutually exclusionary views are postulated by Muslims and Westerners alike: secular materialism, the scientific reason of modernity, and the absence of a moral philosophy, on the one hand, are pitted against religious spiritualism, the nonscientific reason of the Islamic world, and a strong moral philosophy on the other.[6] Such assumptions fuel the tendency of some scholars to imagine future world conflicts in terms of inherent contradictions between Islam and the West and to call for the blanket exclusion of Islamic movements from all positive developments under many pretexts, ranging from "The Islamic-Confucian Connection" and "The Clash of Civilizations" to "The Challenge of Radical Islam."[7]

In contrast, however, other scholars argue for including moderate Islamic movements within existing political systems and for their coexistence with the West.[8] Thus, political Islam and the West are not necessarily incompatible, as the Qur'an can be interpreted to support different political behaviors.[9] Arguments in this vein are exemplified in "Democratization and Islam" and are typically put forward to make the point that the process of liberalization and democratization in the Muslim world requires a reinterpretation of divine texts, as happened historically in the West.[10]

Such literature demonstrates the difficulty that arises in attempts to assess fundamentalist attitudes toward modernity, pluralism, democracy, the secular state, and the West. The problem can be attributed in part to the general lack of interest in sufficient theoretical studies of the political ideologies of Islamic movements. Hence, fundamentalism is typically understood on the basis of its political behaviors, not its political theory. While studies such as James Piscatori's *Islamic Fundamentalisms and the Gulf Crisis* and John Esposito's *Islam and Development: Religion and Sociopolitical Change* are worthwhile in that they provide the reader with useful and balanced information and analyses concerning Islamic movements, only very limited scholarship deals with fundamentalism at a significant theoretical level—for example, Bruce Lawrence's *Defenders of God,* Charles Butterworth's "Political Islam," or Leonard Binder's *Islamic Liberalism.*

Given the need for substantial theoretical work, this study focuses on the textual analysis of the original discourses of major fundamentalist political thinkers like Hasan al-Banna, Sayyid Qutb, Hasan al-Turabi, Rashid al-Ghannushi, and others who have written extensively on modernity, science, legitimacy, empowerment, ideologies, state and society, and the West. It makes the political behaviors of Islamic fundamentalist movements subject to theoretical analysis, investigating the doctrinal frameworks of fundamentalist philosophical thought and political ideologies. It develops further the main theoretical doctrines used by fundamentalists to construct and evaluate philosophy and science, theories of state and society, and international relations and world orders. It also investigates the theoretical origins of fundamentalist doctrines on the Islamic state and ideologies as well as their functions within contemporary existing regimes and as plans for future transformation.

This study is basically textual, providing a systematic exposition of the normative fundamentalist political theory implicit within the fundamentalist discourses studied. This political theory makes possible an evaluation of the changes effected by fundamentalist discourses on the intellectual body of Islamic thought in its early and classical expressions. Principles such as the 'governance' of God and the 'paganism' of the world are presented as issues of value, meaning, and identity, as are the issues that separate Islamic modernism, on the one hand, and radical Islamic fundamentalism, on the other. Thus, a normative political theory is to be employed in order to define the ideal individual, society, state, and world order. The methodological formulation that is used in our inquiry is a composite structure of many methods, including but not restricted to linguistic, historical, and phenomenological analyses. The linguistic analysis explores differences between the radical and moderate political language and clarifies the political ambiguity attached to certain doctrines. This method is then tied to a historical analysis in order to bring back the original interpretations of doctrines like divine governance and human paganism and to draw out their original connotations and current implications.

The assumption here is that ideas have never existed or flourished without a viable context. This book investigates how the fundamentalists employ the Divine Word—that is, the Qur'an—as a source for a new religious discourse empowering the believers to set up a modern legitimate state and also how the Qur'an functions as a political and religious unifying agent. It also shows that the content, style, and language of the Qur'anic discourse became, to the fundamentalists, the formal ideological framework for constructing an Islamic state and a Muslim nation.

Furthermore, this book will examine how the Qur'anic text became a political tract used to evaluate personal, economic, social, and political behaviors of rulers and the ruled, the sacred and the profane, the past and the present. Although fundamentalist discourses are historically developed for certain ends, they have been transformed into metahistorical discourses applicable to all historical epochs and to all societies. The audience for these discourses is increasing because the prevalent form of discourse in the Muslim world has always been the religious discourse. For instance, the discourses of medieval Muslim philosophers and contemporary Muslim reformers, let alone those of the secularists, have never attained a dominant legitimate status in Muslim societies; these discourses were often considered to be blasphemous or irreligious. Problems arose about both the content and, more important, the form of their arguments. For instance, although the medieval philosophers tried to prove the existence of God, their proofs, which were based on reason instead of revelation and which used Aristotelian forms of argumentation, were not popularly considered religious. The discourses of Muslim reformers of the last two centuries also subordinated revelation to scientific reason and were severely attacked as a result.

This book is also concerned with how the content and form of modernist discourses were built on the philosophy of science and, thus, how the renewal of religion became dependent on the cultivation of modern sciences and philosophies. In other words, what these two groups of thinkers have tried to do is to use nonscriptural foundations for reinterpreting scripture. The language, form, and content of their discourses seemed to the majority of people alien and alienating.

Given the modern historical imperialist and colonialist attempts to dominate the Muslim world, I will show that the majority of fundamentalists perceived that the language of the modernists and the domination of the West served to separate the Muslim nation from its history. The conscious and subconscious religious language of the nation, they argue, has been historically loaded with doctrines that could not yield to the language of the West, such as the doctrine of the supremacy of the Muslim *umma* (community). Arabic, as the language of Muslim culture and its discourse, found itself face to face with other, mightier dominant languages and discourses supported and disseminated by mightier and more dominant powers. Thus, the many attempts that were made to create Arabic secular nationalist discourses that might, with the changing conditions of the Arabs and Muslims, replace the religious discourse did not completely work.

This is one of the reasons secular nationalist discourses did not lead to empowering people and legitimizing the state, which became organically and functionally linked to other national states and has yielded to dominant world powers. Although national states like Egypt have had at their disposal a whole range of means to publicize their ideologies—like mass rallies and parties, the press, radio, television, and a good number of paid and unpaid intellectuals and universities—they have not been able to reduce the language and content of fundamentalist discourses. Today, the Egyptian government, for instance, is publishing under the heading of *al-Muwajaha* (confrontation) a series of books written by well-known Islamic thinkers of the nineteenth and twentieth centuries, such as Jamal al-Afghani and Muhammad 'Abduh and 'Abbas Mahmud al-'Aqqad, to counter the intellectual impact of Islamic fundamentalism.

In this book, I also argue that Muslim fundamentalists have been capable of developing discourses that capture the attention of Muslims, because the language and content as well as the form and style of their discourses bring up, in people's minds, the possibility of empowerment, morality, justice, equality, and legitimacy. Thus, when the fundamentalists call for implementing the *shari'a*, they are not calling for reinstituting traditional *shari'a* but are instead empowering people to redirect the course of political life. The fundamentalist demand for legitimacy, for instance, reflects a psychological defiance that challenges local regimes and international powers. Such a feeling cannot be derived from the present; it is, indeed, derived from a specific perception of a superior past that must be intellectually reconstructed. Fundamentalists perceive that the present has favored not Muslims but their enemies. Thus, using the language and forms of the Qur'anic text in the process of building modern fundamentalist discourses serves to provide legitimacy to their economic, social, and political claims against the state and the world.

In the chapters that follow, I will argue that democracy, for instance, which was perceived by modernist reformers as noncontradictory to Islam and thus potentially adoptable, is turned by most fundamentalists, through a process of its identification with *shura* (consultation), into an obligatory political and normative principle in any new Islamic political system. While *shura* is a religious doctrine and, consequently, is validated by the past, democracy is their interest and objective. A Qur'anically developed democracy is, indeed, a powerful tool for popular empowerment. Only through implementing democracy through popular empowerment can Muslims be free from tyranny and set up a legitimate state.

This book will argue that, while most fundamentalists turn pluralism into a religious doctrine through its identification with *al-amr bi al-ma'ruf wa al-nahy 'an al-munkar* (enjoining good and forbidding evil), their objective is to destroy elitist establishments. If no individual can know the ultimate meaning of the metaphysical or political good, individuals or a group of individuals can express themselves individually and collectively and can group themselves in associations and parties. The state monopolization of public space is then illegitimate; people should be empowered to act according to their interests.

While fundamentalists in general do not have at their disposal the high technological and formal aspects of propaganda, their writings are widely read. Some books, like those of Muhammad al-Ghazali and Yusuf al-Qaradawi, now run into their twentieth editions and sell tens of thousands of copies. Fundamentalist views are spread even more widely through sermons, teaching (both inside and outside of mosques), and by other oral forms, especially when printed forms are banned. Many writings are banned, but banning has always increased their popularity and made them more in demand. However, the popularity of Muslim fundamentalist discourses is primarily derived not from the actual distribution but from the context of distribution, where the audience can identify with the doctrines being circulated. These doctrines stir the historical and present consciousness to act on transforming the vicissitudes of the present. Basic doctrines, like *tawhid* and *ijma'* (consensus), are empowering and function as links with a glorious and successful past; modern doctrines, like those of the secular nation-state, are restricting and function as links with failure and a humiliating present. The book shows how religious fundamentalist writings have become for their public a means to transcend both the historicity of the past and the darkness of the present, with a promise for a brighter future.

Organization of the Book

Chapter one, "Two Discourses on Modern Islamic Political Thought," sets forth the ideological and political discourses of both Islamic modernism and Islamic fundamentalism. It compares and contrasts the essential doctrines of the two tendencies in order to develop better understanding of the theoretical roots of Islamic fundamentalism. It focuses mainly on the ideological and philosophical foundations of both modernism and fundamentalism and delineates their major conclusions on knowledge, politics, and society.

I argue that the basic objective of both modernism and fundamentalism is to raise Muslim consciousness and to induce a social and political movement that strives to attain material, political, and spiritual progress. To achieve both, a new, nonhistorical reading of Islam becomes the basic condition for starting a modern process of reformulating Islamic history and reforming Islamic civilization. However, this process, in itself, reformulates the tenets of political Islam and reforms the principles of political rule. The need for serious re-examination and reinterpretation of Islamic literature and, of course, of the long-standing interpretations of Islam is postulated in order to accommodate the demands of modernity.

While modernism advocated Islam as the avenue for salvation, the modernization of Islam is to be conducted in line with the West, both in terms of philosophy and politics. Islamic morality is seen to be the distinguishing mark between Islam and other philosophies. No total or unending confrontation is postulated as a prelude to progress and development. On yet another level, religion's most important function is the calculation of morality. Although *tawhid* is the fundamental comprehensive metaphysical doctrine, it becomes the linchpin in the process of unification and liberation of humankind. However, fundamentalism, especially its radical interpretation, looks at *tawhid* as essentially an instrument of political government and empowerment. To radical fundamentalism, *tawhid* becomes a justification for the domination of others; to moderate fundamentalism, it becomes a justification for not being dominated by others. Fundamental doctrines such as sovereignty are grounded in the Qur'anic discourse, itself utilized to produce a legitimate popular discourse that makes legitimacy a matter of popular consent. Charged with the interpretation of the divine word, the *umma* enjoys the only legitimate power; other powers and authorities are only derivative and hinge on the approval of the community.

Both discourses demystify history and call on believers to shoulder their responsibility in charting their present life and their future as well as in reviving religion. The essence of development lies in human nature. People should not wait for liberation; they should achieve it. Spiritual, intellectual, political, and economic regeneration is the proper domain of human beings who must first liberate themselves and then move to unite with others. However, the fundamentalists insist on complete liberation and solid unification before any real process of regeneration can take place. Their textual analysis of the scripture has a lot to do with their indifference to the possibility of other valid opinions and opposition. But the modernists, whose textual analysis of the scripture relates to nontextual criteria, are more capable, in principle, of absorbing differences. Purification becomes an individual act—not necessarily a collective one. Unity, as well, becomes more accommodating of diversity, since scientific discoveries reflect the possibility of reinterpretation or rediscovery of the truth. Thus, for the modernists, the process of regeneration is always tentative because it depends on a relative science, whereas for the fundamentalists it is, in the final analysis, absolute because it depends on an absolute text (especially to radical fundamentalists). The difference between the two discourses not only is methodological but also leads to the development of different normative systems.

Knowledge, to a fundamentalist, is an act of belief; to a modernist, belief is an act of knowledge. However, both view belief and knowledge as the two basic underpinnings for a sound revival of Muslims. The absence of either leads to imbalance and will derail any process of regeneration. The two discourses are much concerned with regeneration and authenticity. While the modernist entertains the authentic in terms of the new (science), the fundamentalist subjects the new to the authentic (revelation). Authenticity, to the fundamentalists, becomes the yardstick to measure all things, while to the modernists, it is the new. Again, the modernist makes the authentic conform to the new in order to be authenticated; the fundamentalist makes the new conform to the authentic in order to be modernized. Thus, any valid modernist reinterpretation or rereading must be a modern restatement of authenticity, but the fundamentalist one must be an authentic restatement of modernity. The first reading affects our understanding of the authentic text in terms of our modern age; the second affects our understanding of modernity in light of the authentic text. Thus, a modernist may attribute Muslims' weakness to the absence of modernity, while a fundamentalist may attribute it to the lack of authenticity.

Chapter two, "Fundamentalist Discourses on Epistemology and Political Philosophy," addresses the same issues treated in chapter one, but the focus here is exclusively on the theoretical development of Islamic fundamentalism as an independent system of thinking and a discourse. To do this, I construct a common framework representative of Islamic discourses that have been adapted in different shapes and forms to different countries and generations. Fundamentalist discourses on epistemology and political philosophy are worked out as political theory; philosophical and political doctrines are assessed at a theoretical level.

In political philosophy, the fundamentalists also develop the need for setting up a new society on a newly developed thought, while insisting on the Islamization of every social and political theory. Although the fundamentalists reject the traditional modes of understanding entertained by the public or the elites, as shown in the methods of theology, philosophy, Sufism, and jurisprudence, they insist on the validity of the Qur'an and the *sunna,* or the authentic. To fundamentalists, these are the source materials for a comprehensive Islamic revival to empower people.

Islam is presented as the alternative to all other systems and as the only ideological stand that should be used in order to renew local, regional, and international behaviors, both morally and politically. This view has, however, obscured the vision of major fundamentalist thinkers, though not all of them, on how to deal practically with existing institutions and regimes.

Chapter three, "Fundamentalist Discourses on Politics," deals with the conditions that make a fundamentalist theoretician or movement adopt or reject pluralistic democracy. It contextualizes, at length, some general academic and political discussions on pluralism and democracy in the West, particularly in the United States, and in the Arab world, particularly in Egypt. Chapter three also deals theoretically with the foundations and development of pluralism and democracy, with references to the more comprehensive political framework that was elaborated in the previous chapters. It shows the roots of pluralistic and democratic thought within fundamentalism, and it also demonstrates the basis of two contradictory fundamentalist discourses: one that is radical, antiliberal, militant, and antidemocratic, and another that is moderate, liberal, nonmilitant, and democratic. Furthermore, chapter three discusses the reasons the liberal development of the relatively democratic discourse of Hasan al-Banna and the Muslim Brethren could not be maintained under successive, repressive Egyptian governments and why it was more logical that this discourse was transformed into an antiliberal, fundamentalist discourse, of which the most exclusive is that of Sayyid Qutb and the theoreticians who followed him and set up armed radical groups.

I argue that the development of the radical discourse has originally been a reaction to the political, economic, and international conditions of Egypt and the response of successive governments to the basic issues of freedom, social justice, and religion. However, the radical discourse nowadays cannot be understood only in terms of its origins, since it has become a theology of politics. I further argue that what distinguishes a radical ideology from a moderate one revolves primarily around the conditions and principles of transforming a political agenda into daily life.

Fundamentalism employs diverse methodological and practical processes to intellectual and political formulas. For instance, radicals view *shura* not merely as a religious doctrine but as public will and, ultimately, the divine will. The individual must submit to this will; in fact, his freedom depends on it. While this will may opt for a political contract with a ruler, it cannot, because of what it represents, allow pluralism and basic differences. To radicals, the establishment of an Islamic state becomes the fulfillment of this divine will. The institutionalization of *shura* and *ijma'* provides the state, which expresses the general will, a normative role in making basic choices in people's lives. Thus, the state acquires formal legitimacy that makes it accountable only to God or obedient to the *shari'a*. Because the *shari'a* is also institutionalized in the state, legitimacy becomes an issue of formality. For legitimacy can be withdrawn only when the state acts contrary to the *shari'a*. Moreover, the state is the public controller of public morality. In this fashion, religiosity becomes a public act, itself under state control, both morally and politically. Parties, associations, and other civil institutions have no intrinsic validity in this scheme. Such views necessarily demand exclusivity, the negation of pluralistic understanding of religions, and the politicization of Islam. In this context, the establishment of inclusive, pluralistic civil democracies seems theoretically invalid and practically unworkable.

On the other hand, the moderate fundamentalist trend views the absence of pluralistic societies and of democratic institutions as root causes for violence. However, this trend has been excluded from political participation even while it calls for the liberalization of political processes. It has been involved in and has accepted the notion of pluralistic civil society. Its inclusionary views posit no eternally divine struggle between Islam and the West, and it interprets much of what is Western in Islamic terms: it is Islamizing democracy and pluralism. The moderate fundamentalists blend the culture of the East with that of the West, while conflicts between the East and West are reduced to politics and economics instead of religion or culture. The two cultures can coexist because of their common monotheistic origins.

Moderate fundamentalist thinkers view the government's legitimacy as being derived from people and postulate as well the division of power into executive, legislative, and judicial spheres. More important, a political contract is the legitimate means for assuming power. Islam is, however, the constitutional reference when people adopt it. Therefore, I argue that if radical fundamentalism is resistant to dialogue and cooperation with the Arab regimes and the West, in general, moderate fundamentalism has opened up to dialogue, democracy, compromise, universal rights, freedom, pluralism, and civil society.

Chapters four, five, and six develop three theoretical models of an Islamic state that is essentially based on *tawhid* and *shura*. Chapter four, "The Discourse of Hasan al-Banna on *Shura*, Democracy, and the Islamic State," explains al-Banna's discourse on the foundations of the legitimate Islamic state, the main goal of the Muslim Brotherhood in Egypt and elsewhere as well as of many other Islamic fundamentalist movements all over the Islamic world. It shows how al-Banna identifies Islamic rule and *shura* with constitutional rule and multiparty politics. These issues are discussed in the context of three main principles: first, Islam and politics; second, the Islamic state and the *shari'a*; and, third, democracy and *shura*. An analytical conclusion of al-Banna's views of these matters follows the explanation of his discourse.

Al-Banna's political discourse is grounded in his view of metaphysical *tawhid* and its political articulation, the *hakimiyya* of God. Instead of stressing absence of compromise and the denial of rights to the other, al-Banna argues for the theoretical possibility of harmonizing Western and Islamic political thought and makes *hakimiyya* a human act. To him, divine governance is a comprehensive doctrine applied in all circumstances—moral, legal, economic, political, and international. However, its good practice is essentially communal. *Hakimiyya* means the rule based on scriptural Qur'anic precepts that are removed from their social, economic, political, and historical contexts. This is why all fundamentalists, whether radical or not, advocate the fulfillment of divine *hakimiyya*, which means, at minimum, replacing existing governments with Islamic ones. However, it does not mean closing oneself off and rejecting dealings with the community. In fact, al-Banna's approach dealt openly with and tried to influence Egyptian politics and played according to the then-prevalent rules.

Although, to al-Banna, divine governance becomes an absolute political doctrine, so does the doctrine of *shura*. In fact, the good realization of the former becomes dependent on the good exercise of the latter. What al-Banna's development of *shura* has done is to absorb democracy within Islamic political and even religious thought and, consequently, to take the initiative from its secular advocates. It has also provided legitimate religious means to empower people to control any government, since legitimacy is linked to popular approval. By denying any contradiction between democracy and constitutional rule, on the one hand, and *shura* and divine law, on the other, al-Banna becomes able to postulate their correspondence. All of these ideas have become part of the fundamentalist nonhistorical discourse that transforms Islam into a system capable of absorbing what is best in philosophy, politics, economics, science, and history without the need to disclaim the validity of Islam.

Al-Banna makes a distinction between Muslims' understanding of history and history itself. Muslims' understanding of the history of Islam is not Islam itself; therefore, traditional Islamic understanding of Islam can be transcended and replaced with a modern interpretation. Thus, although constitutional rule in the West and *shura* in Islamic history have quite different historical origins, al-Banna finds no theoretical problem in forcing their correspondence. Al-Banna reworks the meaning and formative character of history in order to accommodate modernity and its philosophy, especially because of his assumption that the victory of the West is due to particular doctrines. However, mere additions or transfer of doctrines is insufficient for inducing a revival. *Shura* to al-Banna and almost all of the fundamentalist movements is not only an added doctrine; it is the source of legitimacy for any authority. The introduction of democracy as *shura* into the main political doctrines of fundamentalism is an extremely positive act that counters the authoritarian nature of politics prevalent in the Muslim world.

Chapter five, "The Discourse of Sayyid Qutb on Political Ideology and the Islamic State," starts with Qutb's life, then moves to the analysis of his doctrines and to the ideological and political aspects of his thought. Finally, it shows how he constructs the Islamic state on a theological necessity, and a conclusion assesses the most important features of his thought.

To Sayyid Qutb, the ultimate source of knowledge is God. However, since God's knowledge is unattainable, Qutb contends that revelation is made up of allusions to truths. Nonetheless, revelation is validated by its conformity to nature even though that nature is unknowable. To Qutb, reason functions as an instrument for realizing the objectives of Islam and for receiving, understanding, adapting, and implementing divine doctrines. In the absence of Qur'anic injunctions, Qutb employs utility to justify the validity of doctrines and practices. Thus, the importance of doctrines and practices is related to their utility. For instance, science is perceived as an instrument of power necessary for victory. Qutb's discourse brings together the religious discourse and the dominant scientific discourse as the underlying bases of a new Islamic society. The eternal, textually based, religious discourse is the foundation of society, while science is a practical necessity. No scientific discourse should attempt to provide moral and metaphysical precepts but should instead aim at improving material life.

According to Qutb, in an Islamic system the public will represents the divine will; therefore, the individual or groups cannot legitimately stand against it. What is important to Qutb is not the freedom of the individual, as such, since the individual must always yield to the community. Radicalism looks at the individual as a member of a body whose well-being, as a whole, must come before that of the individual. Thus, a political contract creates a public will for the whole of society. Therefore, no divisions (parties, associations, etc.) are allowed to destroy social unity.

While Qutb's discourse is somehow a product of contemporary political crises, it cannot be viewed merely as a reaction to a hostile environment. It has been the basis of a new political discourse and ideology advocating the institution of Islam. Again, while the radicalism of his fundamentalist discourse is attributed to the crises of contemporary social and political life, his teachings provide normative statements on philosophy, science, history, politics, and economics. While Qutb bases his discourse on the Qur'an and the *sunna*, he politicizes them and makes their political signification the only proper interpretation.

On the political side, Qutb provides religious justifications for socialist principles and for representative government in order to pinpoint the compatibility of Islam with modernity. Hence, he offers democracy as the choice of the people, all the while rejecting the term "democracy." Therefore, most of Qutb's new Islamic political, theoretical discourse encompasses what he considered best in the Western traditions. In this fashion, Qutb reinforces the notion of the validity of Islam for all ages, for its principles may accommodate modernity. Contemporary Muslims are freed to revive Islam and to construct a new discourse that might accommodate any immediate or contemporary issue.

Chapter six, "The Discourse of Hasan al-Turabi on the Islamic State and Democracy," gives al-Turabi's argument that the doctrine of a modern Islamic state cannot be realized without turning the Islamic system into a democratic system. It shows the three basic components of al-Turabi's political discourse—namely, the congruence between the divine and the human, man's liberation and freedom, and *shura* and democracy. Al-Turabi's emphasis on the role of religious fundamental texts, as basically a point of reference for unity and cooperation and as a convocation to democracy, is well elaborated in terms of the effects of these texts on Islamic political theory, on the construction of a good society, and on the making of a representative government.

Al-Turabi's revivalist discourse centers on ending the normative character of the past as both a history and a system. The Qur'an and the *sunna* are exempted because they function as metaphysical and metahistorical formative and constitutive fundamentals of Islam and its main authentic sources. In fact, they constitute and guarantee an unending process of renewal based on interpretation and reinterpretation. Al-Turabi's quest for reinterpretation hinges on developing an intellectual and formative discourse that rediscovers the appropriate meanings and significance of the texts in the conditions of modern living—a discourse that must reformulate the religious roots, or *usul al-din*. However, his reformulation casts religion as ideology because it is not directed at a more substantive understanding of the divine but, instead, at more control of politics and society. Religiosity, though important, is superseded by political doctrines such as the Islamic state and the unity of the community. *Tawhid* manifests, for instance, in the individual's commitment and actions toward the Islamization of state and society. Deep theological commitment to Islam must involve the economy, society, and the state. Practical Islamic activism signifies the deep-rootedness of belief, while shallow and ceremonial, nonactive commitment to Islam weakens belief.

To al-Turabi democracy is transformed into a religious act; *tawhid*, when applied in a democratic society, becomes a form and formalizes *shura* into a substantive principle. Al-Turabi transforms the religious discourse into a political discourse; thus, political belief, for instance, depends on the sound application of divine governance. This is why al-Turabi denies the utility of traditional jurisprudence and calls for the development of a modern religious jurisprudence as part of an ideologically derived political discourse. In this design, the rendering of categorical and lasting interpretation of a text requires a continuous ratifying process by Muslims and the continuous existence of an Islamic state.

Al-Turabi argues that, because the traditional Islamic state and society have disintegrated, there is an urgent need for another appropriate, interpretative discourse to build a new state and society. An eternal interpretation is an interpretative impossibility, since interpretation is conditional and tentative. In his attempt to find a proper channel for a relative interpretation of the text, he finds the power of society; however, a Muslim society does, indeed, need an Islamic state, which becomes the symbol of collective self-awareness and empowerment and the possibility of a relatively correct textual understanding. Al-Turabi theoretically frees Muslims from the finished product of early and medieval thinking and ways of living and permits the modernization of Islam and Islamization of modernity. Through a process of historical neutralization, he harmonizes modern Islamic political thought with Western political thought and legitimizes the possibility of developing a mutual political discourse and a meaningful dialogue.

Before concluding the introduction, I should note here that the term "Islamic fundamentalism" is used to denote a multitude of Islamic political movements aiming at essentially reviving, both politically and religiously, the fundamentals of Islam—the Qur'an and the *sunna* of the Prophet—which function as the only authoritative texts in the formation of an Islamic state. Fundamentalism is a term that was developed in the West in order to describe the belief of some evangelists in the Bible as the literal and eternal word of God. Later, this meaning was expanded to include all sorts of religious groups that attempt to live according to their revelations; thus, there is Jewish fundamentalism, Christian fundamentalism, and Islamic fundamentalism. And although fundamentalism has been loaded with negative connotations, it is employed here to describe the movement that calls for the return to the fundamentals of Islam—that is, the Holy Qur'an and the *sunna*. Islamic fundamentalism, as opposed to other fundamentalisms, is politically revolutionary, not conservative. It is both a philosophy and a way of life that brings together politics and theology and makes the latter dependent on the former.[11]

A final note is on transliteration. The system used here is a simplified version of that of the *International Journal of Middle East Studies*. The sign ' stands for *ayn*, the sign ' for *hamza*.

1

Two Discourses on Modern Islamic Political Thought

Fundamentalism and Modernism

Most modern Western political thinkers have demystified the state and related its legitimacy to serving worldly concerns, such as satisfying the needs of its citizens and society at large. The vast majority of classical, medieval, and modern Muslim thinkers have not, however, removed the aura of mysticism from the state. Though they accept that a main task of the state is to order worldly concerns of its members, this in itself is not seen as a sufficient moral or political ground for citizens' submission to a specific ruling power and system. While organizing human affairs, resolving conflicts, conducting relations among states, and even promoting survival are valid occupations of the state, they do not legitimize one political system or another, unless linked to supranational Islamic orientations.

Muslim thinkers have offered more specific grounds for justifying the necessity of attaining an Islamic state. These grounds include establishing a moral society on the basis of God's *shari'a* (law) for the service of the oneness of God. Good politics, then, aims at the attainment of an Islamic system grounded in both a philosophy of normative principles and a method of applying a set of prescriptive remedies to social and political problems. Put differently, the legitimacy of an Islamic state is rooted in a general philosophy of life and a particular moral and political philosophy. In modern times, two major dominant Islamic discourses, fundamentalism and modernism, have been developed as modern interpretations of Islam aimed at remedying the ills of and reviving Muslim societies.

This chapter sets forth the ideological and political discourses of both Islamic modernism—referred to, sometimes, as reformism—as advocated by Jamal al-Din al-Afghani (1839–1897), Muhammad ʿAbduh (1849–1905), Muhammad Iqbal (1875–1938), and ʿAli Shariʿati (1933–1977) and Islamic fundamentalism, as advocated by Abu al-Aʿla al-Mawdudi (1903–1980), Hasan al-Banna (1906–1949), Sayyid Qutb (1906–1966), and Ayatollah al-Khumayni (1903–1989). This examination will present the theoretical roots of Islamic fundamentalism, which will be detailed further in the following chapter.

These theoreticians have been selected not only because they represent the two trends but also because of their formative role in their creation. Al-Afghani, for instance, the most outstanding Muslim modernist and activist, set the agenda for modern Islamic thought throughout the Muslim world. He was thus known as the sage and awakener of the East. He called for a reworking of Islamic thought to include Western science, democracy, and constitutional government. Rulers and opposition alike tried to tempt him to join their camps, and he vascillated among them before ultimately dying in Turkey after suffering from jaw cancer. ʿAbduh, a disciple and friend of al-Afghani who joined him in exile in Paris in 1879 after they were expelled from Cairo, attempted to interpret Islam in terms of modernity and developed the doctrines of *al-maslaha* (interest) as utility, *shura* (consultation) as parliamentary democracy, and *ijmaʿ* as public opinion. Al-Afghani and ʿAbduh published *al-ʿUrwa al-Wuthqa* (the tightest bond), which became very influential throughout the Muslim world. ʿAbduh became the mufti of Egypt in 1899 and tried to reform Al-Azhar by introducing modern sciences into its curriculum. Rida joined ʿAbduh in 1897 and became very close to him. Rida published the very influential magazine *al-Manar* until 1935, and many credit him with the development of the modern view of an Islamic state. Iqbal, who received his Ph.D. from Trinity College in England in 1905, was the most well-known Pakistani reformer. He is probably the most philosophic among the modernist reformers who tried to blend the culture of the East with that of the West. He became very influential throughout the Islamic world, especially on the Indian subcontinent, and was elected to the Indian parliament in 1936. He was also a member of the All-India Muslim League. In Iran, Ali Shariʿati, who held a doctorate from the Sorbonne, spent his life lecturing and established a strong organization, Husayniyahyi Irshad, that focused on developing intellectual activities and spreading the message for social justice. The organization became one of the centers for opposition to the Shah, and Shari'ati was repeatedly imprisoned by the regime. He was found dead, apparently from a heart attack, in England, but rumors suggested that he had been assassinated by Iranian agents. His main contribution is his interpretation of Islam in terms of modernity and as a social, economic, and political philosophy.

In the fundamentalist camps, the political thought of al-Mawdudi, the most renowned Pakistani fundamentalist and the founder of the fundamentalist Jama'at-I Islami, exerted tremendous influence on Muslims throughout the world. His idea of Islam as a system and method, and his doctrines of paganism of the world and governance, became central issues that distinguish fundamentalism from other trends. In Egypt in 1927, Hasan al-Banna founded the first full-fledged Islamic fundamentalist movement, the Muslim Brotherhood, in the Arab world; it spread throughout the Muslim world and became the prototype that most Islamic movements tried to imitate. While working as a teacher after receiving a bachelor of arts degree from Dar al-'Ulum, he strove to link political and economic issues to religion and argued that Islam was a complete moral, economic, social, political, and philosophical system. Al-Banna called for active commitment to Islam through political actions that seek the establishment of the Islamic state. The assassination of al-Banna in 1949 led to splits within the movement. It was Qutb, however, who developed the ideological basis of Islamic activism that later manifested itself in radical and violent groups. Qutb, who was imprisoned for over a decade and finally hanged in 1966, viewed societies as being responsible for the "un-Islamic" actions of their government and, therefore, as paganist as their rulers. He called for a total revolution against all human systems.

Unlike Qutb, in 1979 al-Khumayni achieved an Islamic revolution in Iran and established an Islamic state, the Islamic Republic of Iran. He based the legitimacy of the government on the guardianship of the jurist and called for almost total adherence to the Imam's representative: Khumayni, himself. Finally, al-Nadawi, whose numerous writings have spread all over the Muslim world, is still probably the most important fundamentalist writer on the need for Islam as a civilizational force in world politics. He influenced many Muslim audiences in different countries, including Sayyid Qutb while on a visit to Egypt in 1951. Because of his influence in rearguing the modern world's need for Islam, he was granted the Saudi King Faysal Award in 1979 for the service of Islam. Al-Nadawi, an Indian and formerly a member of Nadwat al-'Ulama' and al-Jama'a al-Islamiyya, currently lives in England.

This chapter consists of three parts. Part one deals with the ideological and philosophical foundations of both modernism and fundamentalism; part two focuses on modernist and fundamentalist normative political principles. Part three delineates some of the major conclusions about knowledge, politics, and ideology. The objective of this chapter is to show the philosophic level of both fundamentalism and modernism and to dispel many erroneous and imprecise notions concerning fundamentalist and modern discursive thinking.

Fundamentalist Islamic thought has generally been treated as a reaction to passing political, social, and economic phenomena—a treatment that carries some truth and includes, in fact, Western philosophies. However, it does not follow that fundamentalism lacks deep-rooted principles and should be dismissed as religious fanaticism.[1] For instance, depicting the Muslim Brotherhood, the most distinguished and powerful fundamentalist organization, as a militant group believing in the "literal interpretation of the Koran and the Sunna," working for "the revival of the principle of *jihad*, holy war," without attempting to arrive at "a restatement of Islamic doctrines"[2] misses essential points concerning fundamentalism.

However, the negative propaganda that fundamentalism has received from both Arab and foreign media, scholars, and governments has precluded understanding the theoretical and practical contributions of fundamentalism. Consequently, this has prevented serious thinking concerning fundamentalism's basic assumptions and doctrines as well as its intellectual prospects. Substantial academic works have been produced on the philosophy of contemporary modernist Muslim reformers such as Jamal al-Din al-Afghani, Muhammad 'Abduh, and Muhammad Iqbal. At the same time, in-depth theoretical studies of fundamentalism lag behind studies on fundamentalist terrorism or militancy. Superficial readings of fundamentalism do not reflect precisely the complexity of fundamentalism and do not account for a variety of fundamentalist discourses developed by major theoreticians such as Sayyid Qutb, Abu al-A'la al-Mawdudi, the founder of the Islamic movement in Pakistan, and Hasan al-Banna, the founder of the Muslim Brethren, who neither advocate a literal interpretation of the Holy Qur'an nor think that Islamic doctrines are in no need of restatement.

Islamic fundamentalism could not be studied only as a set of political movements; it must also be viewed as a set of intellectual discourses and critiques of philosophy, political ideology, and science. Its philosophical tradition includes both a belief in the existence of objective and ultimate truth and a claim of limited human subjective understanding of that truth. Further, fundamentalism attempts to offer a way of life and thought based on its understanding of both God's law (shari'a) and nature. Its political ideology refutes the notions of both an ultimate human authority and man's possessive nature. Thus, fundamentalism upholds the need for setting up virtuous, just, and equal societies. In this sense, fundamentalist calls for an immediate political project, the Islamic state, are linked to achieving these societies. Whether such a philosophy is well grounded or properly developed, and whether one accepts or rejects fundamentalism, should not make it a passing phenomenon.

Philosophical Foundations

The principles of reason and religion and of philosophy and science are the underpinning of the intellectual foundations of both Islamic fundamentalism and Islamic modernism. The comparison and contrast of the different views on these principles reveal the different conceptual understanding of both movements; in fact, that understanding distinguishes one movement from the other.

Reason and Religion

While fundamentalists look primarily at reason, they make the existence of morality a natural, objective reality that is beyond the scope of human reason. Living in harmony with this universal moral system thus requires revelation. For al-Mawdudi and Qutb, God has created in the human being a *fitra* (intuition), which acts as the recipient of revelation and assures obedience to God, who created the universal laws in both their physical and moral forms. Universal natural laws are not value-free but aim at the well-being of this universe. Both universal moral and natural laws are created by God to serve human beings.

According to Qutb, Islam conforms to *fitra* and to the universe, since all are parts of a divine creation. This is why our happiness hinges on correspondence among the parts, themselves, and between the parts and the whole. Conversely, unhappiness is the consequence of disunity: mind against body, humans against humans, humans against society, and, ultimately, humans against nature, as in the case of adopting a nondivine *nizam* (system). While knowledge and happiness are based on their correspondence to *fitra*, Qutb makes happiness equal to fulfilling human *fitra* in nature, which is nothing less than total obedience to God's laws.[3] Thus, it is apparent that, for Qutb as well as for other fundamentalists, nature plays an essential role in laying the foundation of knowledge. Hence, a correct definition of any doctrine must be developed according to an accurate understanding of nature. The nature of Islamic social justice, for instance, cannot be realized comprehensively without being grounded in an Islamic worldview. Social justice is a derivative of *tawhid* (oneness of God).[4]

To the fundamentalists, religion functions as philosophy. Ancient and medieval philosophers argued that the good city, knowledge, and happiness depend on correct metaphysics attained by reason.[5] However, Qutb views the good state, knowledge, and happiness as derivatives of correct doctrines. This kind of linkage—that is, making the validity of any political system dependent on its ability to promote happiness—shows that good politics is the art of seeking the fulfillment of the divine purpose in creating humans. Such a fulfillment requires a correct understanding of nature. It follows, then, that any social order that is incapable of fulfilling human *fitra* is unnatural, unjust, and unsuitable to human beings and to the divine design.[6]

While *fitra* directs humans to the good, fundamentalists still view humans as having diverted their natural drive and forgotten *fitra*, and as having replaced them with thought and desire. Humans have involved themselves in philosophy, and this has led mankind to wrong conclusions, as symbolized in worshiping ungodly things and abstract ideas. Nonetheless, humans look for God as naturally as they seek water and shelter. Put simply, moral laws, residing in *fitra*, are intuitive and natural. Al-Mawdudi, for instance, contends that humans agree that a well-administered society enjoys cooperation, mutuality, advice, social justice, and equality; humans also agree that theft, adultery, murder, spying, jealousy, and so forth are evil.[7]

Conversely, while modernism agrees that moral laws are natural, it argues that they are so because they can be authenticated and demonstrated by reason. ʿAli Shariʾati, for instance, argues that Islam—as opposed to Marxism, which equates moral laws with social customs and economic materialism—attributes moral laws to the primordial nature of humans.[8] Reason, however, is the instrument that locates them. While Jamal al-Din al-Afghani insists on the existence in humans of an urge to rise above bestiality and to improve their lives, he tells us that following the *fitra* without reason cannot be the primary instrument for the pursuit of knowledge and the cultivation of civilization. In particular, progress requires the study of science, itself necessary for knowledge. Solid moral and religious grounds require solid knowledge.[9]

The first major difference that emerges, then, between the two discourses is that, whereas Qutb and al-Mawdudi locate the secrets of human nature in intuition and make them known only to God, al-Afghani, ʿAbduh, Iqbal, and Shariʿati view humans as potential knowers, though they may not attain the ultimate knowledge. This difference arises from divergent functions of reason: *fitra* manifests itself to al-Mawdudi, Qutb, and other fundamentalists in obedience to God but to al-Afghani, ʿAbduh, and others in the pursuit of knowledge.

This is why Qutb, al-Mawdudi, and al-Nadawi divide systems of thought, life, and action into two cardinal categories relevant to their proximity to divine laws: the divine and the humanly created. Those individuals who regulate their lives and behavior according to the system derived from a divine creed are followers of divine religion. However, those individuals who derive their system from anything else are the followers not of divine religion but of human religion.[10] This division is due to the fundamentalists' identification of religion with any system of life based on a metaphysical concept and accompanied by a social and political order. Every system of life is then a religion, and the religion of a group is the system that regulates the life of that group. Put differently, religion is not only an abstraction, a metaphysical doctrine, an emotion, or a belief; it is, equally, the culture or the system that regulates behavior. Communism is thus presented not only as a social system but also as a metaphysical doctrine based on material contradiction and ultimately as a religion."[11]

This is the reason, for fundamentalists, requiring proofs before submitting to God is unbelief. They view Islam as total submission with or without logical proofs. Belief in the day of judgment, for instance, should be adhered to whether a logical proof can be found or not. Although Islam is not opposed to reason, it requires that a logical proof should follow belief and not vice versa.[12] For Hasan al-Banna, logical proofs and syllogisms are accepted because the mind is spoken to in the Holy Qur'an. However, their service is to defend religion against myth and distortion. More important, God's existence needs no proof; rather, belief in it is intuitive. And the question "who created God?" is a misguided question, as humans are incapable of understanding even themselves.[13]

The modernists agree that religion is intuitive rather than volitional, but they postulate the harmony of reason and religion. To Muhammad 'Abduh, there is a general agreement among Muslims that some issues in religion cannot be believed in except through reason—as in knowing, for instance, God's ability to send messengers. If God is good, then He must send messengers to teach and warn humans, or else His punishment does not seem to be warranted. 'Abduh also argues that most Muslims have agreed that religion advances principles that transcend human understanding. Religion does not, however, advance principles that are opposite to reason. For instance, human reason can prove logically that God exists but cannot show His essence because the finite cannot understand the infinite.[14]

According to 'Abduh, religion remains the main element in morality and one of the greatest human forces, for it influences the majority more than reason does. More important, reason is the source for knowing and using religion; however, once belief is attained, the Prophet should be followed.[15] Similarly, to Iqbal, while religion starts with feeling, it has never taken itself as a matter of feeling, alone, and has constantly striven after metaphysics. Religion is not a partial issue, mere feeling or mere action; rather it is an expression of complete humanity. In Islam, the ideal and the real are not two separate or opposite forces, and Islam bridges the gap between the two. The ideal must eventually absorb the real.[16] Shari'ati further defines Islam as a profound spiritual, idealistic, intelligible, and logical interpretation of the universe that is fully attuned to earthly realities and divinity.

Philosophy and Science

The difference between modernism and fundamentalism thus lies in the fundamentalist perception of Islam as an intuitive and self-evident truth as opposed to the modernist acceptance of philosophy in principle and the consequent need for proof. 'Abduh's acceptance of individual pursuit of knowledge falls within this difference. For him, finding rational proofs strengthens religion and facilitates submission to Prophetic teachings. Again, while the fundamentalist denial of the ability of human reason to arrive at truth without revelation hampers developing rational discourses, the modernist call for the cultivation of reason strengthens the development of Islamic rational discourses.

This difference, however, goes beyond just the employment of reason, to include the nature of reason, which itself hinges on understanding the worldview of Islam (*tawhid*). Al-Mawdudi and Qutb define Islam as both an active program for life and a discourse aimed at constructing a worldwide framework based on *hakimiyya* (divine governance). *Tawhid*, as the fundamental component of Islam, is not only a religious principle; more important, it requires eliminating independent earthly human systems opposed to *hakimiyya* and human transformation. An act like this indicates that God's governance of the universe negates the legitimacy of independent human governments.[17] An essential part of the fundamentalists' conception of *tawhid* is then turned into a process of negation of, and opposition to, any human-made system that is not grounded in *hakimiyya*. Any meaningful search for ultimate truths in this universe is, therefore, denied if it is unrelated to God.

The modernists, in contrast, view *tawhid* constructively. They posit it as a starting point that seeks development and understanding. Because not everything is given, human beings have to exert themselves. *Tawhid* is not an instrument of negation and opposition but is, to paraphrase Iqbal, a working force for the establishment of equality, solidarity, and freedom. In Iqbal's view, the state becomes nothing more than an attempt to transform these principles into a definite organization.[18] For Shari'ati *tawhid* views the whole universe as a single living and conscious organism that possesses intelligence, will, purpose, and feeling.[19]

While Iqbal's and Shari'ati's definitions of *tawhid* allow, and even encourage, philosophizing, they do not accept every philosophy. For instance, Shari'ati argues that attaining truth revolves around inventing "a method of investigation" useful for the discovery of truth. Although, according to Shari'ati, Plato's philosophy is more sophisticated than Descartes', the latter is more useful.[20] While accepting philosophy in principle, Iqbal does not accept all philosophies. Iqbal argues that the birth of Islam is anticlassical and that Muslim philosophers did not understand Islam, which they read in light of Greek thought. Islam asks its adherents to use their perception and reason to understand the world; the philosophers, however, despised sense perception and did not develop an Islamically inspired philosophical model. While Islam encourages empirical approaches, science has a partial character and is unable to furnish complete knowledge. Thus, mechanism is inadequate for the analysis of life. In principle, the religious and the scientific, though using different methods, aim at discovering the real.[21] Iqbal's rejection is directed at materialism and speculative philosophy, not at every intellectual or spiritual pursuit.

Philosophy for modernist Muslim thinkers is essentially philosophy of science. When 'Abduh puts forward the argument that Islam cannot contradict reason, he means that it cannot contradict science; the domain of reason is not speculation but the scientific field. While there is no contradiction between reason and revelation, the philosophical attempts to harmonize revelation and philosophical proofs of God's existence and essence are unwarranted; speculations cannot be proven. Science, however, can be ascertained; therefore, 'Abduh's insistence on the harmony between reason and revelation means the harmony between science and revelation.[22]

Like 'Abduh, al-Afghani makes science the ultimate interpreter, both when Qur'anic verses are obscure or when they are contradictory to science. The Qur'an provides very general principles that must not contradict "the stipulation of reason and the achievement of science." And al-Afghani employs ta'wil (interpretation) as the method to resolve any possible contradiction between scientific facts and shari'a postulates, as in the case of the story of creation versus the theory of evolution.[23]

However, fundamentalism conceptualizes the function of science differently. Al-Mawdudi asserts that Islam encourages beneficial scientific experiments. However, the bias of experimental science, which is essentially developed in the West, makes it lacking in universality and places it in the service of nationalism, immorality, and unbelief.[24] While agreeing with al-Mawdudi on his opinion about the materialistic direction of science, nonetheless al-Banna and Qutb view science as a historical part of Islamic contribution to civilization and, consequently, as universal.

Notwithstanding occasional negative remarks about science, the modernists generally look to Western scientific thought, as well as to the newly discovered scientific knowledge, as the core needed for a new and modern interpretive discourse of the traditions of both Islam and the Qur'an. Thus, the modernists' rejection of medieval thought, medieval theology, and ancient philosophy is due to their unscientific nature. For the modernists, science replaced the speculative philosophy that medieval thinkers had extensively employed in the exposition of Islam and the development of science. This is why Iqbal calls for a scientific writing of a new Islamic theology. An important instance that he provides is the interpretation of the Qur'anic verses that describe God as light. Muslim 'ulama' (religious scholars) have interpreted these verses as metaphors for omnipresence. Iqbal's interpretation takes from modern physics the idea that the velocity of light cannot be exceeded and is the same for all observers. Since light approaches most nearly the absolute, the metaphor of light as applied to God must be viewed as a suggestion of the absoluteness of God and not of His omnipresence.[25]

Such an emphasis on the interpretative power of science compelled the modernists to devalue the importance of revelation and to provide very important but shaky new interpretations while critiquing traditional and philosophical methods of religious interpretation. To an extent, moral philosophy and religious precepts became dependent on the authority of science and, consequently, weakened. The modernists are not aware that, even if one assumes the absolute truth of scientific knowledge, science is still incapable of finding moral and metaphysical laws. If God cannot be located in spatiotemporal parameters, as Muslim theologians and others believe, then it does not matter much if one interprets the metaphor of God as light to mean absoluteness or omnipresence. The moral obligation to obey God's teachings does not change or affect the theory of light, which has nothing to do with the metaphysical understanding of God. Whether the light travels in particles or in straight lines has no bearing on God's essence and attributes or even on moral laws.

Despite these limitations, science constitutes a quintessential part of the modernist new theology employed to reinterpret and redirect modern Islamic discourses on philosophy, theology, and political thought, whereas fundamentalists disclaim the validity of science as a theological, exegetical, or interpretive power over scripture. Although more attentive to the possible negative effects of science in interpreting scripture, the fundamentalist alternative denies the role not only of science in the interpretation of scripture but also of philosophy, theology, and even history. Fundamentalists disregard the substantive and instrumental importance of history in interpreting the Qur'an, as the real Qur'anic writing and its transmission, as well as their accuracy, are validated by historical processes. Moreover, discrediting historical processes leads to enfeebling the Prophet's *sunna* (traditions), since the *sunna*'s efficacy also relies on historical transmission. The fundamentalists concur on the accuracy of both the Qur'an and the *sunna*—an assumption that underscores the problem of dismissing historical processes and their significance on various developments of knowledge.[26]

However, the fundamentalists validate borrowing from only the generations of the Prophet Muhammad and the first two caliphs to Qutb or from the first four caliphs to al-Mawdudi and the majority of fundamentalists. The reason for the exemption of these caliphs from the frailties of human existence is that they paid due attention to the real meaning of Islam. As opposed to the modernists, the fundamentalists demystify normative developments in history as well as history itself—with the exception noted above. While they do not deny the existence of some occasional good guidelines, they nonetheless view history as being essentially corrupt and falling short of an ideal Islamic worldview. Demystifying history is, by and large, a profound threat to the orthodox establishment of Sunnism as well as to Shi'ism, whose authorities lie in historical developments of both doctrines and sects. Traditional imperatives, such as the doctrines of great founders of theological and jurisprudential schools like Abu Hanifa, al-Shafi'i, Ibn Hanbal, and Malik or al-Ghazali and al-Baqillani, have been turned into reasonable historical interpretations, but they are not the only ones. Such imperatives lack the quintessential meanings that have been attached to and are turned into nothing more than a *ijtihad* (reasoning) that could easily be changed by another *ijtihad*.

While producing new interpretations, the modernists have not challenged the normative status of Islamic theological and jurisprudential schools. 'Abduh's rejection of the human being's complete understanding of divine things is traditional, both in substance and method. His *Risalat al-Tawhid* (Treatise on oneness) is mainly a layman's reinterpretation of major works on medieval theology without the hairsplitting argumentation and discussion about divine attributes. That science is congruent with religion, or that they are not contradictory, is an argument also put forward by the great scholar al-Ghazali in his *Tahafut al-Falasifah* (Incoherence of the philosophers), similar to the argument put forth against the futility of discussing divine attributes. Again, al-Kindi, Ibn Sina, and Ibn Rushd introduced the sciences of the day into intellectual circles. In other words, the modernists have been instrumental in opening up the closed intellectual circles to the need for rearguing traditions and modernizing Islamic interpretations by using all possible tools at hand.[27]

In a pointed dissension to this, the fundamentalists, in general, see the Islamic and Western past and present disciplines of philosophy, jurisprudence, and theology as superannuated. These disciplines are historically developed and as such have no universal values. Although not aware of it, the fundamentalists are indirect historicists; they view almost all old, medieval, and even modern interpretations as nothing more than temporary readings of—or the imposition of different meanings by different readers into—the religious text. However, the real meaning of the text is reserved only to the Author, and no reader can make a claim to its universal reading. Fundamentalists look at the divergent readings as the outcomes of a complex set of conditions that makes a reader read or interpret a text in one way or another. Divergence of theological, jurisprudential, philosophical, and political schools and sects are the products of specific ways of living which may not necessarily fit contemporary societies and problems. Put differently, what is more important than the logic of a reading and its formal truth is its relevance to the conditions of the reading itself and its pragmatic aftermath. Qutb and other fundamentalists transmute their rejection of historical readings into the possible legitimacy of new readings that are relevant to the problems of this age.

Political Principles

Tawhid has been developed by the fundamentalists to a point where it is used as the cord that ties together politics, economics, ethics, theology, and all other aspects of life. Because God, as the Creator, is the fountain of every material and spiritual thing, He is viewed as the ultimate authority in political life, as well. To the fundamentalists, humans' theoretical, theological, and political submission should be directed only to God. By this, they go beyond the traditional theological submission as understood in the old, medieval, and modern history of Islam. In this sense, they could not but load this doctrine of *tawhid* with ultimate political importance by insisting on subordinating politics and political philosophy to the highest kind of religious doctrines, *tawhid*. This is why they confuse religiosity with proper political behavior. Thus, establishing the state on the basis of divine governance becomes a must for the legitimacy of any political regime.

However, the fundamentalists' rejection of modernity does not make their thought traditional as a matter of necessity. In fact, part of fundamentalists' criticism centers on traditional establishments and their religious and political role. Traditional religious *'ulama'* do not, according to Qutb, comprehend the true Qur'anic spirit. Their imitation of a defunct jurisprudence that is irrelevant to modern living and their complacency toward political power lead to the alienation of Islam from the populace. The secular elites do not fare better, for they have marginalized Islam from the administration of government. Thus, the rejection of both secular and religious elites makes the fundamentalists advocates of a new model for Muslims who properly comprehend both religion and modernity. While underscoring the fragility of Muslim civilization, al-Mawdudi, Qutb, and other thinkers believe that only an Islamic revival, not traditionalism, can be instrumental in motivating an Islamic renaissance. Muslims must aim at inventing a new science and philosophy that must be developed from the essence of Islam, or else there is no opportunity to recapture scientific and political supremacy.[28]

Such a notion is very significant in the explication of the fundamentalist political project, at both the theoretical and practical levels. While the modernists' acceptance of the West led to their adoption of Western political theories, it precluded developing an original political theory or a few underpinnings for theory building. Their attempts introduced some Western political doctrines, like democracy and republicanism, and some practical recommendations to rulers. The nature of their political thought was oriented for immediate political goals but not fully grounded in theoretical advancements. Even the modernist criticism of traditionalism was not directed at traditions, per se, but at its rigid interpretation, which prevented making traditions suitable to Western notions, especially on the harmonious nature of religion and science. History again was not discredited as such but used to show how the Muslims, through various stages of development, dealt with foreigners and their compendium of knowledge.

We must keep in mind that the modernists, themselves, had no claim to any sort of theory building but were very keen on the need to bring together the West and the East, both scientifically and religiously. This is why the modernists did not shy away from adopting ideas from the West. The fact that they did not write a theory allowed the fundamentalists to use the adopted modernist notions to build their theory, such as when they introduced *shura* (consultation) as democracy (discussed later in the book). The modernists should, however, be credited for open-mindedness and for Islamizing essential concepts, such as democracy and pluralism. The revival of an intellectual atmosphere in the Muslim world is due to the modernists, as is the belief in the possible congruence between Islam and the West.

However, the fundamentalists have taken over and produced a multitude of readings whose essential discourse converges on intellectual and political transformation that could be either moderate or radical. The essence of the fundamentalist political discourse consists of four basic doctrines.

Legislation

Dismissing traditional readings and developing new ones have moved the fundamentalists from being just a political movement with specific ideological orientations to being a religious and intellectual movement seeking alternative religious, political, and intellectual readings that replace traditional and modernist Islamic and Western readings. Their alternative readings have centered around the discourse on *tawhid* and divine *hakimiyya* (governance). Al-Banna, Qutb, and al-Mawdudi, for instance, make God not only the source of legislation but also the focus of the new society that should aim at obedience to Him. Emphasizing the need to link even civic ethics to obedience follows suit. To Qutb, *tawhid* is not only human liberation from authority, but it forms the basis of any ethical, moral, and political system. Because Qutb believes that the basis of moral and ethical systems is divine, humans should not impose their systems. The Muslim society must follow the intuitive moral system, as revealed in the universal divine Qur'anic norms. These norms are not humanly derived, and their application is not an imposition on human nature. The divine system, as presented by the *shari'a* is, therefore, necessary for human well-being and for avoiding misery. To Qutb, Islamic *shari'a* is not a social but an eternal phenomenon, postulating the duties and rights of individuals and the state. Thus, legislating the basic principles of government, morality, and legality is sealed off from human calculation. However, these comprehensive, yet flexible, Qur'anic principles are designed to suit all ages and societies. The task of humans is to codify from—or read into—these general principles what is appropriate to society.[29]

Consequently, any deviation from *tawhid,* whether legal, political, or even personal, is a vitiation of true Islam, the fundamentalists argue. Sovereignty, both in a strict sense and in a general sense, belongs only to God, not to the individual, Qutb contends. Radical fundamentalism considers any kind of submission to human, social, political, or individual pressures as *shirk,* or unbelief. However, accepting the weakness of humans and the existence of uncontrollable events and difficult conditions, moderate fundamentalism gives more leeway to interpret the issue of sovereignty (elaborated in a later chapter). For both trends, however, human programs and systems must not contradict divine ordinances. While divine sovereignty covers the mundane and the sublime, its implication is mostly related to politics that orders human life. The law of God is meaningful in terms not only of the beyond but also of the here and now. It penetrates both human conscience and, more significantly, humans' political identity. Although the concern for the next life is part of religion, earthly living is as important, since it is the bridge between the profane and the sacred. Thus, the goal of *shari'a* is to sanctify what is profane so that the duality between the other life and this life is, at least, softened and, at best, terminated. Consequently, human will must be consumed in the divine will—an act that makes human will an expression of the divine and, consequently, humans' political actions and systems, divine actions and systems. Only in this way can an individual evaluate others' behavior and thought. It is only in this way that a fundamentalist can put down charges of belief and unbelief. Thus, when a fundamentalist, especially a radical, considers himself as a representation of what God wanted humans to be like, the ideal human type, his task then goes beyond normal self-understanding. The *shari'a* becomes to a fundamentalist the only meaningful law and an Islamic system the only acceptable system.[30] This argument is used to vindicate the fundamentalists' call for nonreconciliation with Western thought because of a perceived basic incongruence between Islamic ideals and non-Islamic ones.

It is in this context that one can understand al-Mawdudi's argument that it is only through the sublimation of lower instincts, and not through their scientification or rationalization, that humans honor themselves. Will must be used even to turn instinctual worship of God to intentional one. Any detraction from such worship dishonors the human being and leads him to fall again to the animalistic, instinctual state—al-Mawdudi gives the West as an example.[31]

Thus far, the fundamentalists' argument, especially the radical, has been to underline the need for modern and new foundations of an Islamic civilization. Their deliberate dismissal of Western civilization and past Islamic civilization leads them to uphold the need for "Islamic authenticity" as a ground for developing new theories. This applies also to the formal aspect of government, such as proper forms of an Islamic state. While the moderate trend uses some Western doctrines, like democracy, such doctrines are always underpinned by Islamic doctrines like *shura* (a topic that is treated in chapter three).

Revolution

While the modernists reject numerous medieval Islamic theories of Islam, they are not theoretically antagonistic to Western principles and theories and do not pinpoint any basic, inherent animosity between Islam and the West. This is why they have had no hesitation in adopting Western political and scientific theories; Al-Afghani, ʿAbduh, and Iqbal have no theoretical problem, for instance, in accepting republican forms of government.[32]

To many fundamentalists, however, and the radicals in particular, *tawhid* denies the theoretical and practical possibility of dialogue and compromise. Qutb argues that *tawhid* is a revolution against all formal or informal institutions that claim any authoritative or normative role—an act that is considered to be an infringement on the divinity of God. For instance, a legislature that legislates in its own name is seizing God's divine authority to legislate.[33] A massive infringement on this level must lead to eradicating the institution that committed it. According to Qutb, a change like this is no less than a revolution aimed ultimately at conscious transformation of social and political institutions. This notwithstanding, individuals are not forced to become Muslims, though they must not create obstacles to developing a Muslim society and an Islamic state, as these two entities shoulder the responsibility of ending human enslavement to human beings and to material things. This responsibility is not limited to Muslim countries but includes all the countries of the world. Therefore, no compromise on this issue is entertained. According to Qutb and al-Mawdudi, compromise denies the possibility of reconstructing the world and leads Muslims to give up some principles and to accommodate others. Thus, radical fundamentalists theoretically link radical change to creativity, assuming that the old cannot be renovated but must be destroyed.[34]

For radical fundamentalists, such a change or revolution necessitates transforming the positive force of *tawhid* to a position of realistic activism. Revolution must be ready to challenge—nationally, regionally, and internationally—all sorts of powers, systems, ideologies, and philosophies.[35] This transformation cannot take place without first owning the necessary philosophical and political knowledge of the others, because ideas must be confronted by ideas and material objects with their like. An ideology cannot fight a gun; fighting a gun requires a stronger gun. The foremost material obstacle is the governments and societies of the world, as Islam's field of operation is the world, not only the Muslim countries. Therefore, an Islamic revolution must be set up whose objective is the total abolition of the regimes that are essentially based on the government of humans over humans, or simply *al-jahiliyya* (paganism). Individuals must be liberated from the shackles of the present and the past and given the choice of a new life. Such a new life, however, cannot be achieved without providing a new Islamic context in which the individual has a real choice to follow Islam or not.[36]

Another principle illustrating the untraditional political behavior of Islamic fundamentalism is its call for revolution. Muslims have traditionally accepted more or less unjust rulers who nominally adhered to Islamic law. Great jurists and theologians such as Ibn Taymiyya, al-Ghazali, and Ibn Jamaʿa demanded yielding to unjust rulers because the scourges of revolutions outweighed their possible benefits.[37] The fundamentalists now view revolting against unjust and unelected rulers not only as a political doctrine but also as an ethical obligation. In particular, the view of Islam as a revolution, disseminated by Sayyid Qutb in the second half of the twentieth century, represents a radical development within the history of Islamic political thought. Revolution is now loaded with political, ethical, theological, and metaphysical connotations. Its fulfillment becomes a synonym for the righteous application of Islamic teachings. Thus, Qutb and al-Mawdudi postulate Islam as a total revolution against ungodly human conditions, the rectification of which requires nothing less than total annihilation of human delusions about knowledge and power. Again, al-Mawdudi makes God's messengers advocates of radical, comprehensive transformation of all existing institutions. For Qutb, al-Banna, al-Mawdudi, and Khumayni, revolution became a quest for universal change to bring about justice and happiness, which must not be hindered by any authority.[38] In the view of the fundamentalists, the revolutionary aspects of Islam are not contingent upon the nature of Islam.

The rise of fundamentalism is not invited only by a particular environment "produced of a crisis situation characterized by economic difficulties, moral and ideological confusion, and political instability."[39] It is the other way around. The absence of revolution for the fundamentalists indicates the depth of corruption and injustice in the conscience of Muslims, the intensity of crisis, and the loss of true Islam, a religion that is neither submissive nor stagnant. Thus, the fundamentalists' emphasis on the religious nature of activism is indicative of the superiority of praxis over theory and the importance of good action over good theory. For the fundamentalists, then, the actual formation of a good Muslim society takes precedence over the development of a seemingly coherent theory. In fact, such a formation is *tawhid* in action. Indeed, the collective formation of ideas for fundamentalism cannot be described in traditional terms, except when one means the text. But traditionalism is not the text; it is, rather, the interpretations that have been necessarily linked to the text. In a Christian context, one might make a comparison to Martin Luther, whose call to return to the scripture contradicted traditionalism.

For the fundamentalists *tawhid* must revolutionize the conscience and must be expressed in a popular movement. It must also transform the secular into the religious and go beyond the narrow limits of human existence to the unity of humankind. Revolution aims, then, at translating *tawhid* and *wahda* (unity) into a social and political movement against the universal state of moral and political bankruptcy which justifies itself by materialistic progress. However, the fundamentalists view such progress and its moral bankruptcy as a state that is not conducive to the general objective of humankind—that is, happiness. Instead, it is a source of misery that has plunged people into lust, selfishness, infidelity, and disunity. This state of affairs cannot be alleviated by taking a step here or there; its change requires a total mental, social, political, and intellectual revolution that sweeps away materialism along with its manifestations.[40]

Revolution is not, however, a synonym for a coup d'état or a forceful seizure of power; it is an attempt at a total transformation that changes the way people think and live. The fundamentalists view this change to be within the natural development of humankind. It is, according to the fundamentalists, a natural right for people to revolt, and force is justified when obstacles are imposed on this development. In particular, the fundamentalists are concerned with the state's denial of their activities to propagate their understanding of Islam. Freedom to propagate is basic to the fundamentalists who want to call people to their ideas. Any obstruction of propagation is, thus, identified with standing against Islam itself, since Islam is essentially a call for change.

This situation leads to the necessity of setting up a vanguard whose raison d'être is struggle, or *jihad,* against the institutions resisting the propagation of Islam. A vanguard, in the view of al-Banna, al-Mawdudi, and Qutb, must be responsible for making people aware of existing inhuman conditions and the need to reorganize human institutions on the principles of *tawhid* and justice. Assuming power ideally should be the result of popular approval.[41] The fundamentalists presume that making the truths of Islam known is sufficient to induce people to follow Islamic teachings. Their insistence on people's freedom to adopt any philosophy of life springs from their confidence in Islam's natural appeal.

Part of the difference between the fundamentalist view and the modernist view can be attributed to the historical conditions of the two groups. Al-Afghani and 'Abduh, for instance, were writing while the Islamic caliphate was still an international empire; Qutb and al-Banna were writing under either an oppressive national state or British colonialism. However, this might help us understand only part of their motivations. Viewing Islam as a moderate or radical revolution may be the outcome of the political inability of the modernists to revive Islam in the realm of politics. The fundamentalist rejection of the present and the past reflects the modernist inability to produce real reform because of deep-rooted corruption and injustice. Thus, nothing but uprooting un-Islamic societies can be satisfactory to radical fundamentalists; there is no possibility of a Muslim society or an Islamic state without universal changes.[42]

Foremost among the required changes is the denial of historical normativeness, which becomes the basis for renewing religion. Thus, the fundamentalists postulate reworking religious principles in terms of Muslim modern experience. What was good in the past was good not because of its normative status but because of its derivative nature from Islam. The first two caliphs in Islam were good, according to Qutb, not because they had special status but because they were able to exemplify Islamic teachings in their society. They did not force themselves on the people but were elected and were good examples of Islamic political behavior. To apply this to today's circumstances means that only those individuals who are elected by *shura* are good examples of Islamic political behavior. The fundamentalists are not attempting to relive the life of early Muslims but simply to derive certain examples in order to show the possibility of applying the *shari'a*. This thinking should not mean, however, that Muslims ought to imitate that period. The fundamentalist view is that Islam is capable of setting up in every age a new society that should be morally and materially more progressive. Material and moral progress is a preoccupation of Islamic fundamentalism, as it does not call for setting up a new Islamic state in order to reestablish the state of *al-Madina*. A new Islamic state does not necessarily look like the first Islamic state. However, what is common between the first and the new are the moral, political, and religious grounds that created the community and justified the state.

Consequently, statements that give the impression of history brought to a standstill do not reflect precisely the fundamentalist project. The writings that deny the new fundamentalist project and link the present and the future to a lost golden past[43] miss basic differences between the ideals postulated by the traditionalists and those of the fundamentalists. While Qutb, for instance, views the first community as the best example of an Islamic nation, this is so only because the first community upheld *tawhid* and justice. Again, the first caliphate amplified the legitimate exercise and transition of power by communal consent. Thus, though the interpretations of *tawhid*, justice, *shura,* and *ijma*' (consensus) may differ from one time to another, they are potentially applicable to all ages. Their linkage to the Qur'an forms both the religious and political bases of the Muslim community. The death of the Prophet does deny the possibility of setting up a new ideal Muslim community. Fundamentalist arguments are based on the assumed possibility of an ideal Islamic state whose attainability hinges on an ongoing process of rereading the text and its principles in terms of current conditions. If fundamentalists believe in the futility of establishing an Islamic state, what then are they doing? In fact, the opposite is true; their notion of Islamic revival hinges on the rise or fall of the anticipated Islamic state and society. The perfection of government and society is not linked in fundamentalist thought to the existence of a superhuman institution but, instead, to the application of the Qur'an. The superhuman bond is nothing but the Qur'an, and its perfection is the measure of human behavior. That the Prophet Muhammad represented a flashing instance of that perfection is, for the fundamentalists, the outcome of applying the Qur'an. Again, political freedom, morality, and justice are theoretical possibilities that are applicable today.

However, some scholars acknowledge that, while fundamentalists are working in a radically changed environment, they still entertain traditional modes of understanding and behavior. Some scholars argue that fundamentalism assumes that "things can and should go as much as they have for generations past." Again, while it speaks to a changed milieu and is not a blind opponent of social change, it still stresses that "change must be governed by traditional values and modes of understanding."[44]

As we have seen, the fundamentalists reject both elite and public modes. Traditional modes should not mean, however, the Qur'an and the *sunna,* for they are source material for understanding. The fundamentalist modes are, indeed, untraditional both in reading the text and in political behavior. For instance, they reject theology, philosophy, and history. Again, while the political behavior of Muslims traditionally has been acquiescent, the fundamentalists are, by and large, revolutionary.

Fundamentalists like Qutb and al-Banna do propose a new, comprehensive reading of Islam. Simply, this reading is the individual's interpretation of the Qur'an without any authoritative human guide. Although it is difficult in practice, since reading the Qur'an requires the mastery of many disciplines like linguistics and grammar, it only underlines the importance of individual freedom—an act that abolishes the authority of tradition. It opens the door wide for the ideologization of Islam through a political reading or a new political Qur'anic exegesis as a source for Islamic revival.

Thus, an activist political behavior, in the fundamentalist view, takes precedence over submission to social and political traditions. Authoritative exegeses and authoritarian governments were both dropped as proper means of reading the text and dealing with reality, respectively. Of course, certain values, especially the moral, are shared between the fundamentalist Muslims and ordinary Muslims. However, their justification for the fundamentalists lies only in the Qur'anic text, not in society or history.

Consensus

The untraditional and revolutionary interpretations employed by the fundamentalists are more apparent when studying their understanding of two essential political concepts—namely, consensus (*ijma'*) and revolution. Consensus, whose employment was theoretical in matters of jurisprudence and theology, is viewed as the source of political transformation. It has been used traditionally to arrive at one Qur'anic reading or another and has been relegated to the scholarly elites in order to convince the community to follow one interpretation or another. Now, the fundamentalists view it as a source for freeing the community—not only from conservative, traditional readings of scholars but, more important, from the tyranny of both rulers and political traditions. Thus, all fields of Islamic sciences and other aspects of life become the proper interest of ordinary Muslims and subject to their approval. No legitimate legal or political principles can be imposed on the community without its consent. The historically derived, normative status of the scholars and of political authority is denied and replaced by a need for a continuous process of ratification and agreement by the community. No political leader or religious scholar has the right to impose his will on the people.[45]

In the view of the fundamentalists, consensus is a political tool used to check the Islamicity of the state rather than to control heretical views in the community. By freeing consensus from its historical limitations, the door is now open to the fundamentalists to use it as a device to measure political behavior. This also leads to the need for communal involvement in political matters regarding the forms and the content of politics. Now it is only the community that can speak with an authoritative voice; individuals have only opinions. The right to create political institutions, to evaluate political behavior, or to interpret the scripture is communal. Equality of rights and duties is postulated as a necessary condition for proper political behavior. This is why most fundamentalists make popular consensus a necessary condition for electing a legitimate Muslim ruler. Any ruler who comes to power without popular approval, even though he upholds Islamic law, is not legitimate. This view contrasts with medieval thinkers' acceptance of seizure of power, which the fundamentalists see as yielding to political power and betraying God's trust. God's delegation of authority is to all humankind as His vicegerent and is not bestowed on particular scholars, classes, or rulers. Consequently, no seizure of power can be legitimately justified.

This idea of legitimacy is also extended to include both the intellectual and the political realms. While historically the elites looked upon themselves as ipso facto communal representatives, the fundamentalists turn down any suggestion of particular privileges to any elite, be it political or religious. While most fundamentalists acknowledge differences among individuals, they are nonetheless against the institutionalization of intellectual and political elitism. No group of people can rightfully claim to have more rights or to enjoy special prerogatives.

Most fundamentalists play down the importance of consensus in theology, which was the main goal of traditional theology. As noted previously, people should be capable of reading and interpreting the text without an authoritative human intercessor. Legitimate interpretations must not contradict the text, on the one hand, but must be grounded in *tawhid*, on the other. Divine governance, representing the practical embodiment of *tawhid*, must appear in Muslims' unity and must be the principle of revival. Any revival that lacks this governance is indistinguishable from un-Islamic ones, since the moral grounds for an Islamic revival must always be present and embodied in the setting up of a Muslim society and an Islamic state.[46]

Needless to say, such an understanding of *tawhid* leads, in the long run, to some difficulty in understanding the text, itself. Opposing textual interpretations can be provided by different groups to support various political views. Again, while the fundamentalist understanding may seem more liberal than the traditional, it carries within it the possibility of more authoritarianism, since some groups or individuals may claim to be representing the true meaning of Islam at a specific historical epoch—a claim upheld by many radical fundamentalist groups nowadays. This is the reason some other criterion, besides the text, must be employed to prevent incoherent or circular interpretations of the text.

Nevertheless, the rule of Islam is by no means the rule of theocracy; it is the rule of Islamic law, however vaguely defined. Qutb and al-Banna argue against the legitimate existence of an Islamic clergy, who are no more than scholars. A proper Islamic rule is no more than the systematic rule of Islamic law where Islamic ideas spread and where Islamic regulations define the forms of government and society. Thus, the inherent authority of the clergy is denied by all Sunni fundamentalists. To describe the proper Islamic government as a theocracy is, therefore, a misnomer, since it gives the wrong impression about Islam. Neither theory nor practice lends credibility to theocracy in Islam.[47]

The Shi'ite brand of Islamic fundamentalism, as advocated by Ayatollah Khumayni, may more appropriately be called theocratic. Khumayni advocates in his *Al-Hukuma al Islamiyya* (The Islamic government) the legitimate rule of only jurists, because a proper Islamic government must be based on jurisprudence.[48] However, the majority of the fundamentalists rule out the need for a clergy to bestow legitimacy on Islamic government. Its legitimacy springs from adhering to divine governance and from the execution of the *shari'a*. While for Khumayni and Qutb, the *shari'a* forms the basis of government, Qutb views the right to rule as a matter of delegation from the people, but Khumayni views it, directly and indirectly, as issuing from the *Imam*. [49]

While the fundamentalists converge ideologically on many issues, there are still many differences—basic and essential—and these will be elaborated in chapter three. It is noteworthy that, while al-Mawdudi, for instance, suspects the serenity of the majority because of their deficient analytical skills, he feels that an elite must lead the way. He makes the goodness, as well as the corruption, of the people dependent on their elite. However, this does not mean that the elite has any intrinsic status; its role is social and political.[50] It is preferable that an elite starts the process of reformation, or else a popular movement may lead to the termination of the benefits of revolution. Revolutions may lead to more dislocations than corrections. However, Qutb, al-Banna, and others are more trusting of the people, for true reformation cannot take place except by grassroots changes brought about by the people.

Conclusion

It has become obvious throughout this chapter that the basic objective of both modernism and fundamentalism is to raise Muslim consciousness and to induce a social and political movement aimed at attaining material, political, and spiritual progress. A new reading of Islam becomes, for both the modernists and the fundamentalists, the basic condition for starting a modern process of reformulating Islamic history and reforming Islamic civilization. However, the process, itself, reformulates the tenets of political Islam and reforms the principles of political rule. The need for serious reexamination and reinterpretation of Islamic literature and, of course, of the long-standing interpretations of Islam is postulated in order to accommodate modernity and modern human needs.

While modernism advocates Islam as the avenue for salvation, the modernization of Islam is to be conducted in line with the philosophy and politics of the West. However, Islamic morality is the distinguishing mark between Islam and other systems. No total or unending confrontation is postulated as a prelude to progress and development. On yet another level, religion's most important function is the calculation of morality. Although *tawhid* is the fundamental, comprehensive, metaphysical doctrine, it becomes the linchpin in the process of unifying and liberating humankind. However, fundamentalism, especially its radical interpretation, looks at *tawhid* as essentially an instrument of political government.

For radical fundamentalism, *tawhid* becomes a justification for dominating others, while in the moderate fundamentalist view, it is justification for not being dominated by others. Fundamental doctrines such as sovereignty are grounded in the Qur'anic discourse, itself used to produce a legitimate popular discourse that makes legitimacy a matter of popular consent. Charged with interpreting the divine word, the *umma* (community) enjoys the only legitimate power; other powers are only derivative and hinge on Muslims' approval.

Both modernist and fundamentalist discourses demystify history and call on humans to shoulder their responsibilities in charting their present lives and futures as well as in reviving religion. The essence of development lies in human nature: humans should not wait for salvation; they should achieve it. Spiritual, intellectual, political, and economic regeneration is the proper domain of humans, who must first purify themselves and then move to unite themselves with fellow human beings. However, the fundamentalists insist on complete purification and solid unification before any real process of regeneration can take place.

Fundamentalists' textual analysis of the scripture has a lot to do with their indifference to the possibility of other valid, but opposing, opinions. The modernists, however, whose textual analysis of the scripture relates to nontextual criteria, are more capable, in principle, of absorbing differences. Purification becomes an individual—not necessarily collective—act. Unity becomes, as well, more accommodating of diversity, since scientific discoveries reflect the possibility of reinterpretation or rediscovery of the truth. Thus, the process of regeneration for the modernists is always tentative, because it depends on a relative science, whereas the process of regeneration for the fundamentalists, especially the radicals, is ultimately absolute, because it depends on an absolute text. Not only is the difference between the two discourses methodological, but it leads also to the development of different normative systems.

While to a modernist, knowledge precedes belief, for a fundamentalist, it is otherwise. Knowledge to a fundamentalist becomes an act of belief, while to a modernist, belief is an act of knowledge. However, both view belief and knowledge as the basic two underpinnings for a sound revival. The absence of either leads to imbalance and to derailing any process of regeneration.

The two discourses are much concerned with regeneration and authenticity. While the modernist entertains and judges the authentic in terms of the new (science), the fundamentalist subjects the new to the authentic (revelation). The fundamentalist uses authenticity as the yardstick to measure all things, while the modernist uses the new as the yardstick. Again, the modernist makes the authentic yield to the new; the fundamentalist makes the new conform to the authentic.

2

Fundamentalist Discourses on Epistemology and Political Philosophy

The general, modern Islamic fundamentalist discourses in the older tradition of Abu al-A'la al-Mawdudi, Hasan al-Banna, Sayyid Qutb, Abu al-Hasan al-Nadawi, Ayatollah al-Khumayni, Hadi al-Mudarrisi, and 'Abd al-Jawad Yasin could go a long way in outlining the epistemological and political framework that laid the foundations of modern Islamic fundamentalist thought. I have included al-Mudarrisi and Yasin because their thought reflects further development of the basic issues treated by the fundamentalists. In Bahrain, Hadi al-Mudarrisi was instrumental in founding the Islamic Action Organization, which played an active political role in Bahraini politics during the late 1970s and 1980s. The organization called for the radical transformation of the local social and economic order. 'Abd al-Jawad Yasin seems to have played a major role in al-Jama'at al-Islamiyya (Islamic groups) that became the dominant political power in the universities and the means of protest against the Egyptian regime since 1977. One of these groups is al-Qiwa al-Qutbiyya (Qutbian forces), and one of its theoreticians is 'Abd al-Jawad Yasin, the author of Fiqh al-Jahiliyya al-Mu'asira (The jurisprudence of contemporary paganism), who further developed Qutb's argument of "human paganism" in order to make a universal doctrine.

The lives of the fundamentalist thinkers cover many historical periods and areas of the Muslim world—such as Egypt, India, Iran, and Iraq—and represent different socioeconomic backgrounds and diverse political contexts. While they have developed their multifaceted discourses, it is still possible to study and draw from their discourses one unified framework—that is, fundamentalism. Of course, there are major and numerous differences and variations between one thinker and another or, at times, between one discourse and another, especially on issues that relate to political behavior. However, the focus here is on the discourse that unites them theoretically. I have treated major differences and variations later in the book.

Epistemological Framework

Knowledge

Al-Mawdudi, al-Banna, al-Nadawi, Qutb, and other fundamentalists ground their discourses in a presupposition: the poverty and shallowness of reason. Only through divine revelation can humans attain a solid, exemplary moral worth. When *fitra* is enlightened by divine revelation, it becomes a force for humankind's happiness. From the outset, the fundamentalists assume the impossibility of knowledge through reason because human knowledge cannot comprehend, interact with, or act according to ultimate truths.[1]

This is the reason fundamentalists turn any discourse on knowledge into a conjecture surpassing mental understanding and transform knowledge into a mental state of belief. To them, complete knowledge requires rational understanding by reason, spiritual comprehension, and physical action. True knowledge is thus pictured as a possessive power that overwhelms human reason and conscience and dictates action. In his discourse, al-Banna goes as far as saying that Islam as a method of knowledge should determine all human affairs and influence all forms and rules of conduct. To him, submissive worshiping without total ideological and philosophical commitment to Islam hinders the development of Muslims and their religion. Therefore, he argues, Muslims must develop Islamic systems for their nation from pure sources, as the Companions of the Prophet and their followers from the "good ancestors" (*al-Salaf al-Salih*) did. Muslims must neither commit themselves beyond the confines of this general statement nor tie themselves to any historic act or generation. Islam has been careful not to postulate any permanent temporal systems, but its general principles allow for continuous development of philosophical and intellectual systems. This enhances the chances for perfection and deters imperfection. Thus, priority is given to the individual more than to the system, since it is human nature, and not systems, that should be perfected. Human adjustment is required in accordance with the spirit of the ages. Therefore, Islam may benefit from all human systems that do not go against its general postulates and basic principles.[2]

Because ultimate knowledge is untenable, the fundamentalists like al-Banna, al-Nadawi, and Qutb cannot but doubt humans' powers. No human being can claim to understand God, prove the necessity of His existence, or comprehend His nature. Such an argument allows the fundamentalists to disclaim any attempt by humans to question God's wisdom in creation or in death and life. Humans are simply unequipped mentally and psychologically to comprehend the true nature of things.[3]

Al-Nadawi argues that the Qur'anic discourse does not deal philosophically with fundamental issues like creation. Most of its doctrines are related to moral and social aspects of human life. The metaphysical issues are simple and uncomplicated and are related to *tawhid*. Although *tawhid* allows for the temporary inclusion of new scientific theories on nature, historically this was curtailed by introducing Aristotelian thought into Islamic thought and by adhering to limits imposed by jurists and theologians.[4] Because the fundamentalists limit humans' ability to know, due to their weak reasoning capacities, true knowledge can be attained through God's revelation. From this fundamentalist viewpoint, understanding the universal order as a totality, and not as disjointed parts, is the prelude to understanding all parts of the universal order.

Philosophy

From a fundamentalist perspective, philosophy as a method to attain knowledge leads to poor and wrong discourses. Instead of abstract theorizing, the philosophers should, according to al-Banna, al-Mawdudi, Qutb, and al-Mudarrisi, develop discourses beneficial to society. Because philosophy is treated as a descriptive method of the essence of things and not their structures,[5] the fundamentalists view philosophies as barren and mistaken. Abu al-A'la al-Mawdudi, Hasan al-Banna, and Sayyid Qutb have taken a hostile attitude toward philosophy, especially that based on critical analysis and abstracts.

In his discourse, al-Nadawi specifically attributes the intellectual problems of Western civilization to Greek thought, because the latter suffers from several defects: belief in the corporeal and insensitivity to what is not; lack of emphasis on the spiritual; and dependence on worldly pleasures and nationalistic tendencies. All these phenomena can be subsumed under the term "materialism," and the materialistic characteristics of God are manifested in idols and temples. The Greeks could not abstract divine characteristics. Thus, they invented a god for beauty, another for power, and so forth. Such doctrines led ultimately to a materialistic kind of living, and arts such as sculpture, dancing, and music were developed from a materialistic worldview. Materialism negatively affected the morals of the Greeks and led to the spread of moral looseness and political anarchy.

Al-Nadawi also criticizes the Roman heritage, the second component of Western civilization. Although less philosophical and poetical than the Greeks, the Romans depended on power and organization; in fact, they added power to materialism. The Romans were preoccupied with the idea of domination of the world; in politics, they put their gods aside because the deities did not have any political weight. Ultimately, the Roman Empire collapsed with the ascendancy of luxury and moral degradation. However, Rome's decay coincided with the Christianization of the empire by Emperor Constantine, and thus Christianity lost its purity because Greek paganism and Roman veneration of power triumphed over the true spirit of Christianity. Finally, materialism triumphed over all other forms of thought and is still a main feature of Western beliefs.[6]

Notwithstanding the fundamentalists' rejection of philosophy in principle, they built their discourses on direct and subjective intuition. Truth is not to be abstractly known but, instead, must be existentially felt. The fundamentalists belong to the noncognitive school, because they accept the notion that epistemological statements are true or false. They also belong to the nonnaturalist tradition, because they state that epistemological and moral principles cannot be defined by logical and ethical statements. Thus, if the theory of knowledge depends on the nature and scope of knowledge, as well as on its presuppositions, bases, and validity, then the fundamentalist discourse is defined, in terms of its nature and scope, by the observable and the ascertainable. Those unobservable concepts such as order in the universe or God cannot be sufficiently ascertained, because reason, whether phenomenological or functional, is unreliable as a conduit to what is absolute and necessary. The utmost possible theoretical employment of reason, in the view of Qutb, al-Nadawi, al-Banna, al-Khumayni, and al-Mudarrisi, is the application of *ijtihad* (independent reasoning) in matters of understanding and realizing the divine precepts—that is, an interpretative discourse.[7]

Qutb argues that the distinctive mark between the philosophic Western method and the religious Islamic method is that the philosophic method originates in reason, but the religious method originates from the divine and resides in conscience. The divine origin of the Islamic discourses is what gives them their basic credibility insofar as they do not suffer from human imperfection, ignorance, and desire (which are common features of human discourses). Although other religions were originally as pure as Islam, the interference of human elements in their interpretations, which generated paganism and materialism, took away their credibility.[8] The fundamentalists turn reason into a channel for understanding what exists by prohibiting exploration into any theoretical and philosophical discussions that lead away from revelation. This is the standpoint that the fundamentalists employ to reject all human-made philosophies like rationalism and positivism. Human philosophies, to al-Banna, al-Mawdudi, Qutb, and al-Khumayni, are violations of the divine discourse, which assumes the inaccessibility of many parts of nature to reason.[9] Al-Banna, for instance, argues that, although Islam is not opposed to knowledge, which disciplines and directs power, it links knowledge to religious sciences and objectives.[10] Al-Khumayni goes further, using the argument of inaccessibility to prove the necessity for an *imam*; God would not leave humankind without a direct source of truth.[11]

By neglecting the role of pure reason, al-Nadawi, al-Mawdudi, al-Banna, and Qutb highlight the role of practical reason, praxis, or the interpretative discourse. A sign for any real knowledge is, then, its production of doctrines leading to action. A correct discourse is, therefore, one that is based on action justified by the sacred text. The fundamentalists see knowledge not as an end in itself but as a motivating force for action.[12] Al-Banna puts this relationship in the following perspective: the revival of religion aims primarily at the individual who should became a model—or a living discourse—for others. It aims also at developing a conscience naturally capable of both differentiating between good and evil and standing against the unjust. In this fashion, the conscience becomes a good instrument for achieving the good life and the triumph of good over evil. According to al-Banna, it is in the proper disciplining of conscience in accordance with the Islamic worldview that the true interpretative discourse on intellectual development lies and that the secrets of existence may be unveiled. This kind of knowledge leads to total commitment to an Islamic way of life.[13]

By linking knowledge and action, al-Nadawi, al-Banna, and Qutb underscore the importance of action and its discourse as a proof of the soundness of knowledge. True knowledge entails action, and action entails true discourse and the satisfaction of the material, spiritual, and intellectual needs of human beings. Islam does this and provides a basic interpretative discourse on human beings, life, the universe, and God.[14] Al-Nadawi pictures this idea very clearly and states that the human being is God's vicegerent (khalifa), whose main objective in this life is to properly develop material things. The human being is viewed by al-Nadawi as an active, not theoretical, vicegerent of God, whose actions should aim ultimately at the good.[15] Qutb goes deeper by arguing that Islam aims also at methodological developments as a first step toward substantive changes. Islam's method focuses on developing a nation through a creed; it functions, then, not only as a belief system but also as a revolutionary discourse that goes against all human discourses. Making Islam only a theoretical, inactive discourse, and denying its discourse of change, eliminates—in the fundamentalist view—its divine element and subjects it to human methods. Islamic methods of thinking and activism are, thus, as important as Islamic doctrines and are, in fact, inseparable.[16]

Fundamentalists like al-Nadawi, al-Mawdudi, al-Banna, Qutb, and al-Mudarrisi view Islam as the most perfect method of knowledge, because it subsumes, under the doctrine of unity, the unity of the intellectual and the spiritual with the material, and the known with the unknown. Grounded in tawhid, the doctrine of unity denies the legitimacy of any theoretical or practical disunity and views the whole existence as one creation. Any individual or state that negates unity is branded by many fundamentalists as being in a state of jahiliyya.[17] This state, which is ruled by a jungle mentality, according to al-Mudarrisi, devalues human worth and pushes it backward, notwithstanding the high technology of the twentieth century. He further argues that both methodology and philosophy of power dominate

Western thinking; both the Marxist and the capitalist are charged with the same crime—domination. Vietnam is cited as an instance.[18]

Al-Nadawi describes in detail the turning of the world toward international paganism. For him, Christian Europe has turned into materialist paganism and left aside all sorts of spiritual teachings and religious morality. Now it believes, at the individual level, only in pleasure and material interest; in political life, in power and domination; and in social life, in aggressive nationalism and unjust citizenship. Europe has revolted against human nature and moral principles and has lost sight of valuable goals. It has also lost religious conscientiousness and fallen into materialism. It is, according to al-Nadawi, like an unbridled elephant that steps over the weak and destroys whatever comes in front of it. The whole world looks as if it is a train pulled by paganism and materialism. The Muslims, like many others, are only passengers who control nothing; the faster the train moves, the faster humanity moves into paganism, moral degradation, and spiritual bankruptcy.[19]

Nature

Nature, both as a concept and as a fact, plays a crucial role in formulating truth, according to fundamentalists such as al-Banna, Qutb, and ʿAbd al-Jawad Yasin. To them, the truth of Islam stems from its harmony with natural norms and human *fitra*. Islam is both an integral part of the universe and an expression of true nature, and so the fundamentalists discredit any human philosophy as being an unnecessary intervention based on ignorance of human nature and the role of science.[20]

On the practical level, al-Banna explains the Islamic nation's need for science; science is, in fact, a religious duty and provides Muslims with power. However, Islam has not differentiated between the science of this world and that of the hereafter. Studying the universe must lead to better understanding of religion and to increase Muslims' power. This power, however, must ultimately be tied to belief and unity. Otherwise, the final objective of power lacks moral justification: it destroys itself as well as others.[21]

As argued before, the fundamentalists do not reject science but, instead, reject its claim to metaphysical status and restrict its function to transmitting facts, observations, and experiments. The fundamentalist rejection of metaphysical philosophy centers around the idea that philosophical foundations are generalizations of facts derived from individual sciences. Fundamentalists detest the perceived attempts made by both science and philosophy to replace religion. However, they believe that there is a basic difference between philosophy and religion. While philosophy comes about as a result of human attempts to explain the universe, it becomes passive knowledge. Conversely, while religion results from revelations and interacts with human feelings and engulfs all facets of life, it functions as a linkage between the human being, the universe, and God.[22] Qutb explains this by saying that the religious discourse speaks to the innermost existential aspect of human existence and provides it with tranquility and stability. A discourse like this does lead us to look at knowledge as well as action as part of an overall divine design whose fulfillment is the center for true knowledge and ultimate happiness. Exempting a few scientific fields like statistics, chemistry, and biology, Qutb further argues that all philosophical schools, historiographies, ethics, and comparative religions, as well as sociology and psychology, are deficient in being able to analyze the development of the human soul, the movement of history, and the origin of the universe.[23]

Because Muslim fundamentalists such as al-Banna, al-Nadawi, and al-Khumayni assume a close relation between thinking and the social environment, they do not view any civilization as a general human heritage. This view leads them to reject the description of Western philosophy and civilization as part of Islamic civilization or a universal civilization. They see the channeling of Greek philosophy into Islamic thought—by Muslim philosophers such as al-Kindi, al-Farabi, Ibn Sina, and Ibn Rushd—as a false attempt at the renewal of Islam.[24] Al-Nadawi argues that the pure oneness of God was overshadowed by polytheism, ignorance, and heresies; thus, the Muslim nation lost its distinctive mark. Humankind was overcome by whims, philosophies, and systems that did not secure its happiness.[25]

Fundamentalists like al-Nadawi and Qutb argue that, because the Muslim philosophers disregarded developing purely Islamic doctrines, Muslims were not able to derive pure Islamic doctrines from Islamic philosophies.[26] Qutb explains the fundamentalists' problem with philosophy in the following way. When some Muslim philosophers were enticed by Greek philosophy, especially that of Aristotle, they thought that the Greek discourse reached maturity and perfection. Instead of constructing an Islamic discourse, according to the general rules of religion, they used the general rules of philosophy in order to construct the Islamic discourse. Philosophy corrupted the harmony of religion by, first, introducing different theological disputations into Islamic literature and, second, including in their teachings diverse paganistic and Christian elements that were unfit for *tawhid*. Philosophical arguments were used by different political trends, turning them into theological schools.[27]

Religion

Al-Mawdudi, al-Banna, Qutb, and others present religion as the alternative to philosophy because its *manhaj* (method) and *nizam* (system) are harmonious with the universe. By this presentation, fundamentalism, especially the radical trend, reduces all methods and systems of life and action into a basic, twofold division: what is God-given and what is human-made. The God-given is derived from a divine scripture, and those individuals and institutions that organize their lives and actions accordingly are God's followers, or *hizb Allah* (the party of God). But the human-made is derived from human systems; their followers constitute *hizb al-Shaytan* (the party of Satan). Religion in this sense is a method of belief that includes a system of metaphysics, politics, society, and morality.[28]

Al-Banna believes that God has provided in Islam all of the necessary rules for the good life of a nation as well as for its renaissance and happiness. While world ideologies, specifically socialism and capitalism, have some benefits but many harmful effects, Islam for the fundamentalists has captured what is beneficial and shunned what is harmful in both ideologies. However, the renaissance of the East (*nahdat al-sharq*) cannot be kindled by imitating other nations; instead, it depends on Islam, itself. Every nation, according to al-Banna, has a constitution, and the fountain of the Islamic constitution is the Qur'an. Again, every nation has a law, and Islamic laws must be derivatives of Islamic *shari'a* and in accordance with its constitutive principles.[29]

In fact, the fundamentalists, led by al-Mawdudi, al-Nadawi, al-Banna, and Qutb, conceive religion as a system of life defined both by doctrines and, more substantively, by political, social, and individual behaviors. For them the religion of people is not the mere profession of faith but is the way they act; consequently, people's behavior becomes the yardstick of faith. True faith must include, then, the realms of both conscience and public life.[30] It is simply a living, motivating force. Islam is not a theory that deals with postulates; it is, more important, a method that deals with the real. Action must then come before theory. Those individuals who challenge Islam by asking Muslims to produce a theory want to subjugate Islam to their own theory. However, Qutb, for instance, argues that a valid theory can only be a by-product of life, itself, or of activism, and not otherwise. When Islam was established, Qutb goes on, it fought paganism all over. The Islamic creed was also set up not as a theory but essentially as an organic society that was active and organized. All of this led finally to the establishment of the greater community.[31]

From this perspective, it seems useless to the fundamentalists to separate the diverse aspects of life, because sound social activities should be tied up ultimately to a metaphysical doctrine—i.e., *tawhid*. This doctrine is adhered to, the fundamentalists contend, even though religion offers only allusions (*iha'at*) linked directly or indirectly to great truths. This interpretation leads the fundamentalists to transform *tawhid* into a doctrine covering all spiritual and social activities and leading, in fact, to basic changes in the individual, society, and state.[32] In this context, al-Banna gives the example of the Muslim Brotherhood in Egypt. Its activities range from liberating the Muslim world and establishing a free Islamic state to eliminating poverty and crime. All of this requires a deep religious belief, strict organization, and constant activism.[33]

Political Doctrines

Tawhid also plays an essential role in formulating the fundamentalists' political discourse. Because their political discourse is constructed around the doctrine of *tawhid,* their ideology is transformed into a doctrinal one. Insofar as *tawhid* is a political doctrine, it entails political submission to God. Such a rendering provides the fundamentalists with a doctrinal yardstick to evaluate political behavior and to produce political doctrines.

Paganism of the World

Modern life reduced humans to animalistic living. To the fundamentalists, modern life is based on the philosophy of power and the logic of dominance and exploitation. All of this has led to barbaric and bloody wars.[34] Fundamentalists like al-Banna, Qutb, and al-Mudarrisi believe that Europe and the West, in general, have given up their high ideals, virtues, and humane principles and replaced them with materialistic paganism, or *jahiliyya*. This paganism has resulted in social confusion, moral degeneration, economic tension, and spiritual bankruptcy.[35] All of the ongoing international political conflicts are the result of competition over material life, and there are no substantive differences between the competing parties. Even "communist Russia," al-Nadawi goes on to say, was nothing more than a by-product of Western civilization. Asian nations are following suit, but their conflict with the West is over the leadership of the world.[36]

In the final analysis, the fundamentalists viewed ideological conflicts between international capitalism and socialism as a power struggle rooted in economic interests, though socialism advocates justice and capitalism supports free enterprise.[37] Al-Mudarrisi puts the fundamentalist view on capitalism and Marxism in the following context: While capitalism opens the way for monopoly and free trade by the few and allows private property, Marxism humiliates and enslaves the people through their need for food yet provides some justice for the entourage of the regime. Marxism kills any motivation for production, and the principle of equality for all is a myth, although the people are equal in poverty, except for party leaders, who live better than their counterparts in the West. And, continues al-Mudarrisi, capitalists are exerting the worst forms of imperialism against the peoples of the world in order to secure the development of their economy. Although it is unfair, for instance, to destroy the economy of people in Africa in order to improve the standards of those living in Europe or America, this is exactly what both Marxism and capitalism do.[38]

From this angle, radical fundamentalists such as al-Mawdudi, al-Nadawi, Qutb, and al-Mudarrisi view all existing societies on earth as paganist (*jahili*) societies.[39] They use *tawhid* as a device to evaluate the Islamicity or the *jahiliyya* of any social institution or political order. What worries the fundamentalists most is that the Muslims are imitating Western civilization in its worst forms: destruction, degeneration, sectarian divisions, civil wars, and racial discrimination. Al-Nadawi sees that the imitation of the West goes beyond these characteristics and subjects the Muslim world to the scientific, industrial, commercial, and political dominance of the West. Muslims have also become allies and soldiers of Western paganism. Some Muslims even look to the West, the leader of the new wave of paganism, as their protector and the enforcer of world justice.[40]

Notwithstanding this scenario, many—but not all—fundamentalists take upon themselves the task of saving humankind by first removing themselves from *jahiliyya*. Politically, this means repudiating any political order that is in violation of divine teachings. In fact, any political order that has this characteristic is in violation of God's *shari'a* and in a state of transgression against His *uluhiyya* (divinity). The *jahili* society, which is set up on any principle that does not take into account divine guidance, must be confronted and modified in accordance with the divine method and system. Qutb has no qualms in calling for subjecting, at any cost, the realities of the world to Islamic standards, because submission to such realities contradicts Islam, whose main objective is destroying paganism.[41]

The Universalism of Islam

For the fundamentalists, the paganism of the world is negated completely only when Islam's universalism (*'Alamiyyat al-Islam*) spreads all over the world. This universalism is represented essentially by the submission of all people to God's divinity. Fundamentalists such as al-Mudarrisi, Qutb, and Yasin do not view this dominance as a transgression against human freedom, because Islam raises humans to their natural place as ends in and of themselves. Islam constructed its relations on respect of humans for their fellow humans in accordance with general principles of *shari'a*.[42] Al-Mudarrisi explains this idea by viewing human nature as having both a moral/spiritual aspect and a physical/material aspect. The latter aspect humans share with animals; the former, however, is unique to humans. Islam balances the two aspects by raising humans above their material aspect and by linking value to what is right and to the human being qua human being. Things are valued in terms of their service to humankind and not as things in themselves.[43]

To Qutb, al-Nadawi, and al-Banna, the universalism of Islam manifests itself in rejecting privileges given to any race, nationality, language, or land. It also manifests itself, as well, in its call to worship one God, to spread justice, to enjoin brotherhood, and to believe in all of the prophets and divine books and in the Day of Judgment.[44] Al-Khumayni adds that Islam is the religion of those who fight for what is right and just and who call for freedom and independence.[45]

However, what makes universalism very important to the fundamentalists is their belief in Islam as the only system that meets the
needs of human *fitra*. Islam's universalism corresponds, in fact, to its
shumuliyya (comprehensiveness), since Islam first regulates all aspects of life and allows for renewed solutions to new problems. Then,
it is also a complete system, having social and political laws and regulations. Al-Nadawi dwells at length on the revolutionary changes that
"true" Islam can bring about. First, it eliminates the persuasive, ritualistic paganism, including the pleasures of life and material things,
and replaces it with self-sacrifice, love for humanity, and adherence
to truth. Second, true Islamic belief leads to honesty and dignity, which
make Muslims unyielding to any political or religious, tyrannical
power. Submission to power without proper political, moral, and legal objectives is unacceptable.[46]

Qutb, al-Banna, al-Khumayni, and al-Nadawi believe that Islamic
law contains the fundamentals of a superior and virtuous social and
political order that deals with the individual, family, society, nation,
and state. Consequently, this moral, social, and political superiority
permits fundamentalists like al-Banna, Qutb, al-Nadawi, and al-
Khumayni to claim the right and the duty of Muslims to call the
world to the truth.[47] Al-Khumayni's argument is very straightforward:
While darkness overshadowed the West, when the North American
continent was still populated exclusively by Native Americans and
the Roman and Persian empires suffered from tyrannical and racial
rulers, Islam put forward divine laws that even the Prophet submit-
ted to. These laws covered human affairs, from birth to death, from
politics to social affairs and worship. Those individuals who talk about
the imperfection of Islamic laws and the need to borrow from the
West are either ignorant or imperialist.[48]

Calling the world to the truth necessitates—in the view of al-
Nadawi, al-Banna, Qutb, and Yasin—the transfer of world leadership from the West, which misused the trust, to the Muslims, who
must struggle to induce that transfer. The struggle should take place
first within the individual, family, society, and state, and then within
the world. If the Muslims struggle accordingly, the fundamentalists
argue, then the Muslims constitute the only real power that can legitimately take away the leadership from the West, destroy the *jahili*
system, and remove political persecution.[49] Al-Banna defends this
notion from possible criticism for its practical impossibility by argu-

ing, idealistically, that the Muslims must start anew as the Prophet did: the Prophet had nothing but truth and will, which he used to defeat many empires.[50]

Islamic universalism is underpinned by the doctrine of God's *hakimiyya*, which postulates the absolute sovereignty of God over the universe. Thus, no legitimate lawgiver exists but Him. Humans must apply His divine legislation and refrain from postulating the basic principles of what is right or wrong. Humankind, for the fundamentalists, must simply be ruled by the basic principles of the *shari'a*. Furthermore, because the doctrine of *hakimiyya* is a derivative of *tawhid*, the latter spreads into all aspects of life and constitutes the only acceptable political basis for any system.[51] Al-Mawdudi elaborates this by saying that "the sovereignty of this kingdom vests in Him. He alone has the right to command or forbid. Worship and obedience are due Him alone without anyone else having a share in it." He adds further that "nothing can claim sovereignty, be it a human being, a family, a class or group, or the human beings in the world taken together. God alone is the sovereign and His commandments are the Law of Islam."[52]

Such a view allows radical fundamentalists such as al-Nadawi, Qutb, al-Mawdudi, and al-Khumayni to call for fighting any human, philosophical, or political system that does not make *tawhid* its fountainhead. As a philosophical system, Islam stands against unbelief and atheism; as a political order, it stands against Western democracy and communism. Thus, radical fundamentalists like al-Mawdudi, Qutb, and al-Nadawi again make this distinction: either people follow divine method and system or they follow human method and system. The first group constitutes the virtuous society; the second group is the nonvirtuous, or the *jahili*.[53] Qutb is more philosophical on this issue and argues that, not only is there a close connection between the nature of any order and distinguishing doctrine and, consequently, between the political system and belief, but, more important, the former should be vitally produced by the latter. It is, therefore, useless to assume the existence of a social and political order without such a doctrine. Islam's main distinguishing doctrine is *tawhid;* Marxism's distinguishing doctrine is dialectical materialism. From this point of view, it seems to Qutb that there must be explicit or implicit concordance between the distinguishing doctrine and the social order.[54]

Of course, numerous fundamentalists—among them Rashid al-Ghannushi, the leader of al-Nahdah in Tunisia; Dr. Hasan al-Turabi in Sudan; Sheikh Muhammad Hussein Fadl Allah, the leader of Hizbullah in Lebanon; and even Hasan al-Banna—do argue for the adoption of democracy. But democracy to them includes not the doctrine of ultimate sovereignty but that of the exercise of power and human sovereignty. It manifests basically in elections, not in the belief that "the ultimate authority in political affairs belongs to the people." Ultimate sovereignty is only God's; humans' sovereignty is related to the exercise of power within the limits of *shariʿa*. This topic is discussed in chapter three.

Revolution

In the view of the fundamentalists, the change from a *jahili* state to a virtuous one requires a process capable of destroying and uprooting *jahiliyya*. It is nothing but a total revolution based on an Islamic *daʿwa* (call). One of the major facets of *jahiliyya* which must be confronted, according to the fundamentalists, is un-Islamic political developments.[55] Revolution is a moral and social duty; it is not restricted to fighting the enemies of Islam but is also embodied in political, ideological, and metaphysical dimensions. Thus, Islam is turned into a religion of revolution which covers all aspects of life and of metaphysics, ethics, politics, and economics; its discourse also becomes revolutionary. Hence, revolution is turned into a world claim justified by calling for comprehensive justice. The enormity of this responsibility leads the fundamentalists to adopt measures such as *jihad* (struggle) and *daʿwa*.[56]

Qutb argues that the mission of Islam is not to reconcile itself with paganist doctrines and realities; in fact, no reconciliation with paganism is possible. At the top of this paganism is human legislation for humans without divine sanctions. Islam's mission is, therefore, to establish a human life and to set up an earthly system according to Islamic law.[57] This is why radicals like Qutb, al-Mawdudi, al-Nadawi, and Yasin argue that *jihad* is launched in order to establish God's *uluhiyya* and to negate any other *uluhiyya*. Those individuals, institutions, or systems that stand against establishing God's *uluhiyya* are, therefore, aggressors against God; their removal becomes a must for fulfilling divine *hakimiyya* and *rububiyya* (lordship). The role of revolution is, then, to liberate humankind from the governments, societies, and systems that are structured on positive laws and legislation instead of on divine ones. The alternative must, therefore, be a pure and uncompromising Islamic government, society, and system.[58]

Although not all fundamentalists push such an exclusive attitude, one cannot but notice how such an attitude has affected Islamic fundamentalism, in general, in terms of its relations with the outside world. Hasan al-Banna, though not as radical as Qutb, argues that Islamic *jihad* is not a message of aggression and ambition but is sanctioned for the protection of *da'wa*, as a guarantee for peace, and as a fulfillment of the divine mission of justice and right.[59] This topic is also discussed in more detail in chapter three.

The practical agenda of radical fundamentalists like al-Nadawi, al-Mawdudi, Qutb, and al-Khumayni includes inducing such a change by the material and moral defense of the *umma*, annihilating any obstacle to Islamic *da'wa*, and establishing divine governance. Hence, every system based on unbelief and *taghut* (tyranny) must be destroyed; no justification of the status quo is allowed by radical fundamentalists. The radicals stress the importance of *tawhid* as a political doctrine and turn, like *al-Khawarij* (seceders) its fundamental formula, "no god but Allah," into a revolution against worldly authorities that apply their own laws and legislation.[60]

Ayatollah Khumayni, like Qutb and others, uses Qur'anic texts in order to make his point and argues that the Qur'an is full of descriptions such as *shirk* (polytheism) and *taghut* for those systems and governments that are not Islamic. Muslims are, therefore, responsible for eliminating them and for preparing the proper environment that enables a new, virtuous generation to destroy the thrones of tyrants. All Muslims, then, are obliged to bring about an Islamic political revolution.[61]

If *jihad*, as traditional Islamic jurisprudence views it, is the exertion of utmost efforts, it requires long-term actions that include scientific, industrial, and spiritual preparations. From a fundamentalist perspective, all this necessitates, in turn, an intellectual and mental revolution.[62] Al-Nadawi divides these preparations into, first, proper education about Islamic goals of Islam as opposed to *jahiliyya*, so that no confusion is entertained, and, second, cultivation of the scientific and technological power necessary to fight the *jahiliyya*.[63] Thus, adds Qutb, old concepts must not be reconciled with Islamic ones but must be abolished altogether. In the place of old concepts and societies, Islamic ones should emerge in order to execute Islamic law. Only by doing this can a Muslim society and an Islamic state emerge.[64] Replacing a Roman or Persian tyrant with an Arab one is not what paves the way for salvation, for tyranny is tyranny no matter what its nationality or religion. Only when "no god but God" is actualized can humanity be liberated.[65]

Justice

To fundamentalists like Qutb and al-Banna, the revolutionary role of Islam does not stop with the establishment of an Islamic state but extends to the realization of justice on the whole earth. Social, legal, and international justice must replace all existing kinds of injustice. Because Islam's target is humankind and the world, fundamentalists aim at spreading justice and providing security to all peoples and religions. This can take place only when Islam becomes the overall basis of an international order. From this point of view, fundamentalists make the doctrine to enjoin good and forbid evil (*al-amr bi al-ma'ruf wa al-nahay 'an al-munkar*) an Islamic duty that includes protecting the weak from injustice. Such moral idealism makes Islam clearly distinguishable from all other systems.[66] Al-Banna outlines this idealism using four characteristics: unwavering will, fixed commitment, great sacrifice, and correct knowledge of and belief in the truth. Every nation that enjoys these characteristics can set up a high civilization and renew itself, but the nation that lacks any of these characteristics is ultimately doomed to nothingness. Al-Banna makes this firm moral edge a condition for any future success, even for correct worship, and discounts the significance of sheer numbers. Weak morality then results in both material and political loss.[67]

However, al-Nadawi, Qutb, and al-Mawdudi want to reduce the fear of establishing an Islamic state by providing certain fundamental rights that might encourage other individuals and peoples to accept or, at least, to tolerate such a state. Thus, they argue that Islam provides humans as humans, regardless of their religion, with basic rights, such as life that cannot be taken away without due process. Also, for the same reasons, they call for developing good relations with other religions and the possibility of good cooperation.[68]

To do this, al-Nadawi, for instance, pictures the current affairs of the world very negatively and argues that current political ideologies that rule the world are more oppressive than those of the old religions that used to rule over empires. Newer ideologies are less tolerant of those who do not follow them; their political oppression is worse than that of the middle ages. If a national party or a group of people wins nowadays, it prevents the loser from any legitimate action and persecutes him as a matter of fact. Al-Nadawi cites the Spanish, Chinese, and Korean civil wars as examples to support his view. Islam, however, attempts to bring justice to humankind and to prevent exploitation.[69]

Al-Mawdudi portrays similar views and explains differences between an Islamic and a non-Islamic state. First of all, the Islamic state is not only an administration; it seeks to fulfill high ideals, including purity, goodness, success, and prosperity. Impartial justice, objective truth, and honesty are the bases of politics, whether between states or between individuals. Power is only a trust from God which is used for fulfilling obligation and establishing justice.[70]

To the fundamentalists, establishing justice requires peace, and maintaining peace requires the dominance of one group or state over the others. Although the fundamentalists do not picture it in this crude way, they nonetheless say the same thing. In fact, before world peace can be realized, peace must be found first in the individual, family, and society. The peace of the individual, which is the real seed of positive peace, gives the supreme power to the spiritual part of the human being to discipline desires and purify the soul. As such desires are balanced and controlled by spiritual yearnings, an equilibrium between the spiritual and the material is made. This peace extends to the family and becomes the focal point of love, mercy, and tranquility. In turn, the peace of the family constitutes a building block for a peaceful society.[71]

Al-Banna argues in his book *Al-Salam fi al-Islam* (Peace in Islam) that Islam holds the notion of the organic unity of humankind and preaches its call without distinction. Citing Qur'anic verses on the topic, he concludes that Islam does acknowledge distinctive differences among peoples, but these differences must be viewed as avenues for cooperation, not for enmity. Again, all religions are one in terms of origin, and the believers in holy books are saved. Using religion for disunity goes against the nature of religion; therefore, the mission of humankind is to be united by religion. Islam is described by al-Banna as the law of peace and the religion of mercy.[72]

Al-Mawdudi and Qutb argue that building societies on the principle of conflict is un-Islamic. Group dynamics should center around, interact with, and coexist within the framework of justice, harmony, development of standards of life, and, above all, divine guidance.[73] In a similar manner, the true peace of the world must revolve around the moral precepts of Islam, including justice. Islam's peaceful coexistence with others depends, then, on fulfilling basic conditions, foremost among which are freedom of worship, nonaggression against Muslims' propagation of their belief, removal of obstacles that stand against the *da'wa,* and realization of comprehensive justice. In the radical fundamentalist view, then, peace cannot be dealt with outside Islamic metaphysical foundations, such as *uluhiyya* and *tawhid,* its political bases, such as justice, equality, and freedom, and its social doctrines, such as balance, integration, and cooperation.[74]

Put differently, Islam's main goal, from the fundamentalist perspective, is the unity of races, peoples, and societies; its necessary concomitant principle is eliminating the multiplicity of systems, institutions, and sources of conflicts and confrontations, such as nationalism, patriotism, racism, ideologies, and economic interests.[75] However, the fundamentalists differ among themselves as to the methods of achieving such goals. Some, like Qutb and al-Mawdudi, tend toward radicalism, while others, like al-Banna and al-Ghannushi, are inclined toward compromise and moderation. Further discussion of these differences follows in chapter three.

Conclusion

Obviously, the fundamentalist discourses on knowledge and political philosophy show a comprehensive framework of knowledge as well as problematic constructions. While to the fundamentalists, *fitra* is the source of knowledge and is used as a yardstick, it is still beyond definition. While it may look like the Cartesian intuition and, thus, appear individual, its power is weakened by the circularity of the argument. Human nature is the instrument of attaining the truth; humans' rationalism may corrupt their true nature.

Again, like Descartes, who created a dichotomy between mind and body, the fundamentalist discourses are similarly loaded with intellectual and political dichotomies. The first manifests itself in the duality between the old and original knowledge based on the Qur'an and the new and modern knowledge based on human experience. The fundamentalists first establish their discourses on the unity of knowledge and nature as having a fixed essence, independent of reason. This view makes knowledge substantive and objective and constitutes the old part of their discourse. Its opposite, the new, manifests in their belief that human knowledge cannot extend to the true essence, because human thought is tightly linked to its historical conditions. Human knowledge is subjective, cannot be absolute, and might be, at times, erroneous. If this idea is applied to the fundamentalist discourses, they are, themselves, historically developed and lack the normative status.

But how could fundamentalist discourses legitimately be used to evaluate the discourses of others, which are also historically developed and, therefore, can claim equal standing to the fundamentalist discourses? There is no solid answer to this. New interpretations of Qur'anic and *sunna* texts that are used by the fundamentalists to deny the validity of other ideological and philosophical views might be used as well by all parties to justify this position or its opposite. A particular textual interpretation, then, is in need of an exterior justification—not the text itself or the *fitra* that might be corrupted. Modern science and even technology, which are used to modernize interpretations of the sacred text, are also disqualified to be the pivotal underpinning of any discourse, because, while true in themselves, they are human products and cannot provide ultimate interpretative legitimacy to any discourse. The fundamentalists sound postmodern when discounting the finality of any interpretation and when doubting the methodological certainty of rationalism, empiricism, positivism, historicism, and even the traditional Islamic methods of jurisprudence, theology and linguistics. The Muslims are then left with a self-justifying text that stands on its own.

This dichotomy spills over into another duality between religion and science. Religion postulates permanent and unchangeable principles; science develops contemporary and changeable principles about the needs of society without epistemological claims. Consequently, the sciences, including history, do not play any normative role in formatting fundamentalist thought because no historically developed process can assume a normative role—except that of the Prophet and the four rightly guided caliphs. The latter exception is weakly argued, however. Again, it is based upon the close historical proximity or interaction between the caliphs and the Prophet. Simply, the normative role is the result of history as well as textual quotations from the *sunna*. Besides this connection, there are not many rational grounds for justifying this exceptional age of normative construction, not only of philosophical views but also of political doctrines, such as *shura*, election, *ijma*, and so forth, which will be taken up later.

In political philosophy, the fundamentalists also developed the need for setting up a new society on new thought while insisting on Islamizing every social or political theory. Although the fundamentalists reject the traditional modes of understanding entertained by the public and the elites, as shown in the methods of theology, philosophy, sufism, and jurisprudence, they insist on the validity of the Qur'an and the *sunna* as the source materials for a comprehensive Islamic revival. While democracy is accepted by major fundamentalist political movements, it is, however, turned into either an operational activity of election and referendum or an Islamic *shura*. (For more discussion, see the chapters on al-Banna, Qutb, and al-Turabi, in particular.)

On yet another level, Islam is presented as the alternative to all other systems and as the only ideology to be used to renew local, regional, and international behaviors, both morally and politically. This view has, however, obscured the vision of some major fundamentalist thinkers on how to deal practically with existing institutions and regimes. In fact, their view of the necessity to transcend space and time has led to idealistic postures preventing meaningful interactions with realities.

All of this leads to the fourth and last dichotomy presented here. Although *tawhid* is profoundly a unifying doctrine in principle, in practice it may lead to duality. In the view of many fundamentalists—with notable exceptions like al-Banna and al-Ghannushi—the world is divided into *dar al-Islam* (the realm of Islam) and *dar al-harb* (the realm of war). Chapter three treats this topic in more detail.

3

Fundamentalist Discourses on Politics

From Pluralistic Democracy to Majoritarian Tyranny

Islam's appropriateness to pluralism and democracy is of major interest to Western scholars and politicians as well as to Muslims, in general, including the fundamentalists. The possibility of combining modern Islamic thought with democracy and pluralism seems to be a rising and controversial topic, as quite a few Muslim fundamentalist thinkers have been introducing democracy and pluralism into Islamic thought. In the Islamic world, the quest for democracy and pluralism is very apparent: a substantial number of political and intellectual conferences were held to study the possible ways to democratize and liberalize politics, society, and thought. A majority of fundamentalist theoreticians are now engaged in the Islamization of democracy and pluralism. They argue that social and political tyranny and oppression are the main catalysts for defeat and underdevelopment of the Islamic world and are detrimental to the rise of Islam.

The disintegration of the Soviet Union added to the urgency of establishing democracy, upholding human rights, and accepting pluralism. Secular and fundamentalist thinkers, alike, attribute the unhealthy and harsh conditions of economic, social, and political life to the absence of democracy and pluralism. A new political process, which stresses the importance of political democratization and liberalization, is on the rise and is entertained in the media, conferences, universities, and other institutions. A few conferences—such as those held in Morocco in 1981 on the Democratic Experience in the Arab World, in 1983 in Cyprus on the Crisis of Democracy in the Arab World, and in Amman in 1989 to discuss Political Pluralism and Democracy in the Arab World—show clearly the emerging interest in democracy and pluralism. Other conferences have taken place, and many studies have been conducted on the same issues.[1]

Nevertheless, the West, in general, has focused primarily on Islamic fundamentalist dangers, without taking into consideration the oppressive nature of most Middle Eastern regimes and political discussions over democracy and pluralism. Sensational titles in magazines and newspapers—such as "Will Democracy Survive in Egypt?" or "The Arab World Where Troubles for the U.S. Never End" or "The Clash of Civilizations"—have further frightened and pushed the West away from the East. While quite a few Western academics concerned with the Middle East deal with the real concerns of the Arab people, the West prefers to look at these concerns as being negligible insofar as they are indigenously developed.[2] However, current events in the Muslim world, particularly in Egypt, Algeria, Tunisia, and the Sudan, have produced political and academic discussions on the compatibility of Muslim fundamentalist discourses, especially the doctrines of an Islamic state, with democracy, human rights, and pluralism as well as with the emerging world order.

This chapter aims at highlighting some of the important debates that have been going on in modern Islamic fundamentalist discourses about democracy and pluralism. It argues that, while a majority of Western media and scholars, along with a majority of their Middle Eastern counterparts, treat fundamentalism as exclusivist by its nature and definition, and while a few widely publicized fundamentalist groups are truly exclusivist and adhere to the notion of change through radical programs and uncompromising revolutions, most mainstream and major fundamentalist groups are pluralistic, democratic, and inclusivist, indeed. The origins of exclusion are neither Islamic metaphysical perceptions of the universe nor abstract interpretations of some theological doctrines of Islam. Furthermore, exclusion is not limited to Islamic fundamentalist groups; it includes the champions of the new and the old world orders. Only with Islamic fundamentalism, however, is the doctrine of exclusion transformed into a part of a new Islamic theology of metaphysical perceptions and abstract doctrines of belief.

Islamic fundamentalism is actually an umbrella term for a wide range of discourses and activism which tends to move from a high level of moderate pluralism, and thus inclusive democracy, to extreme radicalism, intolerant unitarianism, and thus exclusive majority rule.

While some fundamentalist groups are pluralistic in terms of inter-Muslim relations and relations between Muslims and minorities, others are not. Again, while some fundamentalists are politically pluralistic but theologically exclusive, others are accommodating religiously but direct their exclusivist programs to the outside, the West, or imperialism. Even at the scientific level, Western science and technology are argued for by some fundamentalists as Islamically sound, while others exclude them because of their presumed un-Islamic nature. More important, while most fundamentalists call for pluralistic democracy and argue for it as an essentially Islamic point of view, the radicals brand it as unbelief.

Why then do the fundamentalists, given their agreement on the usage of the fundamentals of religion, the Qur'an and the *sunna*, as well as a philosophical and political framework, have these basic and substantive divergent views? The answer (which will be elaborated later in the chapter) is that the inclusive democratic and exclusive authoritarian policies of most Middle Eastern states, along with international powers, reinforce and, in fact, create that dual nature of fundamentalist political thought and behavior. While Arab regimes hold the international order responsible for harsh situations that they put themselves into, the fundamentalists attribute economic, social, and political failures of the states to the regimes, themselves. They view these regimes as conductors of multilayered conflicts between the dominant world powers against the ambitions and hopes of indigenous populations—in this case, the Muslims and their most vibrant spokesmen, the fundamentalists.

Fundamentalists, in general, believe that their governments do not serve the ideological, political, or economic interests of their peoples but serve, instead, those of the dominant world powers. Imperialism, colonialism, exploitation, materialism—all of these are charges brought against the West. Liberalization, whether economic, political, or cultural, as well as social justice, political freedom, and democracy are major demands of both radical and moderate fundamentalist groups. Modern national states have been considered by fundamentalists as the link between what is unacceptable and inhumane in both Western and Eastern civilizations: Western materialism and Eastern despotism. An Islamic state, they believe, can withstand and even correct Western materialistic domination and Eastern political authoritarianism. This notwithstanding, the way a fundamentalist theoretician or movement creates its discourse and argues for the active method of setting up that state, the manner of conducting politics therein, and the basic ideology of the state can provide us with leads to classify any theoretician or movement as exclusivist, nonliberal, and a radical antagonist of pluralistic democracy, or as inclusivist, liberal, and a moderate protagonist of pluralistic democracy.

This chapter, then, seeks to answer two basic questions. First, what are the conditions that make a fundamentalist theoretician and movement develop a discourse on, or reject ideological and political doctrines of, pluralistic democracy? Second, what is the role of comparable inclusive or exclusive policies of Middle Eastern states, as well as the international order, in reinforcing one doctrine or another? The first part of this chapter contextualizes at length some general academic and political discussions on inclusion and exclusion, and pluralism and democracy, in the West (particularly in the United States) and in the Arab world (particularly in Egypt). The second part of the chapter deals with the theoretical foundations and development of inclusion, exclusion, pluralism, and democracy, with references to the more comprehensive political framework that was elaborated earlier. Then the inclusivist and pluralist discourse of the still most profound fundamentalist movement, that of the Muslim Brotherhood in Egypt, is explicated. This discourse, however, has become the basis for two contradictory discourses: one that is radical, antiliberal, exclusivist, and militant, and the other that is moderate, liberal, inclusivist, and nonmilitant. The chapter shows further why the liberal development of the inclusivist discourse of Hasan al-Banna and the Muslim Brethren was not possible under the governments of ʿAbd al-Nasir's regime and those of his successors, and why it was more logical that this discourse was transformed into an exclusivist fundamentalist discourse, of which the most exclusive is that of Sayyid Qutb and the theoreticians who followed him and set up armed radical groups.

I argue that the development of the radical discourse originated in a reaction to the political, economic, and international conditions of Egypt and its method of handling basic issues like freedom, social justice, and religion. However, the radical discourse nowadays cannot be understood only in terms of its origins; it has become a theology of politics that stands on its own. The chapter concludes with a theoretical assessment on the future of the ongoing dialectics of pluralism and democracy.

The World, Pluralism, and Democracy

Both fundamentalist theoreticians and activists, in addition to Muslim and Western academic and press circles, have discussed the issues of exclusion, liberalism, and democracy under liberal democracy. Timothy Sisk outlines the basic interests of the West with the rise of fundamentalist Islam. He asks, "How, and if and when, can pluralism and democratic institutions survive, compatibly with the rising tide of Islamic fundamentalism?"[3] He places fundamentalism in its global, comparative context and views it as a world phenomenon. He also separates tendencies toward liberalism and democracy into two categories: a progressive, fundamentalist view that accepts liberal democracy, and a nonliberal fundamentalist view that seeks social justice, though not in direct conflict with democracy.

In *New Perspective Quarterly,* the whole issue of pluralism and tolerance is discussed under sensational titles that make the reader shy away from reading the articles on Islam. Thus, for instance, who wants to travel "From Beirut to Sarajevo" to fight "Against Cultural Terrorism" or to witness "When Galileo Meets Allah"?[4] However, the editor of the journal puts his concern this way:

> Islam, alone in a plural world, remains monotheistic in faith as well as, in many places, in practice. In today's globalized cultural space, Islam will inevitably be faced with a host of challenges that will pit "the word" not only against the mere language of Western literature, like Salman Rushdie's novel, but also against nondogmatic beliefs, for example, Hinduism, to say nothing of the radically freestyle tolerance of Europe and America that so riles the mullahs. *Faced with these challenges, will Islam turn toward pluralism and the West back toward faith?* [emphasis added].[5]

The answer came from Akbar S. Ahmad. He argues that only one civilization, Islam, will stand firm in its path. The Muslim world provides a global view with a potential alternative role on the world stage. Islam seems to be set on a collision course with the Western world. While the West is based on secular materialism, the scientific reason of modernity, and the absence of moral philosophy, Islam, argues Ahmad, is based on faith, patience, pace, and equilibrium. He draws a picture of nonconciliation between Islam and the West; it is "a straight-out fight between two approaches to the world, two opposed philosophies."[6]

Ahmad's exclusionary view of civilizations is not just Islamic but also has its equivalence among prominent Western intellectuals such as Samuel Huntington, who argues that the future will witness a clash of civilizations. In his "Islamic-Confucian Connection" as well as his more celebrated article, "The Clash of Civilizations," he considers the conflicts that have taken place since the peace of Westphalia in 1648 up through the Cold War as "Western civil wars." Now the "cultural division of Europe among Western Christianity, Orthodox Christianity and Islam has re-emerged."[7] Disregarding any differences in interpreting Islam as well as in its historical schools and modern, diverse tendencies in religion and politics, Huntington—who served at the White House on the National Security Council under President Carter and witnessed the collapse of the Iranian regime under the Shah and the establishment of an Islamic state—proclaims that Islam is

> a militant religion in which there is no distinction between what is religious and what is secular. The idea of "render unto Caesar what is Caesar's, render unto God what is God's" is totally antithetical to Islam. This theocratic proclivity makes it extraordinarily difficult for Islamic societies to accommodate non-Muslims. It makes it very difficult for Muslims to easily fit into societies where the majority is non-Muslim.[8]

In addition to showing very little knowledge of Islamic history and philosophy, Huntington disregards the comparison of Islam with other religions, which, though they look at politics and religion as Islam does, are nonetheless included into the Western culture but not the Eastern. Although Judaism, for instance, is more like Islam than like Christianity, it has been nonetheless included, accepted, and incorporated into Western culture. Until recently the West excluded and persecuted Jews politically and culturally, with Zionism being a direct consequence. In fact, exclusion was often mutual; that is, many Jews did not want to be assimilated by Western culture. Particularly after Hitler, "anti-Semitism" became a term of opprobrium in the West, and Zionist propaganda gave added impetus to this interpretation. Protestant America (as opposed to the Vatican), with its emphasis on the Old Testament as an integral part of the Bible, was potentially very receptive to Zionism.

In general, the Islamic world has been included, but only negatively—that is, by military force employed by the colonial powers in the past, and now by dominant world powers that use the threat of economic sanctions and sophisticated weaponry. Why, then, do these powers not try to include the Islamic world economically, morally, and philosophically, especially if one of the features that distinguishes the West is its inclusive pluralism? Or is non-Islamicity of Muslims the condition for their being included?

Judith Miller advocates a nondemocratic, exclusivist attitude toward the Muslim world, since Islam is incompatible with the values of pluralism, democracy, and human rights. This means that Western policy makers should not support democratic elections, since they might bring radical Islamic fundamentalists to power. She exhorts the American administration and others to reject any sort of conciliation with, or inclusion of, radical, political Islam, because "Western governments should be concerned about these movements and, more important, should oppose them. For despite their rhetorical commitment to democracy and pluralism, virtually all militant fundamentalists oppose both. They are, and are likely to remain, anti-Western, anti-American, and anti-Israeli."

Miller further rejects any distinction between good and bad fundamentalists. Accepting Martin Kramer's idea that militant Islamic groups are incompatible with democracy, since they cannot be by nature "democratic, pluralistic, egalitarian or pro-Western," and Bernard Lewis's argument that liberal democracy and Islam are not bedfellows, Miller concludes (along with Lewis) that autocracy is the norm and postulates that "Islamic militancy presents the West with a paradox. While liberals speak of the need for diversity with equality, fundamentalists see this as a sign of weakness. Liberalism tends not to teach its proponents to fight effectively. What is needed, rather, is almost a contradiction in terms: a liberal militancy, or a militant liberalism that is unapologetic and unabashed.[9]

Fortunately, not all American thinkers, policy makers, and diplomats think similarly. Edward Djerejian, former assistant Secretary of State and U.S. ambassador to Syria and Israel, puts the matter differently. He states that "the U.S. government, however, does not view

Islam as the next 'ism' confronting the West or threatening world peace. That is an overly simplistic response to a complex reality." He goes on to say that

> The Cold War is not being replaced with a new competition between Islam and the West. It is evident that the Crusades have been over for a long time. Indeed, the ecumenical movement is the contemporary trend. Americans recognize Islam as one of the world's great faiths. It is practiced on every continent. It counts among its adherents millions of citizens of the U.S. As Westerners we acknowledge Islam as a historic civilizing force among the many that have influenced and enriched our culture. The legacy of the Muslim culture, which reached the Iberian Peninsula in the 8th century, is a rich one in the sciences, arts, and culture and in tolerance of Judaism and Christianity. Islam acknowledges the major figures of Judeo-Christian heritage: Abraham, Moses, and Christ.[10]

The United States differs, according to Djerejian, with those groups that are insensitive to political pluralism, "who substitute religious and political confrontation with engagement with the rest of the world" and who do not accept the peaceful resolution of the Arab-Israeli conflict and pursue their goals through repression.[11]

Some scholars on the Middle East and the Islamic world go beyond this general statement. Augustus R. Norton, in his "Inclusion Can Deflate Islamic Populism," argues that democracy and Islam are not incompatible, since democracy is the demand of the people of the area to be included in the political system. While skeptics deny the usefulness of democracy for the people because the regimes are inefficient and suffer from legitimacy claims and the fundamentalist political movements are anti-Western, anti-Israeli, and antidemocratic, Norton pins down the claims against the skeptics by saying that "to argue that popular political players are irremediably intransigent and therefore unmoved by tenets in the real world is, at best, naive and, at worst, racist. . . . So long as the fundamentalist movements are given no voice in politics, there can be no surprise that their rhetoric will be shrill and their stance uncompromising. In contrast, well-designed strategies of political inclusion hold great promise for facilitating essential political change."[12] Norton concludes his article with a sober reflection: "The rulers have no intention of stepping aside, but they must be encouraged to widen the political stage and to open avenues for real participation in politics. For the West, and especially the United States, the issues are complex and vexing, but the basic choice is simple: construct policies that emphasize and widen the cultural barriers that divide the Middle East from the West, or pursue policies that surmount the barriers."[13]

William Zartman argues that the two currents of political Islam and democracy are not necessarily incompatible. The Qur'an might be interpreted to support different political behaviors. A synthesis might emerge between Islam and democracy where constitutional checks can be employed. He suggests five measures to democratize and make sure that democracy will triumph, including: "Practice the forms of democracy whenever scheduled, let the most popular win, and let them learn democracy on the job."[14] In "Democratization and Islam," John Esposito and James Piscatori argue that the process of liberalization and democratization in the Muslim world requires, as it did in the West, a process of reinterpretation of the divine texts. While Islam lends itself to different interpretations, some important fundamentalist thinkers have already started the process of accommodating Islam with democracy and liberalism[15]—itself an inclusionary process.

While the above discussion indicates the existence and emergence of a fundamentalist tendency to include some principles of Western civilization—such as liberalism and democratization, as well as a free economic system, which in themselves represent features of an inclusionary mentality of political Islam—it also shows that there is a major and influential tendency among Western politicians and scholars alike to reject, on the one hand, Islamization of democracy and liberalism and, on the other hand, to insist on the Westernization of raw materials and markets under the pretext of national security or the clash of civilizations. The same tendency that stands opposed to the ascendancy of fundamentalism through democracy, because of the assumed fundamentalist authoritarian nature, supports authoritarian regimes for the sake of maintaining a nonexistent democracy— an indication of an exclusionary attitude and intolerance directed at Islam under the guise of fundamentalism and a sign of a twisted logical structure.

It seems so far that most international and regional actors have a vested interest in pushing away fundamentalists from any legitimate role in internal, regional, or international affairs. The argument against the fundamentalists outlined above has its counterpart in the Middle East. In "Liberalization and Democracy in the Arab World," Gudrun Kramer shows why Arab regimes are not yet ready for democracy. However, democracy is now one of the common themes among political movements and differs in nature and extent from one movement to another, ranging from the adoption of a liberal, pluralistic, Western model to that of "an Islamic model of participation qua consultation." However, the two movements "converge on the issues of human rights and political participation." And although some regimes have adopted certain classic mechanisms to liberalize and democratize, such as the *infitah* (open-door policy) and the multiparty system in Egypt, the limitations are nonetheless classic, as well. Kramer points out that "formal constraints also limit the scope of legitimate political expression and action, usually a party law restricting the bases of party formation and a national charter defining the common and inviolable intellectual and political ground." Thus, for instance, the moderate Muslim Brethren in Egypt are not allowed legally to form a party but, nevertheless, are allowed by the regime to participate informally. Kramer goes on to say that "even an Islamic political order may be able to incorporate Western notions of political participation and human rights." Furthermore, "liberalization," she adds, "will inevitably give more room for maneuvering to political actors critical of the West and openly hostile towards Israel. While the public demands a greater distance from the West and a tough stand vis-a-vis Israel, the socioeconomic crisis intensifies dependence on Western governments and international agencies."[16]

The Arab regimes are no longer capable of relying on repression. What supports this argument is that the Egyptian government has decided to counterattack intellectually against the current tide of political Islam by having the General Egyptian Institute for Books publish a series of books under the general title "Confrontation," or *al-Muwajaha*. The series focuses on republishing books of scholars and intellectuals that have in common the goal of refuting the doctrines of radical groups by using the moderate religious and political thought prevalent in Egypt in the late nineteenth and early twentieth centuries—such as those of Jamal al-Din al-Afghani, Muhammad 'Abduh, 'Ali 'Abd al-Raziq, Taha Hussein, 'Abbas al-'Aqqad, and others. The specific objectives are outlined in the following points:

- to circulate the opinions of the pioneers of "enlightenment" (*al-tanwir*)

- to positively focus on the moderate views of Islam

- to refute the radical ideas in relation to Islam's view of govern ment and state and the application of the shari'a.[17]

However, this intellectual governmental activity is only a belated and subsidiary supplement to the doctrine of confronting the fundamentalists—that is, the "security confrontation" doctrine that has been adopted officially by the Arab and Foreign Affairs Committee of Majlis al-Shura, the highest judiciary council in Egypt. The solution, to be developed through the consolidation of security apparatuses, comes first and foremost; it is followed by a religious confrontation that should be launched by the religious officialdom, and, finally and most surprisingly, the legislature must produce a state-of-the-art law against terrorism. But no substantial mention is made of rectifying the severe economic conditions of poverty, loosening political manipulations through liberalization and democratization, or respecting human rights. When the report of the Committee suggests paying greater attention to the social development of poor rural and isolated areas, with special focus on the youth, the objective is to control the hotbed of fundamentalists. The committee also proposes a further supplement to the law, already passed by the Egyptian parliament, restricting the multiplicity of professional unions and the communication of local parties with foreign parties without official permission.[18]

The religious confrontation, led by the late Sheikh al-Azhar, seems to give credit to the measures taken by the government and also to provide indirect legitimacy to political Islam, in addition to weakening the modernist and secular tendencies in Egypt. In a long interview, Sheikh Jad al-Haq Jad al-Haq categorically rejects the separation of the state from Islam. He argues that Islam is made up of *din wa dunya,* or, loosely translated, both a religion and a way of life— basically identical to fundamentalist interpretation. Prophet Muhammad did not differentiate between the political and the religious. Again, the ruler should be appointed by *shura* (consultation), which may be conducted through different methods and technologies. After accepting the ideology of the Muslim Brotherhood as being Islamic, Jad al-Haq objects only to the use of violence by some radical groups. However, the Azhar considers the Egyptian government's policies as Islamic and defends its actions against criticisms by radical and moderate fundamentalist groups.

In 1994 Sheikh Jad al-Haq convened the first General Conference for those shaykhs in charge of official mosques for the specific objective of counterbalancing the activities of radical groups. Fifteen hundred shaykhs attended the conference and participated in its sessions along with, very interestingly, the ministers of foreign affairs, interior, religious endowments, information, housing, and agriculture. The interior minister emphasized the organic link between the security confrontation and the religious one through the collaboration between the mosques and the media to curb terrorism. The information minister affirmed that the media had plans to uncover terrorism but that these plans depended on the true explanation of Islam. While refusing to lift media censorship and to license private television stations, he affirmed the role of the Azhar as an "information authority" to confront "foreign fundamentalist" dangers. An information revolution has been going on, especially now since fundamentalists outside Egypt correspond with those in Egypt by fax.[19]

The Azhar plays—with the tacit approval of the government—the role of a modern court of inquisition. Naguib Mahfouz, a Nobel Prize winner, has announced his readiness to rescind his book, *Awlad Haritna* (The children of our neighborhood) if the Azhar convinces him that it contains any blasphemous remark against Islam. Although Ri'aft al-Sa'id, a secular, leftist intellectual, condemns the fundamentalists for banning the book—in fact it was banned thirty-four years ago by the Azhar under Nasir's presidency—he asks the government to face "the terrorists" not only by security measures but also by curbing their media. As one of the "enlightened thinkers"—a term used by Sa'id to describe himself and his intellectual colleagues—he calls for the suppression of whatever media freedom is left to Islamic thinkers, because radicalism starts initially as an idea.[20] This overlooks the fact that inclusion, tolerance, pluralism, and democracy also started as ideas.

The case of an associate professor at Cairo University, Nasr Hamid Abu Zayd, who was not promoted to the rank of professor but was brought to a secular—not a fundamentalist—court in Egypt because of his heterodox views, shows how the government fights not only the intellectual "terrors" of fundamentalism but also those of modernism. Because he has been convicted of the charge brought against him, he is considered an apostate who should be separated from his wife. The charge focused on his books, which showed "animosity to the texts of the Qur'an and the *sunna*," "non-belief," and "recanting Islam."[21]

While the government uses its legal apparatus to exclude major modernist figures and trends, it also uses this apparatus to exclude moderate fundamentalism. An Egyptian newspaper, *al-Sha'b*, published an article on capital punishment, stating that the Egyptian government has moved from civil and penal law to emergency laws. This allowed employing the "iron fist" policy to contain fundamentalists. During the Mubarak presidency, from 1981 until 1993, the policy resulted in the political execution of forty-eight individuals, almost double the number (twenty-seven) of those who were executed for similar political reasons during a whole century in Egypt, extending from 1882 until 1981, including both the Nasir and Sadat presidencies. In 1995, the number went up to fifty-eight.[22]

A member of the parliament stated in a parliamentary session that Egypt lives on the margin of democracy, for democracy means the peaceful and voluntary handover of power, a feature that does not exist today. The state minister for parliamentary affairs responded by saying that it is unbelievable that the parliamentarians should talk about the succession of power, because elections—not governmental decrees—bring about political authority. Of course, the minister insulted the intelligence of the parliamentarians with this remark. The party that receives the highest votes becomes the ruling party, he added. It is well known, however, that the truth is otherwise: the ruling party gets the highest votes. This notwithstanding, both officials forget, for instance, that one of the most popular movements, the Muslim Brotherhood, is excluded from official representation in government, parliament, or party systems, although at times it is tolerated when running under the labels of other parties.[23]

When the Egyptian government wanted to conduct a national dialogue, it basically launched a conference with itself. Thus, twenty-six of the forty individuals who were appointed by President Mubarak as a preparatory committee to set the agenda for the conference on political dialogue were from the ruling party, al-Hizb al-Watani. Worse than this, 237 out of the 279 conferees were from the ruling party; major political blocs were excluded. Though one might understand the exclusion of the radical groups that rejected inclusionary policies, one cannot really understand the government's exclusionary policies toward the Muslim Brotherhood, which has exhibited both intellectually and politically inclusionary tendencies through its accepting pluralism and democracy as well as the legitimacy of the regime.

So who is dialoguing with whom? The Muslim Brotherhood sought to be included in the much-publicized national dialogue during 1994. While the government refused the official representation of the Muslim Brotherhood in that dialogue, nevertheless the Brotherhood tried to be included through its unofficial representatives in professional unions, such as lawyers, medical doctors, and engineers. The Muslim Brotherhood's view on the dialogue can be represented by what Ahmad Sayf al-Islam Hasan al-Banna, the general secretary of the Lawyers' Union and Hasan al-Banna's son, said about the organization's willingness to participate in the political dialogue if the government were to include it. Later on, the government rejected its participation and pressured political parties to disassociate themselves from the Brotherhood. The Brotherhood's view was that, though excluded as a political party, it could still be included as a representative of civil society. Instead, the government resorted to the repression of the Brotherhood in sweeping security measures that resulted in the death of a pro-Ikhwan (Muslim Brotherhood) lawyer while under arrest, an act that produced a strike by the Lawyers' Union and direct confrontation with security forces in 1994.[24]

Ma'mun al-Hudaybi, the spokesman for the Egyptian Muslim Brotherhood, said in an interview that excluding the Muslim Brotherhood from the dialogue along with independent fundamentalist thinkers such as Muhammad al-Ghazali was an example of excluding those who did not adopt or conform to governmental views. While the government does permit some thinkers to attack religion, it does not allow any open criticism to be directed at slanderers. He characterized the cause for violence in Egypt as being the result of governmental policies of exclusion. Excluded from peaceful participation in political and public affairs, some groups were bound to be turned into radicals, because of the closed-door policy. He expressed the Brethren's opinion that they were oppressed because of a governmental prohibition on holding public meetings, an act considered by the government as a mutiny against the state.[25]

Following the same line of reasoning, Muhammad Salim al-'Awwa, a moderate fundamentalist thinker, lawyer, and university professor, explains the problem of exclusion: the government imposed novel kinds of laws—such as the law against terrorism, emergency laws, the law of shame (al-'ayb), the values court (for the violation of social norms), and so on—in order to cripple society from moving ahead. Again, political parties in the Arab world have been of two sorts: governmental parties that were made by and serve the government but did not represent the majority, even when claiming to do so; and other kinds of parties, which may be unlicensed, such as Egypt's Muslim Brotherhood, or recognized by the government, such as the Muslim Brotherhood in Jordan. The second kind should be encouraged and allowed to be represented in political institutions. However, this was not the case.

Would the establishment of a recognized fundamentalist party in Egypt resolve the problem of radicalism? 'Adil al-Jawjari argues that the concept of *shura* provides the Islamic movement with the method that allows for peaceful coexistence between the government and an Islamic party. The alternative to radicalism must be a party where fundamentalists can vent their grievances and participate in the political life of Egypt. The containment policy that is being imposed from above by the government has proved its futility, and the only meaningful and peaceful solution is establishing a legal fundamentalist party where the rights of minorities, political pluralism, and other essential issues become part of the party's constitution.[26]

Although the Muslim Brotherhood published a manifesto in Islamabad—not in Cairo, because the Brotherhood's name cannot be undersigned publicly in Egypt—condemning violence and terrorism, which has been its proclaimed public policy anyway, it seems now that neither dialogue nor political life is developing or leading to any real, positive change. The Muslim Brotherhood is being further excluded from normal public life, and the likelihood for its inclusion in the public political life with the current regime seems impossible. It might be appropriate here to cite a few articles of the manifesto:

· The Brotherhood affirms its stand to condemn any sort or source of violence and affirms the need to put an end to it. The Qur'an calls on people to use wisdom in propagating God's path.

- The Brotherhood condemns using revenge and vendetta and calls for implementing the *shari'a* that prohibits bloodshed and maintains honor in addition to the sacred things that people cherish.

- The Brotherhood adds its voice to all those who want to see a real end to violence. The Brotherhood declares that any solution that does not include real popular participation is defective.

- Restrictions on popular participation in politics should be lifted, and freedom of party formation and expression of all political forces should be permitted in order to achieve comprehensive social, economic, and political reforms.

- All popular and political forces are required to stand united together in order to extricate themselves from the vicious circle of violence and seek real reforms that fulfill people's hopes.[27]

Fundamentalist Discourses on Pluralism and Democracy

Inclusivist Discourses

The ideological and political discourse of the Muslim Brotherhood's founder and first supreme guide in Egypt, Hasan al-Banna, lays down the bases of inclusionary views of the theological and political doctrine of God's governance, or *hakimiyya*. While it has been used at times, both historically and presently, to exclude whatever is considered un-Islamic and, for some, even non-Islamic, al-Banna transforms it into a source of both legitimacy and compromise. This feature has been followed and developed, more or less, by the majority of moderate, fundamentalist, political movements. Taking into account the circumstances of Egyptian society during the first half of this century, and given the relative freedom that the Egyptians had therein, the question of a forceful seizure of power was not on the agenda of the Brotherhood. Although interested in the Islamization of government, state, and society, al-Banna aimed essentially to be included in the then-existing political order and competed as well with other political parties.

His call for inclusion was not a fabricated slogan but was applied, indeed. Al-Banna, himself, ran twice in elections along with his party, the Brotherhood. Some of the Brotherhood's founding members were simultaneously members of other political parties; the same applies to contemporary Brethren. The peaceful involvement of the Muslim Brotherhood in Egypt's political life is well documented. The Brotherhood was involved in the struggle of the Azhar during the twenties and thirties and sided as well with the king against the government. During that period, al-Banna cooperated at times with Isma'il Sidqi, the on-and-off prime minister, and was engaged in teaching and lecturing. The Brotherhood built its headquarters from voluntary donations, after which it built a mosque and schools for boys and girls. In 1946, the government provided financial aid, free books, and stationery to the Brotherhood schools, with the ministry of education having paid all their educational and administrative expenses. Al-Banna also established holding companies for schools, and this became a success since most of the Brotherhood's membership was composed of middle-class professionals and businessmen. Only a year after the establishment of the Brotherhood in Cairo, it had fifty branches all over Egypt. Worried about the spread of Christian missionary schools in Egypt, the Brotherhood called on King Faruq to subject this activity to state supervision. But after a meeting with a priest in one of the churches, al-Banna wrote that men of religion should unite against atheism. During the same year, the Brotherhood decided to set up a press and publish a weekly journal, *al-Ikhwan al-Muslimun*.[28]

Al-Banna also included boy scouts in his organization. The scouts' pledge was essentially of a moral tone, not political or revolutionary but rather centered around faith, virtue, work, and the family. Al-Banna never denied that the Brotherhood was a movement that sought the revival of religion and had its own political, educational, and economic aspirations. This did not mean, however, that the Brotherhood would isolate itself from society. In 1936, the Brotherhood participated, for instance, in the coronation of King al-Awwal Faruq. During 1948, the membership of its scouts exceeded 40,000 and had spread by then all over Egypt, working to eliminate illiteracy and cholera and malaria epidemics. By 1948, the Brotherhood had set up five hundred branches for social services and had established medical clinics and hospitals and treated about 51,000 patients. Al-Banna also set up a women's organization in the forties, whose membership in 1948 reached five thousand—a high number according to the standards of the time. It played a central role during what is referred to as *al-mihna al-ula* (first ordeal) during the years 1948–50, when it catered to the families of the thousands of Brethren in jail. The active membership of the Brotherhood was around half a million, and the supporters another half million; by the time of its dissolution, there were one thousand branches in Egypt.[29]

In politics, the Brotherhood did not originally resort to violence but played the game as long as it was allowed to do so, turning to violence only when this became prevalent in political life. It was not only the Brotherhood that established secret apparatuses, but these apparatuses were a common denominator with other parties as well as with the state, which used political assassination to resolve many problems. This violence manifested itself against the Brethren in the assassination of al-Banna, the jailing of thousands of the membership, the dissolution of the organization, and the liquidation of its assets.

Until this point, the Brotherhood had played by the rules. More important, the Brotherhood has always accepted the legitimacy of the existing regime, and al-Banna described King Faruq as the legitimate ruler. Al-Banna developed his organization into a political party with a specific political agenda in order to compete with other parties that were, in his opinion, corrupt. In 1942, al-Banna along with other Brethren ran for election, but the prime minister at the time persuaded him to withdraw. In exchange, he was supposed to receive more freedom for his organization and a promise from the government to shut down liquor stores and prohibit prostitution. Later that year, Premier Mustafa al-Nahhas, however, closed down all of the Brotherhood branches except its headquarters. Again in 1945, al-Banna and five other Brothers ran for election but lost. The Brotherhood competed with the Wafd party, the communists, and others. Al-Banna became a powerful player; for instance, he was called to the palace in 1946 for consultation regarding appointing a new prime minister. At the time, the Brotherhood was especially encouraged to stand against the communists and the Wafd.[30] Again, his condemnation of Egyptian parties was based not on their neglect of religion but on their widespread corruption and collaboration with the British. His denunciation of Egyptian pre-Nasir parliamentary experience was, therefore, a rejection of Egyptian party life and not of the principle of constitutional life or multiparty politics. He expressed his belief that Egypt's constitutional life had failed and was in need of reorientation.[31]

During the seventies, the Brethren were used by Sadat in order to boost the legitimacy of his government, though they were still not allowed to form their own political party. They broke with him over his trip to Jerusalem in 1977 and the Camp David agreement and its aftermath.[32] Their protest led to the imprisonment of hundreds of Brethren in addition to members of other radical groups (which will be discussed later). But the Muslim Brethren has not officially sanctioned or used violence to achieve any political or religious objective. Since 1984 the Brotherhood in Egypt and elsewhere, and similar movements like al-Nahda in Tunisia and the Islamic Salvation Front in Algeria, have sought their inclusion in the political process and have been involved in setting up civil institutions. Because in Jordan the Brotherhood has functioned as a political party since the fifties, some of its members became well placed in the government and the parliament.

Inclusion and recognition in the state's hierarchy, as well as the Brotherhood's attempts to become part of state administration, made *hakimiyya* basically a doctrinal organizing principle of government and a symbol of political Islam, all the while allowing inclusionary and pluralistic policies. Al-Banna's emphasis on the proper grounding of political ideology does not exclude individual and collective, social and political reformulations of Islamic political doctrines in accordance with modern society's needs, aspirations, and beliefs.[33]

While Islam contains basic legal material, for al-Banna its denotations and connotations cannot be restricted to or derived from only past historical paradigms. More important, he attempts to show that Islamic thought must account for and deal with modernity as a worldview, not only as a law. Both the law and the worldview must deal with the real world, not in abstract terms but in practical terms. They must, therefore, take into account and include other interpretations, political ideologies, and philosophies. Because Islam is a religion, society, and state, it must deal effectively with religion and the world. This means the inclusion of diverse substantive and methodological, pluralistic interpretations, while maintaining the basic doctrines of religion.[34]

Because the *shari'a* is viewed as a social norm, al-Banna frees its application from past specific methods and links its good practice to maintaining freedom and popular authority over the government and delineating the authorities of the executive, the legislative, and the

judiciary. Western constitutional forms of government do not contradict Islam if grounded in the constitutionality of Islamic law. Constitutional rule is transformed by al-Banna into *shura* by a subtle
reinterpretation in light of modernity and in a spirit not contradictory to the Qur'an. *Shura,* as the basic principle of government and
the exercise of power by society, becomes inclusionary by definition
and employed to empower the people to set the course of political
action and ideology. For al-Banna, because the ultimate source of the
legitimacy of *shura* is the people, its representation cannot be restricted
to one party that usually represents only a fraction of the population. A continuous ratification by the community is required, because
governance is a contract between the ruled and the ruler.[35]

Al-Banna's theoretical acceptance of political pluralistic, democratic, and inclusionary interpretations implants the future seeds for
further acceptance by the Muslim Brotherhood of political pluralism
and democracy, notwithstanding its link to *tawhid* and its political
connotation, unity. From al-Banna's viewpoint, party politics and
political systems do not preclude accepting substantial differences in
ideologies, policies, and programs. An Islamic state, however, does
exclude parties that contradict the oneness of God.[36] The illegitimacy
of atheistic parties is not, in al-Banna's view, an infringement on the
freedom of expression and association. This is so to the extent that
the majority and the minority accept religion as the truth. Such parties would be outside the consensus of society and, therefore, would
threaten its unity. If Islam is chosen as the basis of government and
society, then its opposition becomes a matter of opposition to society, not freedom. Still, this is not a negation of pluralism in Islam,
since foreign ideas and systems of thought can be incorporated.[37]
The state must reflect social agreement and provide a framework for
resolving conflicts peacefully.[38]

Furthermore, al-Banna's system includes different social and religious groups, such as Christians and Jews, who along with Muslims
are united by interest, human good, and the belief in God and the
holy books. Where religion is acknowledged as an essential component of the state, political conflicts ought not to be turned into religious wars and must be resolved by dialogue. In al-Banna's view,
individuals enjoy religious, civil, political, social, and economic equal
rights and duties. The principle of individual involvement—to enjoin
good and forbid evil—is the origin of pluralism, leading to forming

political parties and social organizations or, simply, democratizing social and political processes.[39]

Another important thinker, Taqiy al-Din al-Nabahani, the founder of Hizb al-Tahrir (Liberation Party) in Jordan and Palestine, follows in al-Banna's footsteps. While accepting, in his *Al-Takatul al-Hizbi,* multiparty politics as a contemporary synonym for the duty of enjoining good and forbidding evil, he laments the loss of political movements for many opportunities. This is due to the lack of proper awareness of the role of parties in communal renaissance. For al-Nabahani, a good party life must be based on a set of principles that commits the community to act. Only in this manner can a real party rise and then represent the people and push for major, positive developments. Without popular support, civil actors cannot work properly.[40]

Al-Nabahani imagines a gradual process of development which centers around a three-fold program: first, propagating the party's platform to acquaint people with its principles; second, sharpening the awareness of the people on essential issues through social interactions; and, third, questing for power in order to rule in the people's name. The party must always play the role of a watchdog and must not dissolve itself into state apparatuses. Its independence from the government is essential for its credibility. While the government's role is executive and must represent the people, the party's role is ideological. In this sense, the party must always watch the government. The government should not, therefore, isolate itself from the society but must be responsive. Even when represented in government, the party must stay as a social force that supervises state actions. Put differently, to al-Nabahani, civil institutions are social constructs, and the government must yield to public demands and interests. Nonetheless, this situation must not contradict any Islamic principle.[41]

Al-Nabahani views the institutions of the community at large as the legal source of authority; the government, therefore, must respect the wishes of the community and enact its will. People are free to give or to withdraw authority, especially since a consultative council (*majlis al-shura*) must be the outcome of elections, not of appointment. Al-Nabahani downplays the importance of the executive power and highlights the pivotal functions of elected bodies. They simply represent the people and protect their "natural rights," including the right to form parties.[42]

As a matter of fact, though, Hizb al-Tahrir—both in the East and

West Banks—has not been able, or enabled, since the fifties to act according to its program and play its imagined role. In 1976, the Jordanian government banned the party because its actions were perceived as threatening the stability of the monarchy, especially because of its emphasis on the necessity of elections for the legitimacy of government. As a result of persecution, al-Nabahani went to Damascus and then to Beirut. His party did not get a license, because the Jordanian government viewed the party as aiming at ending the monarchy.[43]

Another fundamentalist thinker previously linked to Hizb al-Tahrir, Munir Shafiq, argues that the relationship between governments and their societies faces major obstacles, such as the lack of social justice, human dignity, and *shura*. These issues transcend the Western ideas of human rights, the sovereignty of law, and democracy, and they form the base for a proper relationship between the ruler and the ruled. He does not accept any justification for the conditions that beset the Muslim life, such as the absence of political freedom and the existence of widespread economic injustice. Thus, any modern resurgence must address these issues by spreading social justice, uplifting human dignity, maintaining basic human rights and the sovereignty of law, and extending the meaning of *shura* and popular political participation through developing representative institutions.[44]

Similarly, Sa'id Hawwa, the Syrian Muslim Brotherhood's leader and an important thinker, argues that in an Islamic state all citizens are equal and protected from despotism and arbitrariness. The distinction between one individual and another should not center on race or belief. As to the exercise of power, it should be based on *shura* and freedom of association, specifically political parties, unions, minority associations, and civil institutions. The one-party system is unworkable in an Islamic state. Furthermore, he adds that the rule of law must reign supreme, and people should be able to have access to courts to redress their grievances. More important, the state must guarantee the freedom of expression, whether on the personal or the public level.[45]

In particular, Hawwa shows sensitivity to the importance of arguing for equal rights for Syrian minorities with the majority. While ultimate authority should rest within the confines of Islamic teachings, and while individuals from minorities can be members of cabinets or parliaments, political representation must be proportionate.

However, the administration of the minorities' internal affairs, such as building educational institutions and having religious courts, is the domain of minorities, themselves, and must not be subjected to the judgment of others.[46]

Other thinkers, like Muhammad S. al-ʿAwwa, a distinguished Egyptian member of the Brotherhood, go beyond these general statements and directly address the issues of democracy and rights. Starting from al-Banna's discourse, al-ʿAwwa elaborates further the absolute necessity of both pluralism and democracy. Islam, in al-ʿAwwa's view, is falsely accused of being opposed to pluralistic societies.[47] That despotism was the general practice of the historical Arab-Islamic state is accepted by al-ʿAwwa as a general description, but this does not mean that Islam, by its very nature, is opposed to pluralism and democracy. He uses historical examples, like the first state in Islam founded by the Prophet, to show that despotism, as a political concept, has not enjoyed any credibility, though it has been tolerated by the general populace. Again, the historical state is not the sole representative of legitimacy, and its model must not be imposed on the people. For al-ʿAwwa, the first step to major changes is the reorganization of the society in a way that allows civil institutions to develop freely without any state control, because the current conditions hinder the development of pluralistic societies where real civil institutions serve the interests of groups. Islamic states have now created their institutions in order to preclude the real representative institutions and, consequently, to force them to go underground. Thus, al-ʿAwwa calls for revitalizing civil society as a means of freeing society from the grip of the state and its unrepresentative institutions.[48]

In al-ʿAwwa's perception, pluralism is the tolerance of diversity—political, economic, religious, linguistic, and otherwise. This diversity is a natural human tendency and an inalienable right, especially when considering that even the Qur'an allows differences in identity and belonging.[49] Al-ʿAwwa identifies six doctrines that make Islam tolerant and pluralistic: first, it does not specify a particular social and political system but provides general ideas; second, a ruler must be elected by the people through *shura;* third, if Islam permits religious freedom then all other kinds of freedom are legitimate; fourth, all people are equal in terms of both rights and duties; fifth, God's command to enjoin good and to forbid evil is a communal, religious duty; and, sixth, rulers are accountable to their communities.[50] However, in al-'Awwa's view, the legitimacy of pluralism hinges on two conditions: first, it should not contradict the basics of Islam, and, second, it should be made in people's interest. In all other respects, individuals and groups may associate with each other in any manner deemed necessary, especially as political parties, which act as a safety valve against limiting freedom and as a means for limiting despotism.[51]

Hasan al-Turabi, the leading and most powerful fundamentalist thinker of contemporary Islamic movements, theoretically breaks many taboos about the state. He drops many conditions about the nature of institutions that may be allowed by an Islamic constitution and in an Islamic state. More than al-Banna did, he imposes Islamic limitations on the power of the state and equates them with those of liberalism and Marxism. The state must not go beyond putting down general rules enabling society to organize its affairs. Accepting the idea that the *shari'a* limits the powers of the state and frees society, he grounds it in the religious command to "enjoin good and to forbid evil."[52]

To al-Turabi, this command parallels pluralism, because its performance is obviously of communal nature. The exercise of *shura* and *ijma'*, people's prerogative, requires primarily the existence of many opinions (*ijtihadat*) so that a community might choose from among them. This task is more urgent today, since Muslims are beset by dire conditions and unprecedented challenges, demanding a new understanding of religion that transcends mere addition and subtraction of particulars to meet the need of providing new organizing principles appropriate for modernity.[53]

Al-Turabi theoretically justifies such a need by arguing that both the specifics and the organizing principles of religion are historically developed and, consequently, subject to change according to the community's needs. The historical nature of these principles means that no normative standing is attributed to them and that their replacement with new specifics and principles is not in violation of religion. While this replacement does involve the Qur'an and the *sunna*, the new *usul* (organizing principles) must be the outcome of a new *ijma'*, itself the consequence of a popular choice in the form of contemporary *shura*.[54] In the view of al-Turabi, if *shura* and democracy are viewed outside their historical conditions, then they might be used synonymously to indicate the same idea. While it is true that ultimate sovereignty in Islam belongs to God, practical and political sovereignty is, however, the people's. For al-Turabi *shura* does not eliminate communal freedom to select an appropriate course of action and a set of rules or even representative bodies. However, al-Turabi cautions against breaking any fundamental Qur'anic principle.[55]

Thus, ultimate political authority is reserved by al-Turabi to the community, which draws a contract with an individual to lead the community and organize its affairs. This is done only through delegating power for the well-being of the community. Al-Turabi accepts any state order that is bound by and is based on contractual mutuality, where the ruler never transgresses against the individual and the communal freedom provided for by the Qur'an. The main Qur'anic discourse is directed primarily not to the state but to the people and, more specifically, to the individual. A proper Islamic constitution must guarantee individual and communal freedom. Proper representative bodies must then be set up to counter the possibility of despotic rule.[56]

Al-Turabi looks at the freedom to organize political institutions as an absolute necessity for an Islamic revival. A reformation that lacks a true philosophic and political reformulation of Islam will not propel the sought-after cultural revolution. Again, mere religiosity along traditional lines would not be conducive to revolution. A revolution, however, must be based on religion, supersede temporary interests, and be underpinned by social consensus, as consensus must be the source of communal interests; the social setting is the environment that enables the individual to enjoy freedom.[57]

While the *shar'ia* is pivotal to al-Turabi, it does not exclude non-Islamic doctrines and institutions, especially if an Islamic society needs them. Al-Turabi exhorts Muslims to keep in mind the objectives of religion. Justice, for instance, does not mean only one thing throughout history; therefore, its individual interpretations must change from one time to another. But there must be no opposition to a Qur'anic text.[58] As an example, al-Turabi explains the true Islamic position on woman by arguing that Islam has provided her with complete independence, as the Qur'anic discourse speaks to her without a male mediator; her belief, like the male's, could not be meaningful without her sincere conviction. If the Qur'an postulates her complete religious freedom, so it stands to reason that she is also free in other aspects of life—in society and state as well as in economics and politics. She has equal rights in public life. While al-Turabi acknowledges the historically lower status and mishandling of women, he attributes all of this to misinterpreting Qur'anic verses on women in addition to the effects of negative social environments. However, these two aspects must be rectified, both theoretically, by a rereading of the text, and practically, by giving women their proper place in society.[59]

This kind of change cannot take place through minor adjustments. In al-Turabi's view, such change requires comprehensive mental adjustments and social restructuring of the community's experiences within a modern program. This program leads to redressing not only the particular grievances of women but also all other contemporary problems. The starting point, however, relates to freeing individuals and groups to pursue what they consider new means toward development, for the historical experience of the Muslims is now defunct and cannot be of major utility. Muslims are experiencing what is not developed by them; simply, it is a new world that requires new thinking.[60]

This call leads al-Turabi to aim at founding a modern jurisprudence that is not based on past history but rather on modern experience. A modern Islamic jurisprudence based on freedom of research, without the past restrictions imposed by jurists and state, seems to al-Turabi capable of providing Muslims with necessary instruments for the onset of revival. In this process, the state's role should be formal—that is, to conduct *shura* and, therefore, to codify communal opinions. It must refrain from forcing its views on the public and must allow a new breed of *'ulama'* to develop and restructure Islamic thinking. Official institutions have no right to seize the communal rights of legislating and thinking.[61]

Al-Turabi postulates further comprehensive freedom as a fundamental right and formative principle in people's lives. More specifically, he denies the government any right to impose even recognized legal views on the community, because such an action constitutes an uncalled-for interference by the state in the community's life and a breach of *shura*. Again, enjoining good and forbidding evil is the source of people's legitimacy over the state.[62] This does not mean to al-Turabi that the views of the community should be one and the same. On the contrary, he believes that the existence of only one public opinion may constitute an obstacle to progress and flexible change. While public opinion expressed in the media or by other means does not constitute an alternative to *shura,* policy makers should take that into consideration. Again, while jurists' *ijma'* on a specific issue is not binding on the community, the state should not dismiss it altogether. However, neither should the community be subjected to jurists or to outspoken public opinions, since a democratic interpretation of Islam requires, in al-Turabi's view, the existence of proper and free relationships among the state, individuals, and community.[63]

According to al-Turabi, without freedom humans lose their true essence and become indistinguishable from animals. The original freedom includes freedom of expression and belief, as God convinces— but does not force—humans to believe. Again, if this is the case with religion, so should it be with political matters. Tyranny, from an Islamic point of view cannot be justified, and the *shari'a* calls on people to voice their views. Today's powerful rulers, however, force the people to follow certain ideologies and political programs, thus marginalizing people and their aspirations. Al-Turabi stands in theory, then, against identifying the individual with the state, because the individual's original freedom cannot be given to institutions and to society; any institutionalization of freedom means its destruction. From al-Turabi's perspective, the only normative, individual commitment is to Islam, which frees the individual from having to yield to imposed principles and ideologies.[64]

Al-Turabi cites a few examples of the powers that Islam has given to both individual and society. For instance, the Muslim society has the power to legislate and impose taxation. While the West, according to al-Turabi, has surrendered such powers to the state, Muslim societies have reserved them for themselves, and there is no delegation as such. Strictly speaking, they are social powers and not political. Their surrender to the state negates the possibility of independent social development and subjects society to the will of the state. As for a modern manifestation of the social power to legislate, al-Turabi gives the example of political parties or legal schools. A political party expresses the individual's cooperation and unity; multiparty politics may be the expression of *shura* in a structured system.[65]

Such freedom, however, must not lead to breaking the Muslim society into combatant ideological groups, such as happened in the history of Islam, whereby the community has basically been split into *Shiʿism* and Sunnism. While pluralism is recommended by al-Turabi, its good practice revolves around its consensual context based on a set of principles that have been agreed upon. This context will also guarantee the indivisibility of society and provide an equilibrium between freedom and unity.[66] The mosque is cited by al-Turabi as a typical place where the true spirit of Islamic democracy is exemplified. Formed by ideological bonds and unified by social and political orientations, it is a prototype for communal unity, solidarity, unified organization, communication, and leadership. Here the democratic aspect of religion is so obvious that even prayer leadership is subject to the selection of the people and cannot legitimately be forced on the community. Also, in spite of individuals' differences in color, origin, wealth, and language, equality permeates all aspects of religious life. This is, in al-Turabi's view, a good example that ought to be copied in the area of politics.[67] Further discussion of this idea will be taken up in chapter six.

The position of the leader of Al-Nahda (Renaissance) in Tunisia, Rashid al-Ghannushi, is not far from the views of al-Turabi. Al-Ghannushi argues for the need to maintain public and private freedom as well as human rights. Both freedom and rights are called for by Qurʾanic teachings and ratified by international covenants. These are not contradictory to Islam and involve primarily freedom of expression and association as well as rights to political participation and independence; they also condemn violence and suppression of free opinions. Such principles, according to al-Ghannushi, should become the center of peaceful coexistence and dialogue between society and the state.[68]

Al-Ghannushi ties the political legitimacy of any political system, however, to its provision of freedom for political parties and different elements of society. They should be allowed to compete peacefully over social, political, and ideological agendas. This system must permit free elections to representative councils and institutions so that they may contribute to state administration. If this takes place, the Islamic movement lends its popular support to, and provides legitimacy to, this system, as the popular authority, grounded in God's governance, is the highest authority in society. Accepting freedom of association leads al-Ghannushi even to accept parties, like the communists, that do not believe in God.[69] The reason behind this, in al-

Ghannushi's view, is that some groups may find it in their best interest to form parties and other institutions that might be irreligious. This does not constitute a breach of religion, since pluralism and, more specifically, freedom of belief are sanctioned by religion. To al-Ghannushi, the sacred text represents a source for, a reference to, and an absorption of truth, while its human interpretations are grounded in diverse discourses representing different understandings under changing social, economic, political, and intellectual complexities. Unfettered possibilities of systematic development should be encouraged.[70]

Openness and dialogue become a must for al-Ghannushi, not only within the Muslim world but with the world, in general, and with the West, in particular. He argues that the world is transformed by scientific advancements into a small village that cannot any longer tolerate war. This matter poses the necessity of serious rethinking about the future of this village, since it has a common fate. This is true if the inhabitants of this village are serious enough to have a common fate. This presupposes, among other things, putting an end to the abstract geographic and cultural division of the world into East and West and to the idea that, while one of them is rational and democratic, the other is perverse and despotic. Such a division is nothing but a recipe for war. Any objective analysis demonstrates that negative and positive values and forces exist in both. The forces of goodness are invited to dialogue and to search for avenues for intercourse.[71]

The views of the fundamentalist trend that legitimizes pluralistic civil society and democracy can be aptly derived from the circulated text of a pact (mithaq) that has been published and distributed by Muhammad al-Hashimi al-Hamidi to other fundamentalists. He states that the success of the Islamic movement, after it gets hold of government, hinges on its establishment of a just and democratic system in the Arab world. Rescuing the community from the tyranny that it has been plunged into necessitates that the Islamic movement should put down limits and a program for justice, shura, and human rights. The program must include the rights of life, equality, justice, and fair trial for all—women and minorities included—as well as the right to political participation and freedom of thought, belief, expression, and religion. His suggestions of the basic principles governing the formation of parties and associations include the freedom to form parties and political associations for all citizens without exception. More-over, parties do not need to be licensed by government. Internal party life must also be governed by democracy. The call for dictatorship and totalitarian rule is prohibited under any circumstance, through either slogan or political propaganda. Furthermore, secular citizens, including communists, have the right to form parties, to propagate their ideology, and to compete for power. Finally, racial, tribal, sectarian, or foreign affiliations cannot be the basis of any legitimate political propaganda.[72]

Along the same lines, the political program of Jabhat al-Inqadh in Algeria calls for adherence to *shura* in order to avoid tyranny and to eradicate all forms of monopoly, whether political, social, or economic. Political pluralism, elections, and other democratic means of political and social life are called for as the means for liberating the community.[73]

Exclusivist Discourses

More than anything else, the discourse of Sayyid Qutb, the founder of radicalism in the Arab world, develops the underpinnings of radical Islamic fundamentalism in that arena. The study of Qutb's thought shows us why many Islamic groups moved to religious radicalism. Qutb himself was both its foremost theoretician and its victim. He was transformed under ʿAbd Al-Nasir's regime from a very liberal writer in Egypt into the most radical fundamentalist thinker in the Arab world, converting his imprisonment and ferocious torture into a radical political theology of violence and isolation. It may be that this was his psychological compensation for the violence and repression inflicted by the regime.

Sayyid Qutb, born to a middle-class family, received his B.A. degree from Dar al-ʿUlum—as did al-Banna. After that, he worked as a teacher and columnist and was associated with Taha Hussein, ʿAbbas Mahmud al-ʿAqqad, and other liberal thinkers. From the time he started writing in journals and magazines, he showed a general tendency to oppose the government and criticize Egypt's state of affairs. He was very daring in his opposition and in his "radical liberalism," manifested in his writing dealing with free love and nudity. His first writings revealed existential, skeptical, and liberal bents. Because of his opposition to government, he was sent away to the countryside;

the two journals of which he was editor-in-chief, *al-'Alam al-'Arabi* and *al-Fikr al-Jadid*, were closed down. Then, in 1948, the ministry of education sent him to the United States to continue his studies on education.[74]

His first book adopting fundamentalism as a way of life and a political agenda, *Al-'Adala al-Ijtima'iyya fi al-Islam* (Social justice in Islam), which appeared during his stay in the United States, was far removed from radicalism and closer to al-Banna's discourse. His stay in the United States during the years of 1948–51 made him review his previous attitude and adoption of Westernization. His dislike of materialism, racism, and the pro-Zionist feelings of the West, which he personally experienced in the United States, seems to have been the beginning of his alienation from Western culture and his return to the roots of the culture that he was brought up in. Upon his return to Egypt—after the death of Hasan al-Banna and the first ordeal of the Muslim Brotherhood—he joined the Brotherhood, became very active in its intellectual and publishing activities, and wrote numerous books on "Islam as the solution." However, until that point, no radicalism or violence were involved. His priority was to rewrite a modern understanding of Islam and the solutions it provided to the basic political, economic, social, and individual problems of Egypt and the Arab and Islamic worlds.[75]

In 1953, Qutb was appointed editor-in-chief of the weekly *Al-Ikhwan al-Muslimun;* it was banned at the time of the dissolution of the Brotherhood, in 1954, after the falling-out between the Brethren and the Free Officers' regime. Qutb was put in jail, then released. The Brotherhood was dissolved again, in late 1954, and many Brethren, including Qutb, were jailed. He was released that year but arrested again after the *Manshiyya* incident, in which an attempt was made on 'Abd al-Nasir's life; Qutb and others were accused of being affiliated with the movement's secret military section. In 1955, Qutb was sentenced to fifteen years in prison; he and thousands of the Brethren and their supporters were subjected to fierce torture that left him with unhealed wounds until the day he died. In this context, he shifted to radical fundamentalism and exclusiveness. Again, isolated from the outside world under daily, tantalizing pressures such as witnessing the slaughter of scores of the Brethren in a jail hospital, Qutb could not but blame those who were free outside the jail but would not defend the unjustly imprisoned and heinously tortured.

These people became, in Qutb's perception, accomplices in the crimes of the regime and, therefore, like the regime, infidels. His most important books, or gospels of radicalism—*Fi Zilal al-Qur'an, Ma'alim fi al-Tariq, Hadha al-Din,* and *Al-Mustaqbal li Hadha al-Din,* and others—were written because of, and in spite of, the torture that he and others tolerated year after year. Qutb was released in 1965; then he was arrested on charges of plotting to overthrow the government and was executed in 1966.[76]

In order to tolerate his pain and poor prison conditions, Qutb transformed his discourse into an exclusivist discourse, so that it was not the state and society that were excluding him but, rather, he as the leader of the believing vanguard who was excluding individuals, societies, and states from the true salvation. The whole world became a target of his condemnation and isolation. The state's vengeful exclusion and repressive intolerance to any sort of popular opposition was counterbalanced by his desperate spiritual, moral, social, and political exclusion and intolerance. This is a clear contextual and historical example of how the parameters of radical fundamentalism developed: it was from his cell, under oppressive and inhumane conditions, that he started developing his theoretical exclusivism.

Qutb argues that divine governance, the essential political component of *tawhid,* must be upheld at all times: when forming a virtuous and just society or providing personal or social freedom, and under all conditions—inside the prison or outside of it. Freedom is perceived in a negative way; people are free insofar as their choice of social and political systems does not violate divine governance and does not hinder religious life. He perceives the state as the moral agent for creating and maintaining morality, both individually and collectively. Because of the divinity of legislation, individuals, societies, and states cannot legitimately develop normative rights and duties, whether related to political freedom, pluralism, political parties, or even personal and social freedom. Universal divine laws, as outlined in the Qur'an, are viewed by Qutb as the bases for all sorts of freedom and relationships. In other words, all people, both Muslim and non-Muslim, must link their views of life with the Islamic worldview, and Muslim and non-Muslim countries must finally submit to the divine laws without exception. The state and civil institutions, as well as individuals, may codify legal articles only if needs arise.[77]

Although this perspective postulates communal precedence over state control, the legitimacy of both is linked to applying divine prescriptions. Qutb argues that, because obedience to government is not absolute, people should revolt when any government violates Qur'anic prescriptions, because it thereby loses its legitimacy. Thus, while ultimate sovereignty, in Qutb's view, is reserved to God, its human application is a popular right and duty. This leads Qutb to argue that the state authority is not based on any divine text but must be popularly endorsed. Only free, popular consent makes social, political, and intellectual institutions legitimate. Adherence to Islamic law must occur from a popular viewpoint, not from an official viewpoint, since it is the people who represent the divine will.[78]

Qutb's view of jurisprudence as a practical discipline severs it from its golden past and theoretical pedestal and links it to contemporary needs. People are then free to reconstitute modern Islamic political theories and institutions. His rejection of the historical, normative compendium of Islamic disciplines leads him to uphold the people's freedom to reorder their systems and lives.[79] Qutb denies, then, the unique legitimacy claims of any specific system or form of government; for instance, he would legitimize any form, republican or otherwise, insofar as its base is consensual agreement.[80] However, theocracy cannot be a sound Islamic system, because no elite may claim divine representation. A proper Islamic state, in Qutb's view, is both communal and constitutional; both the judiciary and the legislature, as well as the executive entity, rule only through delegated powers by means of *shura,*—the central political, theoretical, and practical doctrine of government and politics. Any social agreement that does not contradict *shari'a* is Islamically sound and can be included; elitism, however, is excluded and rejected in principle.[81]

Qutb's discourse so far gives the impression that even radical fundamentalism respects and honors communal choices. While this may be partially true, it still excludes pluralism, free civil society, and multiparty systems, in particular, or simply liberal democratic tendencies. The basis of freedom—the command to enjoin good and forbid evil—must be subjected, according to Qutb, to general communal interests like unity. In turn these interests must control particular political, social, or personal interests like political elitism and economic monopoly. Personal freedom tuned to communal interests and united in broad, unitary, ideological orientations is the source of social peace. To Qutb, a religiously good society rises not on ideologically and religiously conflictual bases but, instead, on goodwill, solidarity, security, peace, and equality.[82]

As an example, Qutb cites self-interest, which he maintains weakens communal solidarity, whereas mutual responsibility (takaful) strengthens that solidarity, itself a religious duty for society. Although Qutb argues that this responsibility is social in nature, it may turn into a political responsibility carried out by the state. This responsibility includes education, health, proper jobs, etc. While the state's interference theoretically must be limited, any failure of society to take care of its own affairs leads, in practice, to the state's moral responsibility to control society. Again, while state institutions are of a supplementary nature to Qutb, they ultimately replace as well as exclude the institutions of civil society. Interest groups are allowed only if their objectives are broad, such as caring for the poor or the sick. Others, like women's liberation movements developed from Western models, are not welcomed or included. He argues that women's freedom to pursue their personal interests without regard to family weakens society. Arguing also that Western political systems are practically and theoretically false, he excludes them and prohibits group formation along Western guidelines. For Qutb, then, a good society is composed of religious groups sharing similar interests and perceptions of life as well as unified political orientations.[83]

Qutb excludes the legitimacy not only of multiparty systems but also of one-party systems, and then replaces the two with a religious vanguard whose job is salvational in the first place. Thus, any ideological group or system that is not based on Islam is not allowed to operate. Minorities are included religiously to the extent that they can keep their faith, but they are excluded politically, not being given any right to form political parties or even a vanguard. Qutb also links any valid free expression to the parameters of Islamic ideological understanding. All those societies and parties that do not conform to such an understanding are described as jahili.[84] Thus, only an Islamic ideology may be represented in a political party (the vanguard, or tali'ah). Qutb's book Ma'alim fi al-Tariq (Signposts on the road) is specific about the mission that this vanguard should carry out in an exclusive and uncompromising attitude with respect to all other ideologies, societies, and ways of life. However, establishing an Islamic system permits the involvement of different institutions in political processes so that the public will is known in the context of an Islamic ideology.[85]

The particular issue that Qutb uses to exclude Western models of unions and federations is their selfish and materialistic nature. However, he argues that *al-naqabat*, or unions, in Islam, which were originally the models for their Western counterparts, are based on brotherhood and solidarity. Thus, Qutb—like Miller and Huntington—sees only a mutual exclusivity between Western philosophies, ideologies, and institutions and those of Islam. The former are *jahili* and, as such, belong to *hizb al-shaytan* (the party of Satan); the others are Islamic and, as such, belong to *hizb Allah* (the party of God).[86]

Once out of jail in 1964, Qutb started forming a party that adhered to the rationalizations described above and included the following principles: Human societies that do not follow Islamic ethics, system, and *shari'a* are in need of an essential Islamic education. Those individuals who respond positively to this education should undertake a course of study on Islamic movements in history in order to set a course of action to fight Zionism and colonialism. Also, no organization is to be established until a highly ideological training is undertaken.[87] Qutb's implementation of this vanguard program ended with his execution by hanging in 1966.

Most of the radical fundamentalist groups in the Arab world, and specifically those in Egypt, have been influenced both directly and indirectly by this Qutbian, radical, exclusivist discourse and by his notions of paganism of the "other." A few examples may suffice here.

In Egypt, the Liman Tarah prison played an important role in the radical education of Qutb and others. Mustafa Shukri, an inmate with Qutb, accepted the latter's views and established the exclusivist Jama'at al-Muslimin (the Community of the Muslims), notoriously known as Al-Takfir wa al-Hijra (Apostatization and Migration), as a fulfillment of the Qutbian vanguard. Shukri denies the legitimacy of pluralism and calls on people to adhere to the Qur'an and the *sunna* only. In his trial before a martial court in Egypt, he explained the exclusivity of his group in its rejection of theories and philosophies that are not textually derived: the Qur'an and the *sunna* are the only criteria of legitimacy and truth; therefore, the government is in violation of divine governance. Furthermore, Shukri brands as unbelievers all Muslims who do not view Islam in this manner and turns migration (*hijra*) from the Egyptian society into a religious duty. In this fashion, he claims that his isolated group is the only true Muslim community.[88]

Salih Sirriyya, the leader of Tanzim al-Fanniyya al-'Askariyya, was also a follower of Qutb. His exclusivity can be seen in his categorization of humankind into three groups only: Muslims, infidels, and hypocrites. Any neglect of an Islamic duty makes the individual an apostate and subjects him to death. Multiparty systems and diverse legal schools negate unity and lead to basic conflicts.[89] While Shukri turned his back to the *jahili* society, Sirriyya allows the temporary use of democracy in order to set up an Islamic state. If the activists are persecuted, then it is possible for such activists to secretly infiltrate the political system and even become cabinet ministers, because the struggle to topple un-Islamic governments and any irreligious organization is a religious duty that ends only on the day of judgment. The defense of un-Islamic governments, participation in un-Islamic ideological parties, and adherence to foreign philosophies and ways of life are cited by Sirriyya as obvious instances of unbelief that should incur death. That sovereignty belongs to God and is used by Sirriyya to divide humankind into the inclusive *hizb al-shaytan,* consisting of all individuals and institutions that do not believe in or practice Islam, and the exclusive *hizb Allah,* consisting of those who struggle to establish the Islamic state. Out of this logic, Sirriyya attempted a coup d'état against Anwar al-Sadat, which resulted in his execution in 1974.[90]

A further example of Qutb's influence is the case of 'Abud al-Zumar, a former army intelligence officer and the military leader of Tanzim al-Jihad, as well as the leader and one of the founders of Jama'at al-Jihad al-Islami. He follows Sayyid Qutb's rationalization of the importance of active opposition to the state. His program of action focuses on an applicable Islamic vision that contributes in uniting Islamic movements within one framework and leads to forgoing individual and public differences. Employing a Qutbian political term, *ma'alim al-tariq* (signpost of the road), he urges the Islamic movement to concentrate on its basic objective, the Islamic state. This requires an uncompromising and exclusive attitude toward all aspects of *jahili* systems and societies. The alternative, in al-Zumar's view, is to employ a radical transformation and a total Islamization of all facets of life and to unstintingly reject secularism, nationalism, and parliamentary life. All this change has to start, however, by dethroning current rulers who do not adhere to the *shari'a.* In line with his exclusive radical ideology, al-Zumar tried but failed to kill President Sadat.[91]

No less exclusive is al-Jamaʿa al-Islamiyya al-Jihadiyya, a branch of Tanzim al-Jihad in Upper Egypt headed by ʿUmar ʿAbd al-Rahman, sentenced for complicity in the World Trade Center bombing and now residing in a U.S. jail. ʿAbd al-Rahman divides even the Islamic movements into two trends. The first trend, headed by the Muslim Brotherhood, accepts the existing Egyptian regime as legitimate and, therefore, adopts pluralism and democracy as legitimate tools of political action to establish an Islamic state. The other trend, headed by al-Jamaʿa al-Islamiyya, denies legitimacy to the regime and publicly follows a course of total confrontation. ʿAbd al-Rahman accuses the Brotherhood of being complacent about the government, as it worked with Sadat and Mubarak, condemned Sadat's death and violent acts, and paid visits to the Coptic Pope. He further rejects the Brotherhood's inclusive and compromising attitude in allying itself with the Wafd party as well as the al-ʿAmal and al-Ahrar. Instead, he calls for replacing the inclusivity of the Brotherhood with the exclusivity of the Jamaʿat by rejecting integration in democratic institutions and by adopting a course of forceful resolution regarding basic issues of identity, ethics, and value system.[92] Also in line with Qutb's argument, he describes any system that adopts foreign principles as belonging to *kufr* (unbelief) and *jahiliyya* and legalizes its overthrow.

This view leads al-Jihad to declare war against the Egyptian parliament, because the parliament gave itself (in Article 86 of the Constitution) the right to legislate and permit democracy, a concept that treats the believer and the nonbeliever equally as citizens.[93] "The ʿassumed democratic system' in Egypt wants us to enter into party politics in order to equate Islam with other ideologies," ʿAbd al-Rahman explains. However, the Islamic movement believes in its distinctive superiority and does not respect the *jahili* positive law. He further rejects any role for representative bodies as avenues for Qurʾanic interpretation and adjudication. Qurʾanic legitimacy stands on its own. Thus, any violation of Qurʾanic texts leads a ruler to *kufr*, punishable by death. ʿAbd al-Rahman, himself, was viewed as the instigator of Sadat's assassination.[94]

Conclusion

It has become clear in this chapter that fundamentalism, though perceived as being one exclusive phenomenon in both practice and theory, is in fact otherwise. Fundamentalism, whether Jewish, Christian, Islamic, or even Hindu, has become a world phenomenon. However, it is only Islam that is identified in an essentialist manner with fundamentalism. Agreements on the framework of Islam (which have been treated in chapter two) might lead not only to the confusion of radical fundamentalism with moderate fundamentalism but also with Islam. If an ordinary, practicing or nonpracticing Muslim is asked whether the Qur'an postulates God's governance in all aspects of life, the answer will be "yes, of course." This belief does not, however, make a Muslim a fundamentalist by definition; conversely, it makes all Muslims fundamentalists by definition.

What must distinguish a radical view from a moderate one is the method used to transform a political agenda into daily life. As we have seen, even fundamentalism employs diverse methodological and practical processes to create intellectual and political formulas. One formula is conceptually based on theoretical and practical exclusivity that permits violent means toward the other. Because radical fundamentalism lives in isolation from society under conditions of social disunity, corruption, exploitation, political violence, and undemocratic regimes, it has transformed its political discourse into an isolationist theology of politics. From this point of view, Islam demands its political contextualization.

For the radicals, *shura* not only becomes a religious doctrine or a mechanism for elections; it also reflects public will, a doctrine much superior to individual freedom or social agreement. More important, it represents the divine will, and any deviation from the divine is a religious violation. The individual cannot but submit to this will; in fact, he is only an appendage to it, with his freedom depending on it. While this will may opt for a political contract with a ruler, it cannot, because of what it represents, allow pluralism and basic differences leading to disunity. The establishment of an Islamic state becomes, for radicalism, the fulfillment of this divine will, and individuals and groups are, consequently, subordinated to the state.

Processed through the lens of the *shari'a,* the institutionalization of *shura* and *ijma'* provides the state, which expresses the general will, a normative role in making basic choices in people's lives. The formal legitimacy that the state acquires makes it, in fact, unaccountable to anything but God or obedience to *shari'a,* itself institutionalized in the state. Henceforth, legitimacy becomes an internal state affair and not a social and public issue, although originally it was so.

And insofar as the state does not go against the *shari'a,* no one can legitimately overthrow it. Because in this context the state supervises public morality and the application of *shari'a,* individual religiosity is subjected to the communal public will, itself transformed into state control, both moral and political. Parties, associations, and other civil institutions have no intrinsic validity in this hierarchy but operate only in a supplementary manner. An elaboration like this seems to demand, in the end, exclusivity. Indeed, there is no possibility of pluralistic understanding of religion, for politicizing Islam as the proper Islamic interpretation cannot be represented except by the state. The establishment of inclusive pluralistic civil democracies and ways of life seems, then, unworkable.

The descriptions that Miller, Lewis, Huntington, and others give of fundamentalism and all other Islamic movements might more appropriately be applied solely to Islamic radicalism. And, using the radical groups as representatives of Islamic and Arab culture is both factually erroneous and culturally biased. Other non-Islamic religious interpretations like those in Hinduism or Judaism suffer from very similar phenomena but are never treated in the same manner. Violence employed by radical groups is not theoretical in origin, but their theory is historically developed. Put differently, they have not been committing violent acts because of their theories; rather, their theories justifying violence have been derived from the real and imagined violence that they have been subjected to. In fact, practice has been transformed into theory, which now has a life of its own. Both radical groups and most regimes are committed to recycling intellectual and practical violence and exclusivity. Violence, secular and religious, has been exercised most of the time in reaction to the tyrannies of political regimes.[95]

In contrast, the moderate trend cites the absence of a pluralistic society and democratic institutions as the real cause for violence. While this trend has long been excluded from political participation, it still calls for its inclusion into politics and formal institutions. Its involvement in civil society and its call for pluralism are still seen as the road to salvation of the community and individuals. Its inclusionary views do not postulate an eternal or divine enmity between Islam's institutions and systems and those of the West. Properly grounded, what is Western becomes, indeed, Islamic. The moderate fundamentalists are able to blend the culture of the East with that of the West, and, in doing so, they are providing Islamic arguments for inclusion—not mutual exclusion, as some secular and religious radicals do in the East and West. The conflict between the East and West is viewed as being primarily political or economic but not religious or cultural. The two have common monotheistic grounds upon which multicultural and religious cooperation and coexistence might be built.

For the moderates, a popular liberating democracy, grounded in Islamic law, is a political bridge between the East and the West. Authoritarianism and despotism are not specifically cultural or Islamic; they have existed in both the West and the East, but are more prominent now in the Arab world. The moderate trend has started to adopt an Islamic interpretation of liberal democracy, as opposed to the popular democracy or, indeed, majoritarian tyranny of radical fundamentalism or the authoritarian nationalism of the Arab world.

Furthermore, if the weakness of fundamentalism—both in its minority radical and, especially, majority moderate trends—might lead to free, liberal, pluralistic, and democratic societies and inclusive regimes in the Middle East, why has this not happened when Islamic movements were at their lowest ebb and their members were packed up in jails? We should keep in mind that the liberal West encouraged, to a large extent, their reemergence as Islamic movements, at least in Egypt during Sadat's presidency and in Afghanistan (the Mujahidin) during the Communist regime.

The important issue of the real motivations behind portraying Islamic movements and the essence of Islam in one way or another carries with it an ideological and even religious view. We need to think about the fine points that Yahya Sadowski brings up about motivation:

The irony of this conjuncture needs to be savored. When the consensus of social scientists held that democracy and development depended upon the actions of strong, assertive social groups, Orientalists held that such associations were absent in Islam. When the consensus evolved and social scientists thought a quiescent, undemanding society was essential to progress, the neo-Orientalists [like Crone, Pipes, and Gellner] portrayed Islam as beaming with pushy, anarchic solidarities. Middle Eastern Muslims, it seems, were doomed to be eternally out of step with intellectual fashion.[96]

4

The Discourse of Hasan al-Banna on *Shura,* Democracy, and the Islamic State

Scholars have put forward a variety of discourses on the nature of modern Islamic states, ranging from the complete conservatism of Saudi Arabia to the total revolution of the Islamic Republic of Iran, as elaborated by the discourses of Ayatollah Khumayni or that of Sayyid Qutb. Between these two extreme models there exist many discourses that are much less conservative, such as that of Hasan al-Banna,[1] and much less revolutionary, such as that of Hasan al-Turabi. Theoretically speaking, all Islamically developed conceptions of an Islamic state are based on similar ideological postulates, such as the need to ground the state in Islamic divine law as the main source of constitutional framework. These postulates include the views that Islam integrates the religious and political, opposes deriving Islamic principles from non-Islamic philosophies and systems, regards religious and ideological compromises as religious concessions, and includes eternal principles capable of dealing with modern, socioeconomic, political and intellectual crises.

The agreement of most fundamentalists over these issues at a theoretical level does not, however, mean that an agreement over a practical discourse or praxis is reached. On the contrary, a spectrum of discourses was developed. For instance, the discourses of Qutb, al-Mawdudi, and al-Khumayni are more radical than those of al-Banna, al-Turabi, and al-Ghannushi. The first three discourses have no notion of gradual change or possible compromise and emphasize the need to overthrow secular governments as a nonnegotiable religious duty. The first three discourses hold tightly and uncompromisingly to both divine governance and universal paganism. However, al-Banna's discourse is more open and less particular about a forceful overthrow of un-Islamic regimes.[2] In fact, his discourse shows readiness to compromise, both practically and theoretically, and relegates ultimate earthly authority to the community. Social agreement is, in itself, an embodiment of divine will. If a community is not willing to adopt an Islamic state, then its imposition does not reflect the nature of Islam. The focus here is on discussing al-Banna's discourse, which is elaborated under three main principles.

Islam and Politics

Al-Banna starts his political discourse by developing a religiously derived Qu'ranic discourse that includes both creed and action. The testimony that there is "no god but God" is for al-Banna a call to establishing divine governance on earth. The perfection of a Muslim's creed must lead him to act on behalf of society.[3] Furthermore, Islam's comprehensiveness makes it fit for human *fitra* and capable of influencing not only the majority of people but the elites as well. In al-Banna's view, because Islam provides the most worldly and just principles, and the straightest of divine legal codes, it uplifts the human soul and sanctifies universal brotherhood. Islam also offers practical ways to achieve all of this in people's daily lives, social living, education, and political aspirations. It is also on these bases that Islam sets its state and establishes its universal call to humankind. While Islam asks humans to satisfy themselves spiritually and materially, it provides them with regulations that prevent extreme behaviors to help the believer arrive at balanced fulfillment. Such a balance is important to al-Banna, because humans do not live in isolation; they are members of a community. The community has, however, its collective reason, which differs from the individual's. Thus, diverse Islamic regulations satisfy different needs: the economic regulations, for material well-being; the political, for unity, justice, and freedom; and the social, for equality. To al-Banna, all these regulations are only fractions of the authentic Islamic method. Only this method can lead humankind to rescue itself from its miserable existence.[4]

Al-Banna adds that what distinguishes Islam from most other religions is its concern with not only worship but also social system. To al-Banna, Islam is thus comprised of creed, worship, and governance and is a collective and state religion. Muslims must then derive their general principles from it. Islam as a social system deals with all social phenomena, and as such the Qur'an and the *sunna* must represent the highest fundamental authority and point of reference. But their interpretations must be conducted through analogical deduction and consensus. In brief, to al-Banna, Islam is concerned with all aspects of life and postulates precise methods, fundamentals, and foundations for humankind. It is simply a general code for all races, peoples, and nations.[5]

According to al-Banna, there is no other system of life that provides nations with the necessary tools needed for renaissance as Islam does. Islam provides, first, the hope needed in the building of nations; second, the national pride needed to create a good image of the self; and third, the power needed for defense. Furthermore, Islam calls for communal and self-preservation through earthly and religious knowledge, ethics, and economy. Again, to al-Banna this call is only a small part of Islamic regulations for the renaissance of nations.[6]

Activism is the sign of good belief, in al-Banna's view, and political action should be in line with Islamic teachings. In fact, separating Islam from politics is not Islamic. Theoretically, Islam is more comprehensive than politics and absorbs it. Individual perfection requires politicizing Islam. In this sense, Islam is a complete, active religion that must relate to all aspects of life. For instance, al-Banna believes that one of the main religious objectives is to provide society with laws of organization. From al-Banna's perspective, Islam must act as a regulator of behavior of both Muslim communities and all human societies. Its general goals are designed to fit all societies, and this can be done through reinterpretations of texts to suit different times and ages.[7] Islam aims, then, at setting up a good nation with a message of unity and sacrifice. It also aims at establishing a just Islamic government, without tyranny or authoritarianism, which serves the people. A government like this helps in establishing a virtuous society.[8]

The function of Islam is based on four principles: first, pure creed that brings humans closer to God; second, correct worship and good religious deeds, such as praying and fasting, that add meaning to life; third, unity that completes the faith and reduces the tension between sects and political tendencies; and fourth, just legislation and good laws that are derived from the Qur'an and the *sunna*.[9] To al-Banna, while there are many philosophical and political systems that compete with it, Islam is singularly different because its main discourse contains what is good in other ideologies and connects them to a higher system of belief. For example, al-Banna cites some good features in communism, which include equality, abolition of differences, and limited property; all of these features are embraced in Islam.[10] As to other revealed religions, al-Banna argues that Islam is the last of them and their complete manifestation. Islam does not negate their ethics and ways of worship and life; in fact, it contains the important teachings of most other religions. What constitutes good religion is good behavior toward the self, the other, the community, and God—not necessarily better argumentations.[11]

Creed, according to al-Banna, is the soul's tranquil acceptance of a notion without any doubt. Thus, in matters of belief, force should not be used to sway people's hearts. Furthermore, because the source of Islamic creed is God's divine text and the Prophet's *sunna*, Islam is not opposed to, but instead is supported by, reason. The Qur'anic discourse speaks of reason as the source of responsibility and makes its existence a requirement for applying the *shari'a*. The Qur'anic discourse also exhorts the human being to think, search, and contemplate, and asks its opponents to produce their evidence. Thus, Islam does not call for limiting the function of reason but, instead, makes reason the instrument of knowledge by providing it with a framework to prevent its aimlessness.[12]

God's essence, for al-Banna, is beyond the comprehension of human reason. Being limited in time and space, reason precludes understanding of the essences of things. This does not mean that Islam is against freedom of thought or the search for truth. To al-Banna, it is a warning to humans against falling into falsehood and total dependence on reason, since reason cannot provide everlasting truths but only partial interpretations that depend on human conditions and the power of an individual's reason. A Muslim must still exert his reason, but such an action cannot constitute a categorical understanding. Al-Banna holds that, when humans disagree, they must always go back to the basic religious texts that are the ultimate source of justification. Because the metaphysical realm is beyond human understanding, the Qur'anic discourse gives humans few basic metaphysical ideas.[13]

Thus, the role of religion for al-Banna is not to set forth a detailed discourse on metaphysics but to focus on specific, existential outcomes. It aims at, first, the revival of conscious awareness of the self's powers; second, cultivation of virtues to uplift the self; third, sacrifice in quest of truth and guidance toward God; fourth, removing humans from ephemeral, material happiness and providing ways for achieving real happiness; fifth, making God the ultimate goal of the soul; sixth, making religion the source of unity and the resolution of conflicts; seventh, encouraging sacrifice for humankind's sake; and eighth, making Islam the focus of development of individuals, societies, nations, and the world.[14] However, in al-Banna's opinion, humans must always fall back on the Qur'an, which is the only authoritative book of creed and social foundations and general codes of earthly legislation. It is a text that aims at guiding humankind to the truth and the good, for the Qur'an makes Muslims custodians of humankind. The believer does not attempt to reform humankind for any material gains but rather guides others to follow in God's path. As such, the Muslim does not limit his call to any geographical area but extends his efforts to encompass the world.[15]

While al-Banna makes the Qur'an the ultimate criterion for knowledge, he finds that differences regarding practical and political matters are natural. One of the reasons that al-Banna uses for allowing diversity is that the power of reason differs from one individual to another. And because reason is the source of interpretation, many divergent interpretations may be postulated. Again, humans' understanding is limited by language and its rules, so that understanding is in turn limited by language and its rules, which also differ from one individual to another. In addition, the level of knowledge affects the level of understanding, and the environment of an interpreter and his power to reason affect both understanding and knowledge. It is very difficult for humans to transcend their own environment even when they wish to do so. Moreover, the credible sources of knowledge may differ from one interpreter to another: while one may accept a specific science or a history as being beyond doubt, another may find no cause for trusting it. Again, sciences or histories may be the same, but their signification may differ from one individual to another.[16]

All of these issues—of renaissance, knowledge, and the good society—require establishing an Islamic state, in al-Banna's view. Otherwise, religion becomes separated from politics, and politics exists outside the realm of religion. The Islamic state cannot be established except by a general religious message, or else its attainment becomes unattractive. The separation of religion from politics is now in practice and has made politics equivalent to corruption. Futhermore, al-Banna argues that when a Muslim community is ruled by laws other than its own, a clash is bound to erupt between it and the ruling power, thus posing difficulties for believers in accepting a secular ruler. Furthermore, most Egyptian laws, which are derivatives of European ones, are contrary to the divine law and shed doubts on the integrity of Islam in the modern world. The laws of a nation should not contradict its system of beliefs, especially when the divine law is not opposed to modernity or change.[17]

The Islamic State and *Shari'a*

Before modern times, specifically during the six and seventh centuries of *hijra*, when the caliphate entered a phase of weakness and challenge, the state as an independent, conceptual, political polity was seriously entertained. Power was split between the executive branch, which dealt with political and economic matters, and the caliphate, which became a symbol of Islamic unity. Later on, and with the rise of moral, political, and economic crises and the invasion of Muslim lands by foreign powers, Muslim communities witnessed many revivalist movements that oscillated between radical revolutions and conservative reforms. In modern times, many movements that call for return to the fundamentals of religion have flourished throughout the Muslim world. Leaders of such movements felt that the Islamic spiritual dimension could aid in developing a clear portrait of the enemy and condemning moral corruption. This is the case especially when a perceived corrupt present is contrasted with a perceived glorious past full of idealism. Such a scenario is, in turn, used to urge Muslims to establish anew their civilization, reconstruct their identity, and absorb modernity and change.

In one way or another, the rise of Islamic fundamentalism must be located within a framework of reactions to educational, political, and intellectual crises from certain cultural and historical perspectives. That the religious and the political are interwoven and cannot be separated is a postulate that has been upheld even by the *Khawarij* (seceders) in the seventh century. They were the first to uphold the doctrine of divine *hukm* (rule) and the ultimate authority of the Qur'an as the sole point of reference for the Muslims. Furthermore, they denied the legitimacy of human arbitration, unless it could be textually supported. They were not ready to submit to the ruling of the community and, instead, isolated themselves from the mainstream and advocated fighting against those who did not adhere to the textual rulings of the Qur'an. Moreover, they gave themselves the right to judge others' beliefs and behaviors and loaded all aspects of human existence with religious connotations. More important, they were uncompromising when it came to either principles or actions. However, the larger community fought them as renegades who did not accept the arbitration of the community.

Similarly, and in modern times, the *Wahabiyya*, following the great medieval thinker Ibn Taymiyya, has called for the purification of Islam by returning to the fundamentals of religion—that is, the Qur'an and the *sunna*. It followed a strict line of thinking in its attempts to reconstruct society and government on the basis of divine *tawhid* and the doctrine of *al-Salaf al-Salih* (good ancestors). What is important about the ancestors is their reluctance to engage in philosophical or intellectual argumentation and their adherence to the basic texts without any major attempt to reinterpret the principles of Islam. They focused more on the spiritual and ethical aspects of Islam, while leaving political matters to politicians and traditional elites. Other important movements in modern times, like *al-Sanusiyya* and *al-Mahdiyya*, started basically as Sufi orders but were later transformed into political movements that struggled against Western interventions in Libya and Sudan, respectively. The two movements considered themselves to be movements of purification that aimed at restoring genuine Islam through political involvement. Again, the two fundamentals, the Qur'an and the *sunna*, were looked at as the road to the salvation of the Islamic community.

At a more involved level, Jamal al-Din al-Afghani stands out both in terms of his intellectual and political influence and for setting forth the modern political agenda for Islamic reforms. He was ready to think over and adopt into Islamic thought any new philosophical, political, or scientific knowledge that could lead to the progress of the Islamic nation. On the political level, he was also ready to adopt those institutions and systems that could serve the Islamic world and save it from its crises. His follower and later colleague, Muhammad 'Abduh, and Rashid Rida, who provided inspiration for Hasan al-Banna, were greatly affected by different aspects of his intellectual and political discourse. While 'Abduh leaned more toward the modernist European aspect of al-Afghani's intellectual discourse, Rida was more adamant on the necessity of returning to the fundamentals of religion to induce an intellectual revival and to develop new Islamic institutions for an Islamic state. The Islamic state became, for Rida, the cornerstone in the renaissance of the *umma* and the guarantee of the ethical foundations of society.

Interestingly, the differences in thought between Muhammad Iqbal and Abu al-A'la al-Mawdudi were similar to those between 'Abduh and Rida. While both tried to reargue Islamic traditions on knowledge and politics through their reconceptualization of *ijtihad,* al-Mawdudi, the founder of *al-Jama'a al-Islamiyya* in Pakistan, was more puritanical. He called for the reestablishment of Islam on purified roots and centered his efforts on establishing an Islamic state that would shoulder the implementation of Islam as a comprehensive way of life and a complete system. Iqbal, however, showed more liberal tendencies in his thought by trying to rework both Islamic traditions and Western modernity into a modernized Islamic concept. To him, the Islamic state became of secondary importance when measured against the awesome intellectual task that the Muslims would have to take on first. Good politics was a by-product of a good intellectual edifice.

However, the Muslim Brotherhood in Egypt, like al-Mawdudi, focused more on the political aspect of Islam as the cornerstone in promoting a modern Islamic revival. It called urgently for establishing an Islamic state as the first step in implementing the *shari'a.* While the Brotherhood centered its intellectual reinterpretation on a return to the fundamentals, they nevertheless selectively accepted major Western political concepts like constitutional rule and democracy as necessary tools for overhauling the doctrine of an Islamic state. However, the Brotherhood's extremely antagonistic dealing with the Egyptian government led some Brothers to splinter off under the leadership of Sayyid Qutb. While Qutb upheld the need for establishing an Islamic state, he rejected any openness to the West or other influences. He made the existence of an Islamic state an essential part of creed; it represented to him and his followers the communal submission to God on the basis of *shari'a.* It became as well the representation of political and legal obedience to the *shari'a,* which was the basis of both legal rules and constitution. The absence of *shari'a* would remove any shred of legitimacy that the state may enjoy and bring it into *jahiliyya.* On yet another level, Ayatollah al-Khumayni restricted further the concept of a legitimate Islamic government: although the *shari'a* was the basis of government, it was only through the rule of the jurists that its existence was legally actualized.

Within the Islamic world today, the demands of the mainstream Islamist movements in Algeria, Tunisia, Jordan, and Egypt follow mostly al-Banna's discourse on the Islamic state, constitutional rule, and multiparty politics. However, radical Sunni movements follow mostly the discourse of Sayyid Qutb, and Shiite political movements follow that of al-Khumayni. A prerequisite for understanding the demand of the majority of fundamentalists is an in-depth study of al-Banna's doctrine of the Islamic state, because this doctrine is the main organizing idea and driving force behind the activities of the Muslim Brotherhood throughout the Arab world. However, this cannot even be entertained—although people and scholars try anyway—without the analysis of al-Banna's political discourse. This in turn requires an understanding of al-Banna's philosophy of life as well as his religious discourse, both of which are derived from the basic sources of the Qur'an and the *sunna* and from the historical role of religion in the life of Muslims. He was not only concerned with political rule but also believed that the impurity of politics resulted from the unethical exercise of power as well as from mishandling multilayered social, economic, and educational crises. A mere change of government did not seem to be what was required or desired for the revival of the ethical spirit of the community. The state was an agency that not only organized people's affairs but transcended such a description to be morally involved in protecting creed and religion's supremacy so that a human regeneration was affected and humankind's lifestyle was amended in accordance with the spirit of religion. The state's function, though limited, must help the people to live a virtuous life by, for example, redirecting the course of education toward God. A view of life that was accepted by the people became the conditioning ground for establishing the desired state. The legitimate exercise of authority or the withdrawal of legitimacy depended, then, on the same conditions, and, once the Islamic state was established, the state could not nullify the original contract between the people and the ruler.

Of course, reestablishing the Islamic caliphate has been regarded generally by al-Banna and the Islamic movements as a revival of the highest political institution. As was the case historically, the caliphate is still viewed as the cornerstone for theoretical political discourses on government and politics. It represents politically the highest goal for Islamic movements and constitutes the symbol of Islamic unity and power. Because it brings together religion and politics, its field of study is not restricted to jurisprudence but also includes theology and the principles of religion (*usul al-din*).

In the history of Islam, great theoreticians such as al-Mawardi in *Al-Ahkam al-Sultaniyya*, Ibn Taymiyya in *Al-Siyasa al-Shar'iyya*, Abu Yusuf in *Kitab al-Kharaj*, al-Ghazali in *Al-Iqtisad fi al-I'tiqad*, Ibn Jama'a in *Tahrir al-Ahkam*, and Ibn Khaldun in the *Muqaddima* started tying the caliphate's functions and qualifications to political and economic development. In this sense, the caliphate must shoulder the responsibility of tuning the community to the ups and downs of history and representing the realities of a given age. However, when it was al-Banna's turn to discuss the caliphate, it had already been abolished by Kemal Atatürk. Thus, in al-Banna's eyes the symbol of Islamic unity was gone. The existence of the caliphate was for him a nostalgic affinity with glory and power as well as the supremacy of Islam. Because the caliphate was a historical seat of authority, its regeneration was an awesome task, as it represented nothing less than the unification of Muslims again in an international state—a difficult achievement, al-Banna knew. Its revival must be preceded by a comprehensive program of reforming the Muslims of his day and must include issues like bringing about complete educational, social, and economic cooperation among Muslim peoples; the formation of alliances and conferences among these peoples; and, finally, founding a league of nations responsible for the caliph's choice.[18]

Resolving such issues, however, was not much easier than establishing the caliphate itself, and this was the reason an alternative institution was called for that seemed more practical and achievable. As an indispensable step for establishing the caliphate, the concept of an Islamic state became as important, both theoretically and practically, as the caliphate itself. Al-Banna and others have argued for the functional legitimacy of the state along the lines of that developed for *imarat al-isti'la'* (government by seizure) and the sultanate. Again, authoritative medieval thinkers—such as al-Mawardi, Ibn Taymiyya, Ibn Jama'a, and Ibn Khaldun—accepted the legitimacy of a government that could maintain unity of Muslims under the umbrella of the *shari'a*. But if the caliphate were ever to come back, then the functional legitimacy of the Islamic state would be either altogether abrogated or functionally subjected to the caliphate.

The Muslim Brotherhood, according to al-Banna, believes that the caliphate is the symbol of Islamic unity and the sign of commitment to Islam. It is a rite that the Muslims must be concerned about achieving, for it is the caliph who is in charge of applying numerous divine legal commands. Al-Banna shows the importance of the caliphate by describing a major event surrounding the Prophet's death: the Muslims discussed and resolved the issue of political succession even before the Prophet's burial. But, because the caliphate does not exist any more, al-Banna calls for some rethinking about the issue of political rule, since it is the center of political contract between the people and their unifying agency. This is why the Muslim Brotherhood makes the revival of Islam dependent on establishing an Islamic system of government. However, the flourishing of Islam cannot take place without spreading the Qur'an and its language as well as achieving a comprehensive political unity among Muslims. At the same time, a modern Islamic government, in al-Banna's view, can take many forms, with new military, economic, and political organizations.[19]

Al-Banna grounds the Islamic government in a few Qur'anic verses:[20]

We have sent down to thee the Book in truth, that thou mightest judge between men, as guided by God: So be not (used) as an advocate by those who betray their trust. (*4:105*)

The answer of the believers, when summoned to God and His Apostle, in order that he may judge between them, is no other than this: They say, "We hear and we obey." (*24:51*)

To thee We sent the Scripture in truth, confirming the scripture that came before it, and guarding it in safety: So judge between them by what God hath revealed, and follow not their vain desires, diverging from the Truth that hath come to thee. To each among you have We prescribed a Law and an Open Way. If God had so willed, He would have made you a single people. (*5:48*)

It was We who revealed the law (to Moses): Therein was guidance and light. By its standards have been judged the Jews, by the Prophets who bowed (as in Islam) to God's Will, by the Rabbis and the Doctors of law: For to them was entrusted the protection of God's Book, and they were witnesses thereto: Therefore fear not men, but fear Me, and sell not My signs for a miserable price. If any do fail to judge by (the light of) what God hath revealed, they are (no better than) unbelievers. We ordained therein for them: "Life for life, eye for eye, nose for nose, ear for ear, tooth for tooth, and wounds equal for equal." But if anyone remits the retaliation by way of charity, it is an act of atonement for himself. And if any fail to judge by (the light of) what God hath revealed, they are (no better than) wrongdoers. (5:44–45)

Let the people of the Gospel judge by what God hath revealed therein. If any do fail to judge by (the light of) what God hath revealed, they are (no better than) those who rebel. (5:47)

Do they then seek after a judgment of (the days of) Ignorance? But who, for a people whose faith is assured, can give better judgment than God? (5:50)

These verses indicate to al-Banna the interrelationship between spiritual and political aspects, thus the linkage between religion with politics. These scriptural references constitute the legitimacy of Islamic rule and its function: promoting the spiritual, political, and economic well-being and defense of the community. Furthermore, its function is extended worldwide, especially since geographical limitations are not, in al-Banna's view, applicable to the Islamic call and, therefore, to the state that universalizes that call. Consequently, the well-being of humankind as a concern of the Islamic call makes the role of the Islamic state both moral and universal.[21] In turn, the universality of the call makes the existence of a universal caliphate a necessity, since it is the institution that transcends localities, borders, and the like. However, and for the time being, al-Banna looks at the geographic Islamic entity, or the state, as more pivotal for instituting the Islamic system. Practically speaking, it is more possible to achieve the Islamic state than to reestablish the caliphate.[22]

In al-Banna's view, an Islamic state is the essential first step for achieving the good Islamic society. Without the state, the society would find many difficulties in voluntarily organizing itself on an Islamic basis, as the nature of many basic Islamic doctrines requires an organizing agency of the first rate. Within modern geographic realities, that agency is the Islamic state.[23] For al-Banna, it is only the state that can function as both an executive agency that remedies all problems and an institution that develops Islamic laws suitable for this age. His perception of Islam as "a complete system regulating all aspects of life and including a system of social norms, government, legislation, law, and education" cannot be realized without the state. Furthermore, because a great deal of reform is of a political nature, then the state must be involved as well. Al-Banna finds that mere religiosity without solid commitment to political, social, and economic activism is useless to the community of Muslims.[24]

More important, absence of commitment to political Islam is *jahiliyya* to al-Banna, because he subordinates the legitimacy of the state to fulfilling basic Islamic goals. Because these goals include a commitment to apply Islamic law and the spread of the Islamic call, religious commitment is then linked to political legitimacy. Thus, the call to Islam is a moral and religious duty that must be carried out privately by the community and officially by the Islamic government. But it is the government that must carry out the broader essentials of the Islamic call—that is, addressing the general moral or spiritual atmosphere within the *umma* and curbing moral and political degeneration and atheistic orientations.[25] In this sense, the government becomes the executive arm of the virtuous society, and, by trust, it enactss the society's moral, religious, and political objectives. Only by following this principle does an Islamic government receive legitimate recognition from Hasan al-Banna.[26] Thus, an Islamic government could not be conceptually and functionally compartmentalized— that is, to function at one time as a secular agency, at another as religious. By following the demands of a virtuous society, the state does not produce conflicting claims but becomes the popular, guiding, social, executive power in charge of executing just laws. Only through such a role could the necessary conditions for the legitimacy of government be fulfilled.[27]

Al-Banna goes back to the state that is founded by the Prophet in order to derive the best prototype of an Islamic state and society. The reason behind this is not specifically the individuals, themselves, or their social and political settings but is, rather, a matter of attitude and philosophy. The principal foundation of that state was unity, which became the backbone of the Qur'anic social system that led to developing authentic religious models. The Qur'anic discourse and its language achieved social unity; the caliphs' unified ideological orientations led to political unity, even at a time when decentralization of government took the forms of local governors, army commanders, and tax collectors.[28] The overall structure of the state was built, however, on a solid creed that went beyond contemporary understanding of government and politics.

This conclusion about the state's function and attitude is entertained by al-Banna because he builds his political discourse on a reinterpretation of the doctrine of God's *rububiyya* (lordship) and *ha-kimiyya* (divine governance). God's universal *rububiyya* makes Islamic revelation the basic text in matters relating to both politics and political philosophy. The history of Islam shows testimonies to Muslims' subordination of politics to religion; for instance, all political expansions were made in the name of Islam.[29] And insofar as Muslims did that, they were victorious, but when they disassociated politics from true religion and lost their religious zeal, they became losers. Consequently, Islam lost the role it had played throughout history. From this, al-Banna deduces that only through a true revival of the Islamic spirit could contemporary Muslims regain both political power and international recognition. For Islam requires from its followers not only the adherence to rituals but, more important, embodying Islam in their active lives. What is also required from the government is not only a symbolic embrace of Islam but an active involvement on its behalf, which constitutes the main source for the legitimacy of government.[30]

In line with al-Ghazali's thought, al-Banna still does not give the government the upper hand in all domains of life but, instead, views it as only an appendix to the *shari'a* and as constrained by it. The government cannot then change the *shari'a* under the guise of its development. It can, however, rework its principles in accordance with changing needs and demands of society. The government's policies should not, therefore, neglect the general and guiding principles of the *shari'a*. For instance, universal principles, such as the necessity of Islamic unity, cannot forever be replaced by narrow bonds of patriotism and nationalism, although the two can be used to strengthen the universal principle. Such an act of replacement distorts the true spirit of the Qur'anic discourse, which aims at unity, not disunity. To al-Banna, denying God's *uluhiyya* over this life and the concomitant disavowal of universal unity lead simply to unbelief.[31] Therefore, al-Banna believes, a major function of the Islamic state is to refuse to yield to those ideologies and philosophies that disrupt the unity of humankind and of Muslims, in particular. In fact, the state must counterattack the political and philosophical endeavors to limit the scope of Islam through imposing humanly developed systems over God's system. If the Islamic state yields to such an act, it would be solidifying *jahiliyya* and contributing to the disunity of humankind and, thus, breaking the postulates of the *shari'a*.[32]

Yielding to other philosophies and ideologies is very disturbing to al-Banna because of his belief that the *shari'a* provides the most flexible and comprehensive universal principles that humankind and Muslims need. These principles could be the intellectual and philosophical underpinnings of an Islamic revival without yielding to alien philosophies and systems. While borrowing leads to political subjection and to the marginalization of Islam, the interpretation of Islam, for al-Banna, leads to a more authentic development of the Islamic system in line with modernity.

Democracy and *Shura*

The *shura's* absorption of, but not subordination to, democracy is an example of not yielding to other philosophies and systems. The modern *shura*, as advocated by al-Banna and others, postulates the necessity of people's involvement not only in political matters but in all issues concerning the community. *Shura* denies the legitimacy of authoritarian rule or political monopoly over the community and makes the community the source of executive power. Al-Banna argues that the ruler, regardless of his social or religious position, must not single-handedly regulate state affairs: in the final analysis, he must resort and yield to people's choices.[33] Further, employing *shura* makes the ruler sensitive to, or at least accommodating of, popular demands. Al-Banna gives us the example of courts in Egypt. In a letter addressed to Interior Minister Ahmad Khashbah, he argues that, if the government takes into consideration people's views and upholds the *shari'a* as the ultimate authority in making and amending laws, the dual judicial system of Egypt must then be amended. Uniting court systems, both secular and religious, under the *shari'a* is a religious must and is in accordance with the nature of the Egyptian people. From an

Islamic point of view, the supremacy of God's law must be maintained in all aspects: political, social, economic, and personal. Current laws, however, go against people's consciousness.[34]

The authority of Islamic law over society and people is grounded, according to al-Banna, in the following verses:[35]

> And this (He commands): Judge thou between them by what God hath revealed, and follow not their vain desires, but beware of them lest they beguile thee from any of that (teaching) which God hath sent down to thee. And if they turn away, be assured that for some of their crimes it is God's purpose to punish them. And truly most men are rebellious. (5:49)

> But no, by thy Lord, they can have no (real) Faith, until they make thee judge in all disputes between them, and find in their souls no resistance against thy decisions, but accept them with the fullest conviction. (4:65)

These verses do not only indicate the supremacy of Islamic law but also provide most fundamentalists, starting with Hasan al-Banna, with textual references to political *hakimiyya* as the major political doctrine of fundamentalist ideologies. These verses are now interpreted by the fundamentalists, in general, and by the radicals, in particular, to indicate the non-Islamicity of contemporary states, since nonadherence to this political *hakimiyya* has been viewed by the radicals as *kufr* and *shirk*. However, the possibility of such a charge has arisen because the fundamentalists have removed these verses from their social and political contexts and have universalized their use metahistorically to include every age and every country. While decontextualizing many verses may be liberating—such as is the case concerning verses related to knowledge and *shura*—yet, at times this process may lead to the opposite result of hardening and narrowing the meaning of the verses within a specific context. Harsh contexts pave the way for harsh interpretations, while favorable conditions make possible accommodating interpretations. Thus, although decontextualization opens up a wide range of possible interpretations, a particular interpretation is nevertheless linked to circumstantial variables. Instead of subjecting a specific event to textual interpretation, texts are in fact interpreted by the context of the interpreter.

Al-Banna, unlike al-Mawdudi and Qutb, does not comprehensively apply the doctrine of *hakimiyya*. In dealing with governments, he favors compromise over isolation and charges of religious unbelief. He also does not push the doctrine to its divisive limits but focuses, instead, on its unitary aspects. He also has no reservation about his organization's working in official apparatuses. Believing in the *hakimiyya* as the substantial underpinning of his political discourse does not make his method impractical. To put it differently, his political discourse is abstract and uncompromising, as in his proposing the necessity and legitimacy of God's *hakimiyya;* his method, however, is practical and compromising, because it is conducted by humans who cannot produce definite final interpretations.

The disavowal of any legitimate theoretical possibility of legislation and political action without proper grounding in the "comprehensive, flexible, and total Islamic legislation" leads al-Banna to ground the appropriateness of actions in correct doctrines. This is why he calls for the derivation of all civil, criminal, commercial, and international affairs from Islamic law. To al-Banna, it is Islamically self-defeating to ground laws for Muslims in non-Islamic laws that deal with foreign cultural peculiarities, not to mention their possible contradiction of Islam. This becomes more acute, since Islamic law, along with its eternal and comprehensive principles, has not precluded the possibilities of individual and collective reformulations.[36] In fact, when Islam was the dominant ideology in the life of the government and the people, history shows, the development of Islamic law was comprehensive and flexible.[37]

Because of the flexible nature of Islamic law, al-Banna argues that its development does not lead to reactionary thinking. He adds that the nature of Islam cannot be reactionary, since Islamic law itself allows progressive individual and collective adaptations to meet the needs of changing living conditions.[38] While Islam postulates specific eternal doctrines and ordinances, this does not mean that everything considered Islamic is divine and, thus, not subject to change. Every philosophy or ideology includes basic unchanging doctrines, but this does not make it reactionary. In this sense, al-Banna feels that labeling Islam in this way exemplifies ignorance of the nature of both divine law and Islamic jurisprudence.[39] Focusing only on a juristic fraction of Islamic law, while neglecting its overall religious roots as its organizing principle, leads to misinterpretation of Islam. The truth is that, to understand Islam, one has to see its multiple functions as part of a religious, social, and political system that includes codes of worship and behavior. Religious beliefs constitute only one part of the Islamic system, and Islam regulates both religion, in the narrow sense, and life, in a general sense. True Muslims, according to al-Banna, could not but subject all aspects of their life to Islam.[40]

Al-Banna exhorts both secular and religious scholars to extend their views of law and to unify what is considered religious and that which is secular. While the constitutive Islamic principles, from al-Banna's perspective, are not subject to agreement and change, the other Islamic rulings are.[41] More important, change does not exclude methodological differences and substantive conflicts, because human beings differ naturally over many issues and do not have recourse to an authoritative, comprehensive, final interpretation.[42] What can be ascertained, however, is the antireligious nature of humans' government over humans by pure human laws that are contrary to Islamic law; this puts the Muslim on a collision course with the government. Al-Banna explains this problem: "If the Muslim wants to amend [the law] so that it accords with his belief, the state declines on the basis of the West's rejection out of fear." However, that law clashes with Islamic law as well as the Egyptian constitution, which makes Islam the state religion; no power can legitimately amend or negate Islamic ordinances of prohibition and permission.[43] Such an action constitutes bankruptcy and *jahiliyya;* the legitimacy of any political authority stems from political rule in accordance with the Qur'an and the principles of Islamic jurisprudence.[44] As a minimum requirement for legitimacy, the government should present the *shari'a* as social law that reflects the views of the people.[45] However, the catch is that its presentation as social law requires its implementation by a representative body.[46]

In order to get over the problem of the priority of implementing the Islamic law over establishing the Islamic government or vice versa, al-Banna specifies no particular method for implementing the law. What is important is its implementation, whether carried out by a secular or by a religious government. Al-Banna posits no problem with Western-style constitutional rule, because in accordance with Islam it maintains personal freedom, upholds *shura,* postulates people's authority over government, specifies the responsibilities and accountability of rulers before their people, and delineates the responsibilities of the executive, the legislative, and the judiciary. Constitutional rule, in al-Banna's view, is thus harmonious with the *shariʿa*.[47] However, al-Banna's adoption of constitutional rule is not a matter of exactly copying a particular Western constitution. The concept is Islamized through a process of philosophical reformulation on religious grounds and is applied through objective institutions. Thus, when al-Banna criticized Egypt's experimentation with constitutional rule, he was calling for its reorientation toward Islamic law and was condemning its failure to perform objectively in Egyptian political life.[48]

On the theoretical level, al-Banna grounds constitutional rule in *shura* by claiming that it is the closest form of government to the nature of Islamic politics. More important, al-Banna finds textual justifications for adopting constitutional rule as *shura* and finds basis for its necessity in a Qur'anic text: "[A]nd consult them in affairs (of moment). Then, when thou hast taken a decision, put thy trust in God" (3:159). Such a derivation is possible, to al-Banna, because this Qur'anic revelation is interpreted as "the basic principle of rule of government and exercise of authority." The Qur'anic power is employed by al-Banna to highlight the power of the community in the making and unmaking of political systems, governments, forms of government, and political behavior. It provides the community with further powers vis-a-vis the state, which must act in conformity with the ambitions and needs of people.

Because to al-Banna the Islamic government represents the central organ of an Islamic system of government, it derives its legitimacy to exercise power from the people. The responsibility of the government is twofold: it is religious before God and political before the people. Furthermore, it is morally and politically responsible for the community's unity and, therefore, must be responsive and defer to communal preferences and wishes. The ruler's power over and responsibility before his people derives from the fact that Islam views the setting up of governments as a social contract between the ruler and the ruled so that the interests of the latter are taken care of. The ruler's reward and punishment must hinge on people's opinions. People enjoy moral supremacy over the ruler in matters of general and particular concerns. Therefore, a legitimate ruler or government must always defer to consultation with the community and yield to its will. Political forms may change from time to time and from one locality to another, but the basic rules of Islam must always be adhered to.[49]

It is obvious that al-Banna upholds people's power over government. This view is not based on the philosophy of natural rights but, rather, is developed in light of such a philosophy and because of textual references to the consultation of the people and to the absence of legitimacy of unlimited governmental powers. However, the whole concept of choice is Qur'anically justified by a reinterpretation of certain texts to conform to the democratic notion of popular governments. While the role of reason is not denied in political matters, it is employed more at the theoretical level to extract political rights and duties. Equality among human beings is postulated by the Qur'an. That this equality means equal political rights and duties is only a rational derivation. Again, this means that no individual or group can claim a privileged position, whether political or religious. Al-Banna does not ascribe equality to any natural quality such as reason but derives it from Qur'anic texts as a means to prove the necessity of rule by the people within divine *hakimiyya*.[50]

Another reason for al-Banna's democratization of *shura* is related to his ability to distinguish divine *hakimiyya* from human *hakimiyya*. The first can never be properly represented; consequently, no individual, group, or institution can properly claim to represent a specific mandate or a divine right to rule. However, the legitimacy of representing human *hakimiyya* must be sought in fulfilling and adhering to Qur'anic instructions (or, in al-Banna's words, "the Islamic constitution") on the proper conditions for carrying out *shura*. This theoretical principle, applying the Islamic constitution, defines to the *umma* at large the kind of *nizam* to be upheld. However, the practical principles that lead to applying *shura* make the *umma* the sole legitimate *sulta* (authority) for government. To al-Banna, this converts *al-amr bi-l-ma'ruf wa-l-nahy 'an al-munkar*, or enjoining the good and forbidding evil, from an ethical concept into a formulation of public, legal, and political right to watch over the government. Moreover, the ruler is made accountable not only to God but to the *umma*, as well. By believing that the exercise of authority requires the continuous ratification and approval of the *umma*, governance is transformed into nothing more than a contract between the ruled and the ruler. In this sense, Muslim politics is democratized.[51]

Al-Banna's view of the *umma*'s need to control the government's exercise of power becomes to the fundamentalists a basic component for the making of righteous politics and the fulfillment of the divine *manhaj*. Only through such a popular power could Islam be reentered into politics and a method of control be effective and subject to change from time to time. But any Islamic system must always be characterized by adopting Islamic rules of *shura* and equality and by striking a balance between the ruler and the ruled, and between the text and the people. Without proper handling of political matters and without proper consciousness, textual authorities, according to al-Banna, may not lead to the Islamic revival that the community is looking for.[52]

Meanwhile, al-Banna provides the state government with almost presidential powers of delegation and execution, in a manner similar to that of medieval Islamic political thought.[53] What is new, however, is the limitation imposed by the *shari'a* as interpreted not by jurists but by people. Two central doctrines are needed for legitimacy: justice and equality. Al-Banna sees both as the philosophical and religious guidelines that the ruler and the ruled must adhere to while legislating or exercising power.[54] *Tawhid*, then, manifests itself politically and morally in equity and justice.[55]

Furthermore, al-Banna argues that a more apparent manifestation of *tawhid* is political unity. It revolves around the Qur'an and its language under one central government. This unity does not, however, exclude the existence of the *umma* in many states, if *tawhid* constitutes the ideological framework and if *shari'a* is the law of the land.[56] That many legitimate Islamic states can coexist is, in al-Banna's view, possible under the practical orientations of modern Islamic thought and due to the conditions of modern existence. Al-Banna stands, however, against any ideological, religious disunity and internal division, which he equates with *kufr*. From this perspective, ideologically based, multiparty politics and opposed political fundamentals cannot be justified. Hence, once ideological unity becomes the basis of multiparty politics, policy differences and programs are acceptable. Al-Banna does not accept the notion that parties represent opposed doctrinal views, since all parties must adhere to *tawhid* and *wahda*. Describing the whole process of Egyptian political life in the first half of this century as divisive and corrupt, al-Banna rejects Egyptian party politics. As an alternative, the *umma* must be directly represented.[57] He explains this by saying that the Egyptian multiparty system was a stumbling block to setting up a strong *umma* under a strong leadership. And at a time when the *umma* was attempting to regain its independence and morale, party politics accepted foreign interferences and was more concerned with individual gains.[58]

More specifically, al-Banna feels that political partisanship probably does not function in Egypt, since it is exploited by foreign powers to interfere in the affairs of Egypt, and the Egyptians have suffered regardless of what party is ruling. Before a party system can function properly, Egypt must be delivered from the occupiers, the British. Furthermore, Egyptian parties are not real parties but reflect personal ambitions and foreign affiliations. As an example, he mentions the Wafd party, which started by demanding independence only to splinter later into the party of free constitutionalists. The Itihad party was the result of a deal between many parties and the king.[59]

Nevertheless, his rejection of this kind of party politics does not lead al-Banna to impose a ban on multiparty politics or to restrict freedom of expression, which must strive to show the truth to which both the majority and the minority must adhere.[60] For al-Banna, political opposition finds justification only when political authorities neither adhere to nor apply the rules of Islam. The Muslim Brothers, according to al-Banna, are neither advocates of revolution nor believers in its utility. In fact, their belief in the capacity of Qur'anic principles to stand against any ideological creed allows the *umma*— through the process of either Arabization or Islamization of political doctrines, like multiparty politics—to transcend any danger to its social and political unity.[61]

On the international level, according to al-Banna, the legitimacy of any world power must stem from its adherence to Islam. But such a situation cannot be brought about except by an Islamic state that positions itself as a guide to other nations.[62] Islam has postulated the superiority of Islamic sovereignty and the necessity of power building so that the just nation should hold power. Al-Banna grounds this view in the Qur'anic injunction that calls on Muslims to enjoin what is right and to forbid what is evil.[63]

In order to bring out the full context of this call, al-Banna hastens to provide an *aya* (verse) that guarantees the rights of non-Muslims and quells their fears about an Islamic state or an international Islamic order: "God forbids you not, with regard to those who fight you not for (your) Faith nor drive you out of your homes, from dealing kindly and justly with them: For God loveth those who are just"

(60:8). In fact, al-Banna believes in the duty of the governing authority to liberate and guide other nations into Islam: "We, the Muslims, are neither communists nor democrats nor anything similar to what they claim; we are, by God's grace, Muslims, which is our road to salvation from Western colonialism."[64]

Conclusion

Al-Banna's political discourse is grounded in his view of metaphysical *tawhid* and its political articulation, divine *hakimiyya*. While al-Banna could, theoretically, have stressed refusal to compromise and denial of the other, he did not—a choice that was taken up later by others. During his time, al-Banna opened the theoretical possibility of harmonizing Western political thought with the Islamic. Unlike al-Mawdudi and Sayyid Qutb, who radicalized the doctrine of *hakimiyya,* he transformed it into a human act. To him divine governance might at times coexist with the worldly *jahiliyya*. "No governance (*hukm*) except God's" becomes, in al-Banna's view, a linchpin that could be employed to claim rights and powers that have been historically denied to Muslims by their rulers. Governance is a comprehensive doctrine that could be used morally, legally, politically, and internationally. Because its power is originally textual and its exercise is basically communal, it has become a powerful tool used by most fundamentalists to evaluate political rules on scriptural bases. But in reality they have judged political governments in terms of the actual exercise of power. Whenever *hakimiyya* is mentioned nowadays, it means this kind of rule based on scriptural Qur'anic precepts extracted from their social, economic, political, and historical contexts. This is the reason all fundamentalists, radical or not, advocate the fulfillment of God's *hakimiyya* by at least replacing existing governments with Islamic ones. But *hakimiyya* does not mean, by definition, withdrawing into oneself and rejecting any dealing with the community. In fact, al-Banna dealt openly with, and tried practically to influence, Egyptian politics.

Although divine governance has become to al-Banna an absolute political doctrine, so has the doctrine of *shura*. In fact, the realization of the former becomes dependent on the good exercise of the latter. What al-Banna's development of *shura* has done is to absorb democracy within Islamic political thought and, consequently, to take the initiative from its secular advocates. It has also provided legitimate religious means toward gaining control of government, since legitimacy is linked to popular approval. By denying any contradiction between democracy, on one hand, and constitutional rule with *shura* and divine law, on the other, al-Banna could postulate their correspondence. This view has become a part of his and the fundamentalists' nonhistorical discourses which transform Islam into a system capable of absorbing what is best in philosophy, politics, economics, science, and history without the need to deny the validity of Islam. On the contrary, this shows to the fundamentalists the true nonhistorical and metaphysical power of the Islamic revelation as an eternal message capable of meeting the needs that arise from development.

Al-Banna has also created a distinction between the Muslims' understanding of Islamic history, history itself, and Islam. Our understanding of the history of Islam is not identical to Islam. This understanding is only one discourse on Islam within specific spatiotemporal conditions. Therefore, according to al-Banna, history and people's understanding of it, as well as their understanding of Islam, have no normative status in themselves. In fact, their correctness depends on their utility to society and Islam. Al-Banna further considers any deformation as grounded in forcing Islam to yield to historical events and their justifications. Meanwhile, though constitutional rule in the West and *shura* in Islamic history had quite different historical origins, al-Banna finds no theoretical problem in forcing their correspondence. In fact, he has no hesitation in calling for adopting Western models of government. An act like this is not un-Islamic; rather, it is Islamic since it helps the Islamic state to run its affairs along divine postulates. Of course, al-Banna rejects secularism and communism, but not every Western doctrine is, to him, secular or communist. Muslims can and should, he feels, benefit from the other and develop their thinking in order to keep pace with basic changes in the world.

What al-Banna has done also is to rework the meaning and formative character of history. He extracts historically loaded terms from their history in order to imbue them with modern meanings. He assumes that the problems that Muslims suffer from are the existence of particular doctrines that made the West victorious. While such doctrines are not necessarily wrong, more than just a transfer is needed to induce any revival. Islamic political theory has been until modern times in need of major development and more practical focus in the formation of a justly constituted authority. Because a text can indicate more than one meaning, in al-Banna's view, it could be argued that it is relative; still, the meaning becomes restrictive and absolute. The interpretation of "And consult with them" is binding on both the ruler and the ruled; any deviation from such an interpretation, or in its implementation, becomes sufficient grounds for charges of illegitimacy and for active opposition to the ruler.

Shura has become, for al-Banna and almost all of the fundamentalist movements, the source of legitimation of any authority, while the continuation of legitimacy hinges on the application of the *shari'a* and popular approval. While great political thinkers such as al-Mawdudi, al-Ghazali, and Ibn Taymiyya have justified seizure of power if the ruler, the sultan, or the prince upheld only nominally the superiority of *shari'a,* one wonders what prevents contemporary Islamic movements from seizing power in the name of Islam! If people do not want an Islamic state and if an Islamic movement succeeds in setting up an Islamic state, could such a state be legitimate from a fundamentalist point of view? In other words, if the ultimate organizing principle is *shura,* then the fundamentalists should accept a secular government if one is chosen by the people; however, if the ultimate government stands on its own, then there is no need to postulate *shura* as being the ultimate organizing principle. One could get around this theoretical difficulty only when the people are devout Muslims and employ *shura.* The historical experience of Muslims shows that, by giving the state the power to employ and to execute *shari'a* in the name of the *umma,* more substantial doctrines of *shari'a* were overlooked in favor of a political interpretation of Islam. What is needed seems to be more than just an overhaul of doctrines that might ultimately be used by political authority.

However, one cannot but commend al-Banna's introduction of democracy as *shura* into the main political doctrines of fundamentalism, at a time when one of the major practical difficulties of real politics is the authoritarian nature of politics exercised in the Muslim world. While the theoretical difficulty mentioned above is still being dealt with (see the later chapters on Qutb and al-Turabi), the existence of an Islamically developed democracy justified by textual authorities seems better than the denial altogether of the important role of democracy in politics.

5

The Discourse of Sayyid Qutb on Political Ideology and the Islamic State

Qutb asserted that he had lived a *jahili* life until he joined the Muslim Brotherhood. While such a life educated him in the sciences and modern aspects of living, it fell short of providing inner satisfaction.[1] Born in 1906 in Musha in the district of Asyut, Qutb received his bachelor of arts degree in education from Dar al-'Ulum, where he became an instructor and published his first book, *Muhimmat al-Sha'ir fi al-Hayat*.[2] He joined the Ministry of Education, working as a teacher from 1933 until 1939. He was intellectually and politically influenced by 'Abbas Mahmud al-'Aqqad and defended adopting Westernization. Qutb's articles, which were published in respected journals, focused on the critical analysis of political and literary issues, with special criticism directed at the government. In 1947, Qutb became the editor of *al-'Alam al-'Arabi* and *al-Fikr al-Jadid*. It was also during that time that he became dissatisfied with Egyptian party politics and resigned from the Sa'dist party.[3]

In 1948, Qutb was sent by the Ministry of Education to the United States, where he studied at many institutions, including the University of Northern Colorado, where he obtained a master's degree in education. While he was there, his book *Al-'Adala al-Ijtima'iyya fi al-Islam* was published; it proved to be the first of his long list of books espousing fundamentalist Islam. Upon his return to Egypt, Qutb wrote for the first time in the Brethren's journal, *Al-Da'wa*, and resigned from his new post in 1951 as Advisor to the Ministry of Education.[4]

Qutb then joined the Muslim Brotherhood, a movement that participated in the revolution of 1952. Later he became advisor to the Revolutionary Council. By 1953, Qutb was devoting all his activities to the Muslim Brotherhood. He became a member of the Working Committee and the Guidance Council and acted as head of the propaganda section of the Muslim Brotherhood.[5] He edited *Al-Ikhwan al-Muslimun* before it was banned in 1954, at the time of the dissolution of the Muslim Brotherhood. The Brotherhood was accused of conspiracy to overthrow the government, and its journals were banned and its leaders and thousands of its followers were arrested and jailed. In 1955, the "People's Court" sentenced Qutb to fifteen years in prison, where Qutb and many others were tortured. Qutb stayed in prison until 1964, then was released and kept under surveillance.[6] Eight months later, Qutb and his brother Muhammad and sisters Hamida and Amina were jailed. He was charged with preparing for an armed revolt and terrorist activities. President 'Abd al-Nasir rejected a worldwide campaign to spare Qutb's life, and he was hanged in August 1966.[7] Posthumously, Qutb has become the leading theoretician and symbol of radical fundamentalism all over the Islamic world.

The Foundations of Sayyid Qutb's Discourse

The Universal Islamic Concept

From Qutb's viewpoint, Islam is a comprehensive way of living which includes all aspects of this life and the life to come. It is so inclusive that it is difficult to imagine a main issue that is not covered by Islam. It includes both religious and worldly affairs, the spiritual and the physical, the ordinary and the extraordinary.[8] All of this, however, is linked to *al-mafhum al-kawni al-Islami* (the universal Islamic concept), which functions as the main constituent of Islam and engulfs all aspects of life. Furthermore, it provides the essentials for building his Islamic discourse on life, truth, knowledge, humans' role in the universe, values, and, above all, an interpretation of the meaning of life.[9]

To Qutb, seven characteristics make this concept superior and substantive: the oneness of God, divinity, constancy, comprehensiveness, balance, positiveness, and realism. The oneness of God, or *taw-hid*, is viewed by Qutb as both the essential component and the main characteristic of the universal Islamic concept. *Tawhid* covers all religions, especially the monotheistic ones like Christianity and Judaism. Islam, therefore, means submission to *tawhid*, which requires following God's path in every aspect of life, whether ritualistic, like prayer, or political, like obeying divine laws and order. It further indicates the need for positive submission to God and negative revolt against submitting to other authorities, be they concrete, metaphorical, metaphysical, or political. Therefore, the only truly Islamic way of life, for Qutb, is the one that ties together all differentiated aspects of life into one solid unit organized around *tawhid*. This is the basic foundation for Islamic politics, economics, ethics, and everything else. The grounding for all of this should be in the text of revelation, not in the traditions or hearsay. A Muslim's belief that there is no ruler and legislator but God should mean that He is the ultimate organizer of life and the universe. Qutb's political discourse is dominated by this idea to the extent that it is extended into all aspects of life, the personal as well as the public, the individual as well as the social, and, of course, the political. In fact, it guarantees to Qutb the coherence of the individual, society, and state.[10]

His view of *tawhid* as textually derived serves to narrow Qutb's understanding of humankind's ways of living into only two attitudes: the divinely Islamic and the *jahili* non-Islamic. This division views any style of living as a system of life; therefore, the individuals who regulate their lives in terms of the divine are God's followers, or *hizb al-Allah*. Conversely, those individuals who follow any other category or human philosophies or nontextually derived religious doctrines are opponents of the divine, or simply *hizb al-Shaytan*.[11] According to Qutb, the divine system of life should be based on a textual, metaphysical doctrine and should include a general political and social order.

Qutb treats every system of life as a religion, based on the idea that a religion or a system is the method that organizes life. Conversely, religion should not be made up of abstract notions but should regulate life, in general, and discipline behavior, in particular. In this subtle way, for instance, Qutb identifies communism as a religion,[12] since any system that regulates life is a religion regardless of its naming. The religion of an individual is, then, his consistent behavior. The conclusion that Qutb wants his reader to arrive at is that those Muslims who do not make Islam their system of life are not truly Muslims. They may have partially followed Islam, but this is insufficient to make somebody a true Muslim, since mere belief without active adherence is worthless and is not conducive to good life. This relates to government, state, society, and political life as well as to the individual, the personal, and so forth.

Qutb's interpretation of religion focuses on praxis rather than theory for the deepening and developing of belief—action being the sign of true belief. Defining religion in this way, Qutb uses religion for encouraging activism in social and political matters and for rejecting non-Islamically derived systems, philosophies, and ways of life. To Qutb, Islam is superior to other religious and nonreligious systems, as its discourse is characterized by vital and direct allusions to great truths that are incomprehensible by human methods. The discourse addresses theoretically and practically the innermost aspects of humanity. Human philosophies limit the truth, because most human encounters cannot be properly expressed and are beyond the comprehension of human thought; these philosophies are, in Qutb's view, full of unnecessary complication, confusion, and dryness.[13]

While composed metaphysically of allusions, religion to Qutb is still the only valid source for knowledge and action. He further denies the methodological and substantive legitimacy and the validity of modern as well as medieval and classical philosophies. For him, there is no special discourse dedicated to any elite, be it religious or philosophical; the Qur'anic discourse is directed at and should be adhered to by all—the common and the elite. The inaccessibility of ultimate universal principles makes any pretension to substantive superior knowledge worthless and pretentious and reduces proper interactions with the true allusions that constitute the bases of credible and possible knowledge, a well-ordered life, and the fulfillment of humanity.

While the second characteristic, divinity (*al-uluhiyya*), indicates to Qutb the unchangeableness of the concept itself, it still keeps the door open to its interpretation.[14] On the one hand, it is unchangeable because God is its author and source, while Prophet Muhammad is the agency of transmission whose mission is essentially to faithfully preach divine doctrines, not human development. The Prophet, like other Muslims, is bound by the same divine law, but he is singled out as a messenger of God.[15] Thus, the Prophet's function was not to philosophize and invent doctrines and philosophies but literally to adhere to the divine law. In this sense, Qutb makes the prophetic discourse a consequence of the Qur'anic discourse and dependent on it. Divine knowledge transmitted through revealed texts surpasses human knowledge, even that of the Prophet, insofar as the divine authority surpasses any human source of knowledge. If this is the case with the Prophet, it is rather easier for Qutb to deny any formative role or even more authentic understanding of religion by theologians and jurists.

On the other hand, divinity of the universal Islamic concept also means that, while it is eternal, its understanding is not and is subject to the conditions of the interpreter and the tools of interpretation. Qutb makes a distinction here between understanding the text and the text, itself. The textually derived Islamic concept is eternally solid; human understanding is eternally fluid. Thus, the possibilities of understanding or reading the universal Islamic concept are extended throughout space and time and becomes linked to the material, political, and economic conditions of the reader and interpreter. Thus, the basic text, or the Qur'an, can be read, interpreted, and understood differently by different generations and individuals. Consequently, past discourses on the meaning of Qur'an should not limit the possibility of diverse modern and contemporary understanding of the text as well as the past, itself. Qutb theoretically accepts different readings and discourses on the text insofar as no violation of the text, itself, is involved. The text cannot be contradicted by a past or present human discourse but only by another text. In other words, what Qutb aims at is establishing the need to reread the Qur'anic text in light of modernity and, hence, developing a modern Qur'anic discourse suitable to modernity.

While the divine concept itself is perfect, human thought is imperfect, lacks permanence, is incapable of transcendence, and falls victim to paganism, Qutb argues. Furthermore, human thought is strongly influenced by its environment and easily motivated by emotions and desire. Thus, for instance, Western thought is not universal but the by-product of specific political and economic conditions. Even its religious foundation is no more than the result of those conditions. Because of this, Qutb believes that he could easily dismiss ancient and modern Western culture and philosophy and exclude them from the development of modern Islamic discourses. Even Medieval Islamic philosophy and theology are excluded because they are Greek and, therefore, in Qutb's view, un-Islamic. The paganism of Greek thought, according to Qutb, is the first foundation of Western thought and the main cause for opposing it as well as its derivatives.[16]

Because the universal concept is divine to Qutb, then it must enjoy constancy, or *al-thabat,* which is its third characteristic. For its basis, the Qur'an along with its divine truths, is constant. Prime ideas on divine oneness, angels, the day of judgment, and the like are not subject to addition or subtraction or to change and development.[17] Furthermore, it is constant in terms of its function as the regulator of human thought to safeguard a proper Islamic way of life and guarantee stability of human, individual, and social values. Qutb is very disturbed by the instability of spiritual, social, and political life.[18] To Qutb, Western concepts of development have done away with any stability for humankind and have replaced the innermost, constant human feelings with interests of material progress, therefore depriving humankind of enjoying material progress from a real human profile. The relationship to God and to fellow humans is reduced to fluctuating issues, but in Islam these basic issues—like humans' position in the universe, their fate, their relation with this universe, and their relation with the Creator—provide Muslims with positive constancy that allows them to enjoy a peaceful and stable life.[19]

Moreover, this kind of constancy provides, from Qutb's view, harmony between the Qur'anic discourse and human life. It functions as an Islamic protector of Muslims against misconceived doctrines, concepts, and systems. It further provides Muslims with the basis of a stable and permanent society, which permits the freedom of development and which has allowed Islam to withstand aggressions against its doctrines and peoples throughout history.[20]

Comprehensiveness, or *al-shumuliyya,* is the fourth characteristic of the universal Islamic concept. Qutb formulates this characteristic against the limitedness and partiality of human thought. A divine, constant *tawhid* cannot but be comprehensive, covering all aspects of life throughout history and transcending the particularities of time and place. Thus, he puts forward this formula: "[T]he Islamic concept is comprehensive whereas man's concepts are partial and limited." Again, while humans are limited in knowledge and experience, their weaknesses and desires are not. It is, therefore, only the Islamic concept that gives humankind an intelligible, interpretative discourse about the phenomena in life and the universe. In Qutb's view, it is the revealed religious discourse that should dominate all aspects of life because of its ability to provide humankind with a meaningful, yet true, discourse about the divine and the human, the social and the individual, the public and the private.[21] As opposed to human systems, Islam does not falsely inform humans or misdirect their activities.

According to Qutb, the fifth characteristic of the universal Islamic concept, al-tawazun (balance), precludes the development of rash and exaggerated attitudes and philosophies similar to those postulated by other religions and systems. It balances the known with the unknown. For instance, while humans surrender to God and accept by faith those issues that are beyond human understanding, like the nature of God's existence or the existence of the day of judgment, the mind is free to investigate those issues that are within the capability of human understanding. Because of its fitra, humankind possesses a natural inclination to submit to the unknown, and Islam satisfies that need by addressing humans' consciousness. However, humans possess also the counter-inclination to know and to make sense of this life, and Islam also meets this need by calling on humankind to extend its knowledge in the sciences that are within human reach. However, the human mind should be careful not to confuse these two aspects of life, because the investigation of the first is futile and impossible, while too much emphasis on the latter leads to confusion. Islam balances the two by giving humans certain points of reference to avoid aimlessness.[22]

The balance of the Islamic concept acts, as well, in drawing the right relationship between the absolute divine will and the stable and observed universal laws and rules, Qutb continues. The laws of nature are, in his view, no more than phenomena of the divine will; there is no necessary relationship between cause and effect, except what has been divinely ordained. What humans can do, then, is to observe and codify laws and consequently realize their objectives and adjust their lives accordingly.[23] For Qutb, the most important benefit of balance is that, in the constancy of the universal laws and the absoluteness of the divine will, the conscience is not without solid grounds and is able, therefore, to adjust its course from one time to another. More important, humans are no longer slaves to nature or afraid of its consequences—such as death—because they then view all of nature, as well as their lives, as part of a totality designed by the divine will. Thus, Qutb argues, part of balance is due to the fact that Islam is part and parcel of nature and an integral part of the universe. In this sense, Islam offers universal concepts, not the narrow and conditioned ones of the human philosophies, which have led for centuries to the loss of a comprehensive thought that integrates all aspects of life and unifies humankind. Human thinking suffers from inventing doctrines that corrupt divine concepts, such as using rationalism and too much dependence on scientific experimentation and its tentative outcomes as a way of understanding the ultimate. This has led to confusing metaphysics with science.[24]

The sixth characteristic of the universal concept, *al-ijabiyya* (positiveness), relates to how humans interact with God, the universe, and life. Mainly, Qutb argues that the divine origin of Islam necessitates activism, not mere inactive belief. God is neither an inactive perfection nor restricted to one aspect or another—like the Persians' gods of light and gods of darkness, Plotinus's idea of God, the God of only Israel, or the mix of divine and human in Christianity.[25] In Qutb's view, the oneness of God embodies a positive concern about the world and the call to Muslims to establish Islamic communities and to deal practically with the individual, the society, and the state. Not only could Islam survive in the conscience, theory, or ideals of the spiritual realm, but it is also a design for an active commitment to bring about the practical fruits of the divine oneness. Its proper understanding turns it into an individual, social, and political motivating force for the improvement of the community.

The last of the seven characteristics is *al-waqi'iyya* (realism), which means to Qutb that Muslims must deal with the real world. Islam does not view the world abstractly but postulates an overall order for improvement. Realism, from Qutb's perspective, does not mean that he accepts any reality but that what Islam calls for is feasible and possible and is not beyond human reach. For instance, the quest for an Islamic state is realistic in that sense and not because it actually exists. Islamic realism is also idealistic in the sense that it attempts to bring up humankind to adopt an ideal. Thus, idealistic realism means that Muslims interact with the realities of this world to uplift humans to their true nature and the divine design. Thus, to Qutb, realistic idealism is the other side of the coin. In other words, though Islam does not call for things that are beyond human capabilities, it still aims at the highest possible human perfection. It is realistic in its demands on humans, societies, and doctrines.[26]

Qutb's Political Discourse

According to Qutb, the most fundamental political impact of revealed *tawhid*, or the universal Islamic concept, is its postulation of *shari'a*, whose political doctrines focus on social justice and revolution. Seeking the establishment of a righteous community through obedience to the Islamic law, Islam revolts against controlling humankind by human laws and systems—an act that Qutb considers to be unbelief. To Qutb, while the proper law governing humankind should be the *shari'a*, it is also the method that leads humankind to establish just societies. Establishing such societies is more necessary nowadays because humankind is losing its true nature, and its problems are on the increase. Qutb's political ideology or theory is then made up of three underpinnings: divine *shari'a* versus human law, social justice versus materialism, and revolutionary Muslim societies versus non-Muslim societies.[27]

The Shari'a versus Human Law

Tawhid, to Qutb, acts both as a liberating tool, to free humans from the domination of unjust authorities in order to establish the Islamic state, and as a social tool, for the development of an Islamic value system and as a system of law. The *shari'a* plays the role of harmonizing the different aspects of life, from setting up governments to prohibiting the legislation of normative values and doctrines. Qutb argues that the revealed Islamic *shari'a* eliminates the possibility of any unwarranted human control by exploiting legislation. The *shari'a* sets both social and political systems on broader moral order and on universal divine laws, as outlined in the Qur'an. Because divine laws are not webbed into the interests and customs of peculiar groups, they do not function, as do human laws, in an alienating manner. But Muslims can, at the same time, base their legislation and its development on the general *usul al-fiqh* (roots of jurisprudence). While articulating particular doctrines depends on the conditions of the interpreter, this is tentative in the case of Islamic law. Human laws have no true reference but people, whose desires and ambitions dictate the principles to be followed. To Qutb, Islamic law is not a social phenomenon but an eternal manifestation of the divine will, defining the moral, social, and political order. In this sense, humankind should follow the order, because it represents the metahistorical and universal basis. Any human legislation that goes against the order has, therefore, no positive and legal standing. Human legislation, then, should be limited to codification and recodification, as required by the different conditions of societies.[28]

Qutb argues that moral and political sovereignty is a divine right; humans' duty is, therefore, to submit to it; otherwise, humans fall prey to polytheism, or *shirk*. Any human action or thinking is correct insofar as it involves no contradiction of the divine law. Sovereignty in principle and legislation belongs to God, and its significance goes beyond rituals and beliefs to include politics and government. While the objective of the law is salvation in the next life, still that cannot be achieved without proper living in this life. The two lives should be integrated, and the instrument for that is the *shari'a*. Because it harmonizes the lives of humans with the divine will, its universal application becomes a duty for all Muslims in order to attain the Islamic order.[29]

Furthermore, Qutb organically links morality and the *shari'a* and underscores the need for obedience by the ruler and the ruled, as nonadherence to the *shari'a* by any government, whether democratic or autocratic, removes legitimacy. Qutb views an Islamic government as, first, the government of law, and, second, the government of the ruled. Rulers are, however, no more than servants of Islamic law. Legitimacy is then of substantive nature and does not stop at the formal level. While the formal aspect of the government's function is to regulate human affairs in accordance with *shura,* and the individual is obliged to obey the government, obedience cannot be unconditional or absolute. Nonadherence to Islamic law removes any formal legitimacy and creates sufficient grounds for disobedience and revolution.

Consequently, legitimacy and law become synonyms for Qutb, who argues that even the formal aspect of legitimacy, *shura,* is part of the law and, hence, is substantive like any other aspect. This is why, functionally, legitimacy starts with Muslims' choice but continues through applying the law. That people should continue obeying the ruler stems from his adherence to the *shari'a*. Thus, Qutb makes a distinction between the ruler's function as the executive of law and the initial source of authority that is based on his merits. The ruler derives initial authority and legitimacy from people, in general; their continued support is, however, linked to proper application of the *shari'a*. But the ruler, as an individual, has no intrinsic religious authority or a divine right derived from God. He derives authority from Muslims' consent.[30] Thus, Qutb participates in the democratic notion of the legitimacy of representative government or "the government of *umma.*" His understanding of people's will is a compromise between popular sovereignty and absolutism. Therefore, the ruler's legitimate authority stems theoretically from two basic components: people's consent and the application of Islamic law.

Thus, Qutb becomes capable of turning down many parts of the formal legitimacy that was advocated in medieval Islamic thought. He does this by a process of dehistoricizing and modernizing Islamic political thought on questions of instituting and removing governments and legitimacy. He thereby negates many of the accepted medieval notions of government and politics, such as hereditary government, rule by seizure, and descent from the Prophet's tribe (*Quraysh*). As a general guide, Islam does not specify any superiority, not even the Prophet's; all Muslims are equal regardless of their ancestry.[31] More important, Qutb directs his conclusions about the past toward dealing with the issues of modern governments and politics. In denying the legitimacy of historical processes, Qutb wants to condemn changes made now to Islamic principles. Rejecting the use of force to attain power in the past is also directed at contemporary Muslim rulers who seize power and are not popularly chosen. Consequently, contemporary Muslims can legitimately free themselves from imposed governments.

Again, Qutb rejects any allusion to the Islamic government being a theocratic government, because there is, to begin with, no single class that should be properly endowed with religious rule. Furthermore, it is only by applying Islamic law that the Islamic government is properly established. Because Islam has created a society that is based on law, Qutb's repudiation of theocracy stems from his opposition to the assumed clergy's authority. Qutb underscores the distinction between "men of religion," or clergy, and religious power: the first has no power; the second is invested in the people. The clergy's rule should not be taken as an Islamic political ideal, for neither theory nor practice supports it.[32]

Qutb looks to the Prophetic rule and its extension, the rule of the first two caliphs, as comprising a universal human model, because of their religious, moral, social, and political achievements. This model provided the bases of exemplary conduct and doctrines addressing topics that ranged from humans' true nature to political, social, and economic duties and rights. However, Qutb is not calling for the reinstitution of that Islamic system or the return to that Muslim society. To him, the Islamicity of any system relates to its adherence to Islamic principles; however, its form may change, and it is subject to the development of society. Consequently, a multitude of forms can be accepted as long as they are grounded in general Islamic principles. Qutb's priority is not the government's form but the cultivation of Muslims who have strong beliefs and are capable of setting up an Islamic society. In a truly Islamic life, organizational systems are, then, secondary.[33]

However, Qutb's elaboration on government's forms makes formal legitimacy dependent on public choice and denies all elitist forms. Representative government becomes, because of its basic principle (*shura*), the cornerstone in forming any state. In one way or another, Qutb is postulating the need for public participation and demands the right to elect rulers. He does that also through dehistoricizing and deconstructing the interpretations of *shura*. For instance, while Muslim *'ulama'* had to nominally approve the ruler's selection, once elected, the ruler had a free hand within the *shari'a*. Moreover, Qutb's argument that *shura* is not specifically defined and that its form is an organizational matter depending on the needs of every age has no doctrinal or historical precedent. *Shura* has been the scholars' domain by advising rulers.

Thus, to Qutb, those societies that do not organize their lives in accordance with the divine law are *jahili* societies, for the very definition of a real nation involves a group of people bound by religion as its nationality. Otherwise, there is no religiously real nation, because land, race, language, and material interests are not adequate.[34] To Qutb, the importance of Islam is its capability of uniting humankind on religious bases and doing away with racial, linguistic, territorial, and cultural differences. Religion should be the Muslims' nationality. Therefore, Muslims must not copy from Christians, who separate state politics from church. The European experience differs, then, from the Islamic, and Islam is different from Christianity in that the latter does not postulate a political code.[35]

Social Justice versus Materialism

In Qutb's view, Islam is at a crossroads, and there are two basic ideologies challenging it: communism, on the one hand, and capitalism, on the other. Because of usury, monopoly, exploitation, and injustice, Qutb refuses to view capitalism as a model that Muslims should follow. Moreover, capitalism has been linked closely to nationalism. Countries like England, France, Italy, and Germany gave themselves, in the name of national interest, the right to exploit, invade, or occupy other countries in the Middle East, India, Africa, or Latin America. Even though socialism and Islam converge on many essential points, such as advocating guarantees of minimum life standards, work, housing, and social justice, an Islamic economic system should be an integral part of Islam.

On yet another level, Marxism and Islam clash head on. Islam is founded on belief in God, while Marxism strives to deny Him. Dialectical materialism is the Marxist core. Ultimately, the conflict presented in economic terms (capitalist, communist, or socialist) is, to Qutb, the conflict between spiritualism and materialism. The former is represented by Islam and religion, in general; the latter is demonstrated by capitalism, socialism, and communism. Qutb argues that Marxism is the most advanced level of mechanical and intellectual materialism, and though the two camps, the capitalist and the socialist, disagree and wage wars for benefits, their difference is a matter of degree, of organization, and of method. Because the materialistic idea of life underlies all of them, Qutb predicts the final victory for Marxism over capitalism when the economies of the West reach stagnation. This is so because communism is nothing but a progressive idea when compared to capitalism. It is progressive because it provides basic material needs for people and addresses the exploited, while capitalism addresses governing authorities and the exploiting class. However, the outcome of both ideologies is unjust because, under capitalism, individuals and their ambitions rule over the community and, under communism, the state rules over individuals.[36]

The alternative to Qutb is Islam, which has stipulated equal opportunity but has made piety and morality rather than material possession the basic values of society. Although it has set forth the right of individual possession and made it the basis of its economic system, it simultaneously imposes limits. An Islamic economic system is neither capitalist nor socialist. What is essential in any Islamic economic system is social justice, and Qutb provides its two primary principles: first, the harmonious, balanced, and absolute unity between the individual and groups; second, the general mutual responsibility between the individuals and groups. The importance of justice stems from its being an ethical doctrine as well as one of the Islamic bases of government. Entrusted with authority that originally belongs to God, the ruler must manifest this trust in, first, obedience to the *shari'a* and, second, social, economic, and political justice.[37] To guarantee administration of justice, Qutb identifies three principles: complete liberation of conscience, human equality, and mutual social responsibility.

Qutb considers morality to be the basis of a stable and coherent society. True social justice exists only when supported, first, by an internal feeling of the individual's worthiness and the community's need and, second, by a creed leading to obeying God and to realizing a sublime human society. Economic liberation is insufficient by itself for realizing a good society or the survival of good individuals in society. Furthermore, liberation cannot be guaranteed by laws alone, because humans are affected by needs and inclinations. What is equally, if not more, important than economic liberation is the liberation of conscience.

Liberating the human conscience from worshiping others but God can be attained only when humankind is freed from submission to all but God, Qutb explains. To do this, Islam disciplines the conscience by inculcating piety and then entrusting it as the guardian of society. Islam makes the human conscience the protector and executor of legislation. This trust is manifested, for instance, in legal decisions, which are usually dependent on the conscience of witnesses whose testimony can put someone in prison or to death. Nonetheless, Islam does not leave the conscience alone and unguided but, instead, considers God as the monitor and witness of people's behavior. For this reason, piety is essential in Islamic life and politics, for when the conscience is liberated from fear, which lowers self-esteem, the individual can be trusted. What this ultimately means to Qutb is that, if the conscience is liberated from enslavement and submission to humans and is full of God's love, the individual will not be afraid of anyone or of losing his livelihood or office. Thus, liberation from fear through obedience to none but God is one of the cardinal principles for building a just society.

Another important point is liberation from enslavement to social values. Qutb is aware that an individual can be liberated from fears but enslaved to social values. Thus, besides the moral and spiritual aspects, liberation also has political and material implications. Private ownership is allowed so that the individual is provided with financial independence from the state, which in turn allows political independence. Ultimately, the individual is capable of challenging any state that disobeys the *shari'a*.[38]

The liberation of conscience becomes, in Qutb's view, all the more essential in order to eliminate injustice and cultivate justice. Qutb believes that administering justice depends on cultivating the conscience. He tells us that, when the conscience has tasted liberation, it finds legal and practical guarantees to assure its continuation. And there will be no need for someone to advocate equality in words, for the conscience has tasted its meaning in its depths and has found it a reality in its life. Because it will not tolerate existing inequality, it will demand its right to equality, struggle to establish this right, preserve it when obtained, and accept nothing less than equality.[39]

Qutb himself acknowledges humans' inequality, and this is why the Islamic right to own property is just; it rewards individual efforts, is suitable to human nature, and motivates individuals to do their utmost. Herein is an acknowledgment that unequal efforts deserve unequal rewards. It is unjust to treat people who are unequal equally. Human faculties—spiritual, intellectual, or physical—are unequal; to assert the opposite is a vanity, according to Qutb. Notwithstanding this acknowledgment, Qutb maintains that every individual should have an equal opportunity.[40]

Although success should depend only on an individual's achievement, regardless of race and other characteristics, real equality should start even before actual existence. Qutb argues that the Islamic community as a whole is responsible for the protection of the weak, the poor, and the needy. Consequently, the state should train people to work so that their primary needs can be satisfied. In the case of those who cannot find work and are unable to meet their needs, the state has to step in and help. To Qutb, the state is not a joint-stock company. An individual has the right to be supported in fulfilling basic needs. Therefore, Qutb views Islamic mutual responsibility not merely as charity but also as a system of preparing people to work and guaranteeing basic necessities to those who cannot. Mutual responsibility is not only an individual duty; it is a public duty, as well. He states that Islam considers acquiring education, with which one can earn and deserve his livelihood, a duty of every individual. The community has a responsibility to facilitate its fulfillment. If the community is incapable of performing this duty, it becomes a state responsibility.[41] Qutb stresses the importance of society over the state; the state intervenes only where the voluntary efforts of individuals and society fail. Therefore, the state, at least in theory, is supplementary to the individual and society, and as long as they can get along without the state, the state should not interfere.

In order to demonstrate to Muslims one of the positive aspects of Islam, Qutb argues that Islam's esteem for life is comprehensive, and its stipulations on rights and duties are precise and conclusive. It has considered the nation to be one body and, on this basis, has set up severe *hudud* (deterrents) for social crimes, since cooperation requires the protection of individuals. Every individual is responsible for protecting the community's interests. In order to highlight the universality of Islamic social justice, Qutb generally views social and international problems as the outcome of injustice among nations. To be true and Islamic, then, justice should be extended to all countries, races, and religions. He states that Islam secures complete social justice in Islamic countries, not only for its adherents but also for all its inhabitants, regardless of their religion, race, and language.[42] From Qutb's view, this Islamic characteristic is unparalleled in any other ideology. Furthermore, Islam has attained a high level of fairness and is free of tribal, racial, and familial loyalties; it has become universal.[43]

Mutual responsibility is also of an economic nature, and Qutb's economic theory is based on his doctrine of social justice. In turn, the latter is part of his political theory based on *tawhid*. Since the well-being of any society requires an economic infrastructure, Qutb attempts to provide an alternative to communism and capitalism. He argues that the function of the government is the enforcement of the law of nature. He accepts the doctrine of natural rights, including that of property. The first principle in the Islamic economic theory is the right of individuals to private ownership. Islam stipulates, however, that ownership is nonexistent except by the authority of the Lawgiver—that is, God. This is the case because rights are not derived from the essence of things but from the permission of the Lawgiver. His reason is that God is the owner of everything, and human-kind is His vicegerent. This vicegerency allows humans to acquire private property, although the acquisition of private property is de-pendent on labor, physical or otherwise. Any ownership of property that is not based on the legal prescriptions of Islam and labor is false possession, because Islam does not acknowledge or guarantee it. Therefore, developing any financial enterprise should be within the framework of Islamic laws. Thus, the benefits of gambling, cheating, monopoly, or excessive gain are illegal and cannot be guaranteed in an Islamic state.[44]

The reason behind this, according to Qutb, is that the individual does not possess the thing, itself, but rather its benefits. Qutb be-lieves that ownership in Islam belongs to the community, in general, and that private ownership is a function of dispensing with condi-tions and limits. Some kinds of property which benefit all people in common are public, and no one has the right to own them. Parts of public properties can be distributed to specific categories of people, like the poor. Such distribution helps improve the living standards of the poor, in particular, and the community, in general.[45] From this perspective, Islam is not against private ownership but is against the unusual accumulation of wealth. To Qutb, the owners of large capi-tal are not free to restrict or spend their capital as they wish, without taking others into account. Qutb argues that, although spending is an individual act, the individual's freedom has to be exercised within a framework. There is seldom a personal act that has no relation to other individuals, although this relation may not be direct or obvi-ous. For this reason, Islam has fixed for the poor a share provided from *zakat* (almsgiving) to improve their survival and livelihood.[46]

According to Qutb, Islam limits ownership because the essential means of production must be owned by the community. Even though Qutb encourages market economy as a means of satisfying the needs of society, he argues that when there is an emergency the state must command the economy. Obviously, Qutb wants to abolish neither pri-vate ownership nor market economy. But neither does he want to al-low unlimited private ownership of means of production or a com-plete command of the economy by the state. As with other issues, the state intervenes when necessary. Qutb states that, in Islam, social, mu-tual responsibility should not lead to any conflict between the rights of individuals and the rights of society, making it incumbent upon the state to protect individuals from selfishness when necessary.[47]

A Revolutionary Muslim Society versus Non-Muslim Societies

To achieve his main objective—the creation of a Muslim nation based on *shari'a* and social justice—Qutb postulates the need for taking prior steps, foremost among which is revolution. As *tawhid* is the basis of an Islamic government and Muslim society, it is also the pivot for revolution. According to Qutb, it should be the basis of propagating Islam (*da'wa*) and political movement. Because *tawhid* is a movement of continuous development, Islam does not accept an evil reality, as such, because its main mission is to eradicate evil and to improve the quality of life. According to Qutb, *tawhid* involves emancipation from subordination to all but the divine law, revolution against the authority of tyrannical lords, and rejection of negating human individuality. Subordination is a crime because God created humankind free and forbade it. "No god but God," declares Qutb, is a revolution against the worldly authority that seizes the first characteristic of divinity, against the situations that are based on this seizure, and against the authorities that rule by human and un-Islamic laws.[48]

Qutb looks to revolution as the main tool in the attainment of a Muslim society that is based on the *shari'a* and social justice. A revolution is the road to conscious transformation of currently existing societies. While it is not meant for converting people to Islam, it still aims at creating the Muslim individual, the Muslim society, and the Islamic state. This is so because an Islamic revolution aspires, as well, to the transformation of humans' enslavement to humans and to matter. As such, this revolution is not directed at a particular society but essentially at all societies that yield to human laws and orders.

This is why, in Qutb's view, a proper Islamic revolution does not compromise with non-Islamic doctrines and orders. The road to change necessitates some creative activism that demands total development and not mere patching up of ways of life and orders and even philosophies and ideologies. Likening the construction of a society to that of a building, Qutb argues that there is a difference between having a plan to construct gradually and patching up a building that was based on another plan. In the end, this patching does not establish a new building. A new building requires first tearing down the old system.[49]

While aiming at a gradual Islamic revolution that could first spread out the message of Islam, Qutb's highest aim is a total revolution that sweeps away the governments of his time and establishes new revolutionary Muslim societies in place of the un-Islamic, patched-up societies. Qutb relies on a gradual transformation of institutions and the spread of Islamic ideology to achieve this ideal.[50] Still, it should shake and destroy the old society in order to build a new one. Not believing in the viability of mild change for a society erected on false or immoral foundations, Qutb insists on the necessity of revolution as the only proper remedy for decaying societies. And for Qutb, all societies are essentially decaying. He uses earthquaking, or *zalzala*, revolution to describe the first step in the process of building the new society.[51] But this *zalzala*, though strong, is not necessarily violent, at least in theory. In Qutb's opinion, it should start with education in a twofold manner: first, by expounding the true meaning of Islam and, second, by refuting the fallacies of Western ideologies.[52]

According to Qutb, because *tawhid* is not a negative philosophical and theoretical declaration but, instead, a positive realistic and active declaration, it involves confronting other philosophies and ideologies. This confrontation requires that Muslims should acquire a knowledge of other philosophies and ideologies. And an active Islamic movement should confront the material obstacles, foremost among which are the existing political authorities. This confrontation by words and deeds applies not only to Arab societies but to all societies, because Islam is not for Arabs alone. Therefore, the ultimate goal of Islamic revolution is to abolish those regimes and governments that are established on the basis of humans ruling over humans and the enslavement of humans by humans—that is, the *jahili* society. Then, the revolution sets individuals free to choose the creed they want. As is obvious to Qutb, this declaration means the comprehensive revolution against the government of humans, in all its forms, systems, and conditions, and the complete rebellion against every un-Islamic way of life.[53]

Further, the Islamic state, according to Qutb, is established on that land where Islamic law rules regardless of whether all or only part of the population is Muslim. But land that is not ruled by Islam is *dar al-harb* (the abode of war), regardless of people's religion. What is significant here is that a Muslim society is Muslim not because it is composed of Muslims but because of the rule of Islamic law. This principle lends support to Qutb's previous argument that the Islamic government is the government of law. Thus, the application of Islamic law in a society, whether composed of a majority of Muslims or a majority of non-Muslims, makes that society Muslim. The Islamic state is defined neither by specific territories nor by specific races, and a Muslim society can be established anywhere. However, some societies that claim to be Muslim are not so because, in his view, they do not uphold the law of Islam. In practical terms, this means that many societies that existed during Qutb's time were not Islamic in his view and, thus, must be changed. Moreover, *dar al-harb* includes any state that fights religious attitudes of Muslims.[54]

While struggle (*jihad*) aims at transforming any institution that opposes and does not allow Islam to be freely practiced, *jihad* is neither suicide nor a campaign of atrocities. Qutb announces that *jihad* has four basic characteristics. Serious realism, the first characteristic, means that Islam faces with *da'wa* and refutation incorrect conceptions and beliefs and faces with power and *jihad* those regimes and authorities based on incorrect conceptions.[55] Qutb cannot accept the argument that Islam launches *jihad* only for defensive purposes, for Islam is not defensive but is a defense of humans against aggression.[56] To him, those thinkers who argue that *jihad* is only defensive are defeated spiritually and mentally, and do not distinguish between the method of this religion in rejecting compulsion to embrace Islam and its method in destroying those material and political forces that stand between humans and their God. In fact, those thinkers who see *jihad* as being only defensive do not understand Islam. It is true that Islam defends the land it exists on, but it also struggles to establish the Islamic order wherever possible and to abolish the *jahili* society.[57]

Active realism is the second characteristic, and it means that *jihad* cannot be fought with words only but requires much more preparation. It does not meet, for instance, a strong military force with an abstract theory. *Jihad* is a movement that can operate in stages and take time and effort as well as organization. Similarly, the third characteristic is a continuous movement that may take many forms and procedures when not in contradiction to Islamic principles. It can take the forms of writing, assisting others, teaching, self-discipline, or other activities. The fourth characteristic is that the regulation of relations between Muslim societies and non-Muslim ones must be based on two provisions: the first is that Islam is the basis of international relations; the second gives Muslims the right to peacefully propagate Islam without barriers imposed by any political regime or force. The freedom to accept or reject Islam is central to Qutb for tolerating non-Muslim societies.[58]

In Qutb's view, the societies that are in need of revolution are the societies that are not bound by the universal Islamic concept—that is, *jahili* societies. By this definition, Qutb includes all existing societies on earth as un-Islamic societies. To him, Christian, Jewish, socialist, and capitalist societies are in need of revolution. Even Muslim societies are included in Qutb's revolution, for while they do not believe in the divinity of any except God, they accept the governance of humans.[59]

Conclusion

From Qutb's point of view, the ultimate source of knowledge is God, who is beyond human philosophy and cannot be understood by human thought. However, the validity of human knowledge depends on its conformity to nature, which is, in turn, unknown by reason. Thus, a human claim to knowledge should be reduced to facts. Consequently, the knowledge of God or others can be known only from God's revelation. Still, Qutb maintains that what is revealed is no more than allusion to truth that is validated by its conformity to nature. Therefore, Qutb has referred to *fitra,* to be found in revelation, so as to argue for the validity or invalidity of any concept or doctrine. This is Qutb's most important argument for attaining and verifying the truth. Nonetheless, the circularity of this argument denies to its components of revelation, nature, and *fitra* any possible verification.

To Qutb, reason's function must be restricted to instrumentality in realizing the characteristics of the Islamic concept and as a judge in matters and values concerned with this concept. Reason is the interpretative instrument of revelation and the universal Islamic concept, for in the absence of Qur'anic injunctions, Qutb focuses on the practicability of discourses and institutions for discerning their validity or invalidity. Ideas per se are not important; rather, their importance lies in terms of utility. Even when they seem to be true, they are no more than approximations that might change from time to time. This is why Qutb rejects the basing of religion on science.

While religion and science cannot replace each other, Qutb's discourse attempts to bring together the religious discourse and the dominant scientific discourse as the underlying bases of the new Islamic society. The eternal, textually based, religious discourse provides the foundations of the society, while the scientific addresses the practical needs of society. While the scientific discourse cannot produce moral or metaphysical knowledge, it is still concerned with the experimental and the useful.

For Qutb, there is no knowledge without presuppositions; all knowledge presupposes a prior understanding of the whole. Qutb criticizes the ideal of objectivity and insists on the historical character of all understanding. Understanding and its discourse are conditioned by time, space, environment, and culture. Although Qutb disregards the possibility of human understanding of, or discoursing on, the ultimate source of knowledge (God), he nonetheless believes in His existence. Our comprehension of the real sources of knowledge is not attainable by observation and accumulation of facts and data, due to the inherent limits of human reason. Although the truth of God's existence has to be justified to an extent, it is ultimately above human authorities and discourses.

While Qutb's discourse should be grounded in the contemporary history of the Islamic world and must be viewed as the product of contemporary political crises, one must not over-generalize and view it merely as a reaction. Now, his discourse is the basis of many new militant political discourses. While the militancy of his fundamentalist discourse can be attributed to the crises of contemporary social and political life, his general discourse should be looked at as normative statements on God, reason, science, history, politics, and economics, the understanding of which requires a closer look at Islamic principles and not only at transient political events. His discourse is impoverished in terms of theology, philosophy, history, and science. While Qutb accepts the Qur'an and the *sunna* as the bases of normative principles, they are nevertheless overshadowed by politics and subordinated to his political discourse. In fact, beyond their political signification, one cannot fathom Qutb's concept of *tawhid*.

Qutb's appeal, however, can be traced to many factors. First, he tries to justify social justice and freedom within the framework of an

Islamically developed discourse. Instead of adhering to democracy and socialism, he explains what he thinks of as important issues for Muslims in an Islamic discourse. Issues such as representative governments are treated without any reference to foreign ideological discourses. Qutb offers religious justifications for socialist principles, for instance. The principles of representative government and social justice become religious and political duties—that is, the principles of government in Islam. By using such justifications, Qutb preempts the advocates of both democracy and socialism and is able to show Muslims that Islam and modernity are compatible. Their compatibility is achieved not by subjecting Islam to modernity but by subjecting modernity to Islam. His discourse absorbs democracy as *shura*, or the choice of people in their governments, and argues that, historically, Muslims have not really understand this. Again, his discourse absorbs social justice and links it to legal, political, and moral issues. Therefore, what Qutb did—and is famous for—was to create a new Islamic, political, theoretical discourse that encompasses the best in the Western traditions, which had been accepted by the majority of people, without negating or subordinating Islam to the West. His discourse reinforces the Islamic notion of Islam's validity for all ages and its capability of accommodating diverse conditions and changing realities. Hence, Qutb urges Muslims not to relegate the Qur'anic discourse to only prayers, funerals, or the personal domain. Instead, they must keep it as their everlasting constitution and basis of life. Furthermore, Qutb provides a new discourse that is not bound by, or subordinate to, past discourses, which could therefore be used by contemporary Muslims to reshape their governments and their ways of life. This new discourse aims at reviving Islam, without depending on its long history, for Qutb dismisses history, itself, as only a manifestation of, not a normative reading of, Islam.

6

The Discourse of Hasan al-Turabi on the Islamic State and Democracy

Hasan ʿAbdallah al-Turabi was born in 1932 in the city of Kassala in eastern Sudan. His family's interest in the traditions of learning and sufism strongly affected his personality. He graduated in 1955 with a B.A. degree in law from the Faculty of Law at Khartoum University. In 1957, he obtained an M.A. degree in law from London and, in 1964, a doctorate in law from the Sorbonne in Paris. In the mid-1960s, al-Turabi served as dean of the Faculty of Law at Khartoum University, was appointed first attorney general of the Sudan, and then was elected a member of parliament. He participated in the writing of the constitutions of Pakistan and the United Arab Emirates. During the period of 1964–69, he headed the Front of the Islamic Pact and the Party of the Islamic Bloc. By the end of the 1970s, he was appointed a cabinet minister.[1]

In 1988, the Islamic National Front, al-Turabi's new organization, joined a coalition government headed by Sadiq al-Mahdi, al-Turabi's brother-in-law. Al-Turabi was initially appointed minister of justice, then minister of foreign affairs and deputy prime minister. Now, Dr. Hasan al-Turabi is the speaker of the National Assembly and the leading theoretician of Islamism in North Africa and the Middle East as well as the leading ideologist and general secretary of the Arab and Islamic Congress in the Sudan; as such, he exerts tremendous influence over the Sudanese government. Although his thought is not well known in the West, his political role is widely acknowledged.[2] In May 1992, he was invited by the United States Congress to speak about Islamic fundamentalism in North Africa and the Sudan, Sudanese-Iranian relations, human rights, and minorities.[3]

The Doctrines

Divinity and Humanity of Islam

Al-Turabi asserts that modern Western superiority to, and dominance over, the Islamic world, both intellectually and militarily, should not mean that the only option left to Muslims is the search for the causes of their defeat or the renewal of their culture in the West, itself. If this were the only option, then following in the West's footsteps would be much easier. Instead, Al-Turabi believes, Muslims should undertake fundamental reexaminations of their culture and its foundations, because only through such a process can Muslims reorient themselves and their civilization toward real and comprehensive awakening. Mere imitation of the West, both intellectually and materially, cannot induce any substantial intellectual or political development. Moreover, he argues, the totality of Islamic thought and culture is no more than a historical and, at times, inadequate experience of Islam. This totality is no more than the attempts of human beings to read and reread the divine text of the Qur'an. At times, it is no more than the superimposition of human conditions and culture on the text. The overall intellectual and historical experience of the Muslims has failed them now at all levels, in military confrontations as well as intellectual rigor. This experience has left them incapable of keeping pace with modernity. This situation is the outcome of the failure of Muslim thinkers and their intellectual edifices to positively influence development by solving Muslims' problems and meeting their dire needs. Muslims live today on the margin of both Islam and the West. Their lives lack both the Islamic religious spirit and the Western technological advancement. Lacking in abstract and scientific sciences, Islamic culture and civilization have long since reached a point of bankruptcy.[4]

Because of al-Turabi's emphasis on the historicism of humans' intellectual development in relation to the text, humans' reading of the Qur'anic text must be historically tentative and incapable of claiming eternal utility. The truth of the reading is relative to its usefulness to social needs and human development. Even then, such usefulness to humankind cannot transform a humanly developed doctrine into an absolute certainty or a categorical imperative that should be applied universally and eternally. In addition, al-Turabi's historicist analysis of

intellectual human products requires restricting any religious interpretation to the conditions of the interpreter, who cannot, regardless
of his intellectual powers, capture the original message of the scripture. Put differently, humans may produce relative and tentative readings or interpretations, which may be good or not, depending on
their practicability. But humans should never proclaim finality for
any human product, including an interpretation. Human conditions
do change, and changes require new readings. The eternal divine text
remains eternal and valid for all ages and places, because its truth
stems not from its correspondence to specific conditions of a particular society but rather from its provision of a set of principles that can
be interpreted and reinterpreted to suit different ages and changes.
Since the divine text remains unaffected by changes in the human
condition, according to al-Turabi, it should therefore be the source
for organizing the philosophies of life, society, and state. It functions,
therefore, both as a text that unifies Muslims ideologically, politically, and socially and as an ultimate canonical authority of probable
modern interpretations. Put differently, since human understanding
of the text's ultimate meaning is always imperfect, the perfection of
the text becomes, itself, a guarantee that Muslims have a metahistorical continuity. Only the formal text, the Qur'an, constitutes a
categorical reading, which is, in turn, viewed as an exposition of quintessential Islam. Qur'anic exegeses are, therefore, tentative and should
be subject to continuous review. According to al-Turabi, the Qur'an,
whose modern usefulness is unfathomed, must be functionally re-
joined to the *umma*'s life. The Islamic society's separation from its
fundamental foundation—the Qur'an—is a major hindrance to any
viable renaissance. Thus, the reworking of the text into all facets of
life is a must for any future development or for the setting of sound
political and philosophical systems.

Historically, the "quarantinization" of the divine text from people's
lives has, in al-Turabi's view, transformed human thinking into a functional replacement of the divine. While people may believe in Islam,
true repercussions of belief cannot be limited to the realm of the conscience or creed but must, more important, involve the practical and
intellectual aspects of life. Otherwise, the Muslims enter into the web
of, and may be accused of perpetrating, a *tahaddi ishraki* (polytheis-
tic challenge), or the upgrading of materialistic and economic factors

and the simultaneous downgrading of God's role. To al-Turabi, the neglect of the divine text in real life makes people then come closer to polytheism.

Thus, for al-Turabi as for many other fundamentalists, any deviation from the divine text or humans' refusal to actualize divine commands leads to a life lived within an impious context, regardless of the knowledge and technology that have been accumulated. While al-Turabi seems to enter into the radical fundamentalist school of Sayyid Qutb and Abu al-A'la al-Mawdudi, because of his linkage of practical issues to creed he actually stops short of doing that. He turns, for instance, Qutb's description of those societies that do not rule by God's commands from *kufr* (unbelief) to *ishrak* (polytheism), where God's commands are associated with those of others. Although this is still a crime, it is not as repugnant and violating as unbelief, since there is still something that connects the human to God, though in a confused manner. Al-Turabi uses polytheism not to charge particular individuals or societies with deviation from God's path but to emphasize the divinity of *hakimiyya* and the importance of belief in this earthly life. More important, he employs polytheism to construct models common in humankind's history. Historical or theoretical precedents, like the pharaoh of Egypt, represent the substance used in the construction of those models. The individual conduct of pharaohs is imbued with creedal connotations and is equated with misbehavior and creedal polytheism. In this sense, the pharaoh and Qarun become models for political polytheism and economic polytheism, respectively.[5]

Al-Turabi portrays previous interpretations of the history of Islam as lacking in understanding of the significance of analyzing the structural role of historical figures and events, whose proper understanding may open the avenue for today's Muslims to view their own culture differently. Furthermore, in al-Turabi's view, it is also the avenue for rewriting their own history and, consequently, producing a new program that might not only change the backward aspects of today's lifestyle but also motivate the Muslims to act from a modern perspective. The rigidity that has dominated Islamic thought for centuries is one of the main features that has halted the progress of Islamic civilization.

Another important feature for al-Turabi is also related to the way Muslim thinkers and jurists have dealt with jurisprudence, the core of Islamic thinking. While earlier Muslims were free and able to construct a major civilization by directing their focus toward the roots, or *usul,* of religion through the development of the roots of jurisprudence, later periods devalued the need to reexamine jurisprudential roots in light of changing circumstances. Instead, they focused on the specifics, or the *furu',* as if they were of divine origin, with very little concern for roots. For al-Turabi, this is an indication that the priority of the Islamic discourses that deal with the form and legitimacy of political order, which originally served the Islamic civilization, has been misplaced, making Islamic discourses obsolete and incapable of serving Muslim societies. Being obsolete also necessitated borrowing from positive Western laws that are in tune with modernity. Such a misplaced political prioritization led to the glorification of jurisprudence, or the thought that should have served the Muslims. In essence, Muslims became the servants of a thought that could not serve them anymore. This, in turn, weakened free thought and allowed the domination of traditionalism, which became identical to religion, itself. The overall, inherited Islamic thought and order have proved their incapability of advancement. What is needed instead is a new and modern Islamic thought that takes into account modernity but simultaneously grounds it in the divine text, not in new or inherited authorities. Individual *ijtihadat,* or reasonings, should deal with profound issues and not merely with unfounded assumptions, linguistic interests, or details that have plagued the history of Islam. Theoretical sciences, or *al-'ulum al-'aqliyya,* are of utmost importance for recreating a viable Islamic thought. Al-Turabi argues that only such sciences are capable of a proper interaction with the divine text and that the transformation of *shari'a* stipulates an unfolding embodiment of law and faith.[6]

Since only the divine text carries within it any normative or eternal value for Muslims, in al-Turabi's view, he looks down at the perceived unchangeableness of Islamic traditions. He describes them as being no more than historical accumulations without any solid or compulsory normative status. Because both the roots and specifics of law are no more than centuries-old accumulations of intellectual, social, and political development and other related problems, al-Turabi dismisses their traditional normative status on historical grounds. General interpretations of Qur'anic verses, for instance, are for al-Turabi nothing but the result of scholarly agreements to give these verses general meanings. Again, the indications of some verses of a particular political structure and form of government are also historical. In this sense, their interpretation, in al-Turabi's opinion, is not useful or practical for the Muslims of today, for scholars' old agreements could be replaced with new ones, which could be as powerful or weak as the old. In other words, no human interpretation or reading could substitute for the original texts; the divine source materials—mainly the Qur'an and, to a lesser extent, the *sunna*—are invaluable in providing both a focus of continuity and a source for change at the same time. Although these are also basic to collecting, developing, validating, and even revealing the text, al-Turabi pays no attention to history and its construction of the texts or the political events that have led to their collection. He further makes the methodological separation between the divine science, or *al-'ilm al-shar'i* (that is, the divine source material), and the natural and human sciences, or *al-'ulum al-tabi'iyya wa al-insaniyya*, though the former is arrived at and authenticated by the latter. Again, while the former is divinely eternal, the latter is humanly entertained and constructed. But the two, aiming at the same objective, are essential for the completion of faith; as examples of combining the two sciences, al-Turabi mentions al-Ghazali and Ibn Taymiyya. However, thinkers must understand the original purpose of the Lawgiver, or else a wrong construction may end up with wrong conceptions, wrong conclusions, and misbehavior.[7]

While al-Turabi postulates the same purpose for the two kinds of sciences, nonetheless he relegates to the human sciences and methods the discovery of what is of utility to humans in this life and excludes the ability to theorize about divine matters related to creation, life, and death. Practicability and usefulness, or praxis, are the signs of valid human thinking or theory building. Mere abstract thinking, lacking any practical aim, seems to al-Turabi to be barren and difficult to ascertain the meaning of. He marginalizes not only abstract thinking but all other sorts of intellectual endeavors that are of no practical use to present-day Muslims. Thus, by implication, traditional Islamic jurisprudence is also dismissed on account of its impracticability for modern living, since practical ambitions oppose theoretical ideals, and historical/traditional sciences obscure people's direct understanding of the Qur'an and the *sunna*. Therefore, al-Turabi underlines the need for new, original "theoretical roots" derived from the texts in order to serve the practical and actual conditions and ideals of contemporary Muslims.[8] Serving the ideals of old societies, whose juristic *usul* resulted from a historical consensus, or *ijma'*, subordinates contemporary Muslims to the ambitions and ideals of past generations and moves them away from the eternal text. Again, Muslims today are just as capable of producing a *shura*, or consultation, or *ijma'* that, though different from past ones, is nonetheless as authentic. For instance, if Muslims were now to use consultation, as practiced historically, they would not be served well, since historically it meant the consultation of elites, whereas today's use of consultation must imply a universal process. Restricting consultation to scholars only, as was the case in the past, is suited neither to modernity nor to the ambitions of the people.[9]

Such dismissing of the past is, in one way or another, one of the features of Islamic fundamentalism. This feature overlooks the fact that traditional jurisprudence did not originally view itself as an eternal interpretation of an eternal text or postulate the possibility of radical change within its structure. That one consensus abrogates an older one is a traditional argument. But al-Turabi, more than others, moves beyond the general call to renew jurisprudence; he calls for renewal of its foundations and bases. Al-Turabi does not, however, take into account the idea that the longevity of the accepted four legal schools of law is due not to any particular claims on their part but to people's following of these schools. Earlier Muslim scholars and founders of schools never claimed everlasting status for their arguments, although they had, as al-Turabi has done, upheld the eternal legitimacy of the source materials—the Qur'an and the *sunna*—and the few political models represented by the first four, rightly guided caliphs. However, al-Turabi's argument, and the fundamentalist endeavor in general, personifies a juristic transformation of historical reconceptualization of *usul* from the text and the rebirth of primordial models. Thus, al-Turabi summons again similar discussions, and his improvement remains within the traditional juristic processes, resulting in the very same *usul:* the Qur'an, the *sunna, ijma'*, and *al-ra'i* (opinion). The innovation lies elsewhere, however; while juristic models were constructed for specific societies, al-Turabi's reformulation aims at constructing an imagined and hoped-for society. Again, while traditional jurisprudence historically reflected the formative power of the *umma*'s consensus, al-Turabi's reconceptualization of jurisprudence serves as a prescriptive model for a new political theory that might propel Muslims to redirect the course of their history and set up a modern society.

What distinguishes al-Turabi's view of jurisprudence from the traditional one is that it aims at bringing about radical and revolutionary changes. But traditional jurisprudence was developed in order to maintain the social well-being of society, since the Muslims considered themselves to be living in an Islamic state. Al-Turabi's jurisprudence aims at constructing, both theoretically and practically, the Muslim society and the Islamic state. Because traditional jurisprudence focused on organizing the society and harmonizing relations among its members, on the one hand, and between society and the state, on the other, the political changes demanded were mostly of minor consequence. In this respect, its political role was mostly restricted to consolidating what already existed and to reducing tension. Al-Turabi, on the other hand, imposes no limits on political action or change in the course of establishing an Islamic state and a Muslim society, especially since such a demand will be fought by the secular state. Radicalism, according to al-Turabi, might be a necessary instrument in weakening resistance to reform and uprooting practical and theoretical indolence. A comprehensive revolutionary change leading to a great Islamic revival could not be induced without undertaking radical measures leading to the elimination of backwardness and underdevelopment.[10] The revolution of intellect and structure frees society from tyranny, or *taghut,* and unjust rule. In this case, al-Turabi imposes no restrictions on revolutionary changes as long as they do not contravene the divine text, which in fact makes the revolutionary changes free of any institutional regulative principle or any practical guide to the level and intensity of change.[11]

Liberation or Freedom of Islam

Such absence of regulative power does not bother al-Turabi at all. His objective in the first place is freeing the forces of change so as to bring about major changes in the lives of people, without of course weakening the essence of creed. This objective seems very difficult to evaluate, given al-Turabi's view of religion. However, any change must take into consideration different kinds of social, economic, and political freedoms, which are, themselves, directed at abolishing *ishrak,* materialism, and submissiveness to individuals or things. Put differently, human submission to divine *tawhid* makes freedom meaningful and paves the way for individuals to liberate themselves from enslavement to others. Without *tawhid*, humankind has no superior doctrine to liberate it, since a human liberating philosophy serves to free people from one ideology only to have them enslaved by another. *Tawhid* is, then, a doctrine that liberates humans from humans and connects them to a higher level of responsibility. The doctrine of *tawhid*, which could not be metaphysically comprehended, becomes most important in terms of its function as a unifying doctrine. Hence, al-Turabi argues, the freedom grounded in the human philosophy of humans is materialistic, unjust, and relative, and it falls short of true *fitra*. However, freedom could be perfected when it is based on a *fitra* that is liberated from submission to human things, carries within it correct beliefs, and is motivated by objectives that go beyond everyday living. For al-Turabi, though the individual pursuit of things is legitimate, yet freedom must not mean animalistic and individualistic actions in order to attain particular earthly gains; in fact, this act poses a danger to the society and constitutes the very opposite of freedom, enslaving humans to their lower instincts and obscuring their vision of true freedom. An individual whose main goal in life is pleasure cannot claim to be free, for freedom comes only from liberty, whose essence is the individual's foregoing animalistic pleasure and living the life of *tawhid*.[12]

The actual, or rather the political, aspect of *tawhid* is not living a specific, traditional way of social and political life; instead, it is living a life that centers around the unity of humankind and, more specifically, the unification of Muslims as a starting point. It is the practical fulfillment of the universal *rabaniyya* (lordship) of God, which ties together patterns of living and worship and liberates them from human methods, systems of worship, and codes of law. The full meaning of unity necessitates its grounding in *tawhid;* failure to do so leads to its grounding in materialism, historicism, and positivism. This human grounding subjects humankind to restriction of its infinite possibilities of unification by inventing chauvinistically narrow bonds, imagined threats, personal leaderships, or other humanly devised points of reference. Put differently, making God the supreme unifying principle moves humankind away from its limiting slogans and principles to restructuring the world along universal lines. Thus, al-Turabi states that the conflicts of individual and political rights with freedoms have not existed in Islamic thought. They have been a characteristic of Western thought, however, because of its history of severe conflicts between the state and society, on the one hand, and the state and individuals, on the other. Such a Western context is not universally valid, and its forceful superimposition on an Islamic context is not conducive to freedom but, instead, deepens conceptual differences. However, this does not imply that al-Turabi is against freedom; on the contrary, he is in favor of freedom—freedom that should be rooted in, and justified by, the divine text. Again, according to al-Turabi, even during the worst ages of Islam, and within an Islamic context (such as when rulers made Islamic rule hereditary), no radical differentiation was made among the state, the individual, and the mosque; or between the individual and society; or even between the private and the public.[13] In this sense, the freedom of individuals and societies can withstand the tyranny of states only when it is grounded in metahistorical points of reference. The stablest point for Muslims is the doctrine of *tawhid*.

Al-Turabi elaborates further by saying that *tawhid* and its *shari'a* historically have acted both as a source of unifying identity and as a method that could be employed by the people against rulers in order to limit state interference in their lives as well as to prevent tyrannical acts of the state against communities. Furthermore, *tawhid* provided metahistorical points of reference that Muslims could use to evaluate historical practices, ideological orientations, and even legal developments. In other words, the goodness of the life of Muslim societies was not dependent, in theory, on the pronouncements of a group of intellectuals or politicians. More important, two of the most important features of political society and social living have never been given up to the state. In theory, again, Muslim societies, as represented indirectly by the circles of religious scholars and orders, were the source of legislation and taxation. In contrast to medieval Western societies, Muslim societies were conceived as being entrusted by God with the original right to interpret, or to derive legal substances from, the text. Thus, in al-Turabi's opinion, the communal prerogatives of legislation and taxation hinge on the acquiescence of the society, not upon the approval of the state. In this manner, Muslim societies never conceived political and constitutional conflicts as individual struggles for liberation or freedom, whether financial or political. Again, while the West gave up its right to legislate and impose taxes and accepted the powers of states and the sovereignty of parliaments, Muslim societies stood up for the freedom of the society as opposed to the tyranny of the state. The individual was not conceived outside the realm of his social environment, especially in that he did not have to give the state the powers of legislation and taxation to then receive back economic, social, and political individual rights.[14]

This does not mean that al-Turabi does not see many problems with those societies of the medieval period, but these problems did not preclude the correct practices of these societies, as opposed to politicians or jurists, whom he blames for derailing Islam from its main objectives. While Qutb and al-Mawdudi blame Muslim societies for their plight, al-Turabi distinguishes clearly between the official level, which is corrupt, and the nonofficial, which is not and which has actually kept the spirit of Islam alive. Social development has not deviated from Islam and has been mostly disengaged from official conduct of the state, which prevented the development of the social structure into a Western-style feudal system.

However, modernity witnessed the superimposition of the dialectical problems of the Western way of life. While Muslim societies are in dire need of change, al-Turabi does not perceive the West to be the model that leads to the softening of conflicts. For al-Turabi, the West is suffering, more than the Islamic world, from all sorts of philosophical, economic, and, to a lesser extent, political problems. While modern Islamic states should have adopted only what is good and relevant to the Islamic world, it borrowed from the West a complete model that included its inherent troubles and tensions. This led to ending the *shari'a* as the model that Muslims could work on and develop from within. A new political life—characterized by sharp economic, political, and ideological tensions and conflicting claims among the individual, the state, and the society—has become a main feature of Muslim societies. Therefore, what has actually occurred is transportation from the West to the East of problems that did not exist initially in the East. Muslim societies lost their original powers without gaining the powers of their Western counterparts. Put differently, contemporary Muslim societies suffer doubly: first, from the negative aspects of their history, intellectual backwardness, and traditionalism; second, from the emergence of new and modern authoritarian states and major conflicts between these states, the society, and the individual. This is why al-Turabi argues that modern Muslim societies are in need of a major reshuffling of priorities, which will turn the social and political agenda upside-down by making *al-tahrir al-Islami* (Islamic liberation) the immediate objective of change. Such a liberation requires a force that will redraw the parameters of conflict, from a mere problem of personal freedom to humans' corruption of their original nature and the reduction of freedom to a personal objective. However, true liberation and freedom should be directed at the elimination of the root cause: *shirk*. True belief eliminates the narrow problem of freedom and brings about true liberation for all—the individual, the society, and the state. Religious liberation leads to political liberation from *salatin al-'ard* (lords of the earth), and this is a must for the proper functioning of the Islamic state through the spread of free religious consciousness. The imposition of a state's political objectives on the believers without a proper Islamic philosophy of life leads the state into outright *jahiliyya* and the loss of legitimacy.[15]

The combination of religious unity and political freedom is, for al-Turabi, proper religious liberation that functions as the ideological equilibrium between different and diverse claims for rights and duties. The *shari'a* is the source of that equilibrium, since it gives equal weight to the rights of the individual versus society, the society versus the state, and the state versus the individual. In this sense, the priority of rights is not the division or balance of power between different human forces; it is religiously derived and, consequently, defined. Religious consciousness—not the material gains of the individual, the society, or the state—functions as the motivating force to settle the issues of rights. In this sense, sheer power could not be the source of rights, even for individuals. Rights are of a more fundamental—that is, religious—nature. For al-Turabi, if the proper consciousness is developed at all levels, then political rights interact with individual and social realities and transform the individual life into a social dimension and the social life into an individual dimension. Only through the proper consciousness could the contradiction between different claims be resolved. The consciousness of an individual becomes representative of social consciousness, and social consciousness represents the will of the people.[16]

Al-Turabi employs such an analysis in order to express doubt about the legitimacy of modern Islamic governments, since most, if not all, lack religious liberation, political freedom, or consciousness. He also means that contemporary Islamic societies are in need of a process of the reification of the political and social into the metaphysical. The posing of today's problems, away from religious consciousness and in terms of economic and political difficulties, may only lead to wrong or unsatisfactory solutions. Al-Turabi views modern Islamic societies as resulting from both traditionalism and modernity. They are more or less combinations of both because the traditional way of thinking is identified by the people with religion. They are modern not because they are developed but in the sense that they are beset by the transported problems of the modern West. Doing away with traditionalism by renewing the roots and understanding of religion may resolve major problems. Al-Turabi stresses also the importance of acquiring the skills necessary for creating an advanced civilization, because mere religious consciousness alone cannot trigger a process of working toward eliminating underdevelopment and setting up an efficient administration. Al-Turabi's assumption regarding the resolution of social and political problems by fulfilling religious liberation, developing the *shari'a*, and eliminating *jahiliyya* curtails potential for reformation and gives rise to uncalled-for hopes. On the other hand, it may encourage believers to forgo any concern about developing this life and to accept backwardness and miserable living conditions and, instead, focus on the other life. A view like this may not be conducive even to the program that al-Turabi is calling for—that is, the revival of Islam, which could not be attained without highly developed modern technology and an economy that would satisfy people's needs and aspirations.

Of course, a great number of contemporary crises could be blamed on the regimes, but their abolishment does not necessarily lead to revival. Again, implementing the *shari'a,* or, more specifically, religious awareness, has not historically abolished rulers' oppression; some medieval, Muslim political thinkers—such as al-Ghazali, al-Mawdudi, Ibn Taymiyya, and Ibn Jama'a—did not see any religious problem with oppression insofar as the ruler adhered nominally to the *shari'a.* While the *shari'a* could be regarded as a source of freedom, other non-*shari'a* postulates must be added to any modern revival, Islamic thinking, and, of course, religious awareness.

Shura and Democracy

Al-Turabi attempts to address such an objection by reinterpreting the doctrine that has been seen in Islamic history as a secondary and nonobligatory principle in political rule—*shura*. Instead, he introduces *shura* as the main central and legitimizing doctrine of political rule. Not only this, but the whole question of the *shariʿa*, to al-Turabi, must be separated from its development and history and reworked in modern times through *shura*—itself in need of a modern interpretation. Put differently, a modern Islamic political discourse cannot flourish on the underpinnings of medieval discourses. While the *shariʿa*'s derivative interpretations were seen as absolutes, medieval social and political practices conditioned such interpretations. Al-Turabi calls, therefore, for the conditioning of the *shariʿa* today in modern experience. Thus, although *shura* has been perceived as a supporting principle in political life, there is no text to limit its interpretation as such. The limitations are social and political, not textual. In modern times, it is closer to democracy. Al-Turabi further argues that, while *shura* and democracy are denotatively similar (i.e., calling for public participation and representation in the making of political affairs), they are, nonetheless, connotatively different. Democracy grounds its ultimate reference in the people, who become the sovereign; in contrast, *shura* grounds its reference in God's revelation, thus making God the supreme sovereign. The advantage that *shura* has over democracy, in al-Turabi's view, is that while human thinking is always fluid, there is a divine text that is always present and unifies the consciousness of people. Democracy has no text but that of human reason, which leads to establishing equal discourses that are equally full of shortcomings. When *shura* tackles or arrives at constitutional, legal, social, and economic principles, *shura* is always made in view of the *shariʿa*, not only in the interest of this group or that. Even when a particular claim is made by a majority, it could be counterbalanced by the *shariʿa*.[17]

To al-Turabi, then, the *shariʿa* is important not only in substantive terms but also in terms of its function as a regulative principle that fills in for the deficiency of human reason, which always acts within the boundaries of its social setting. *Shura* also differs from liberal democracy, where the enjoyment of political rights is mostly figurative and essentially controlled by economic structures. Al-Turabi argues that, without the grounding of human reason in what is beyond reason, defective, sectional, and partial theories and doctrines are produced. The instances that he provides are capitalism, which concentrates wealth in the hands of the few, and communism, which disperses personal wealth but still places real authority with the few. This dialectical result stems from the conditionality of human theories, which precludes the possibility of arriving at any absolute, whether in society, economics, or politics.[18] This is why, according to al-Turabi, all human theories and even religious interpretations are tentative and conditioned by time and space and, as such, can never claim finality.

To al-Turabi, an Islamic order whose discourse goes beyond the mere issue of formal sovereignty and centers around *tawhid* as the organizing principle may have a much more realistic possibility of arriving at perfection. If *shura* is methodologically exercised, equality becomes genuine at all levels, for equality is a divine postulate and is not dependent on the development or the needs of this society or that. As a religious consciousness, it then infiltrates all aspects of life, at home, in academic life, and even in religious circles. Because *shura*, in al-Turabi's view, is the principle that must govern relations between people, no individual may claim any peculiar powers over others, for the text justifies no such thing. Even religious scholars of stature cannot claim any special privileges or hidden status. Their status in forming principles is equal to that of other individuals because *shura* must govern the economic, social, political, and even religious life. In other words, the opinion of a scholar is equal in normative terms to that of an ordinary individual. No group has the rights to impose its views on society.[19]

To al-Turabi, the transcendence of any system to its conditionality necessitates its grounding in the all comprehensive, unifying, and equalizing doctrine of *tawhid*. If *shura* in modern time is separated from *tawhid* it becomes equivalent, in its frailty and tentativeness, to democracy. Thus, any discourse that disrupts the connection between *shura* and *tawhid* derails the objective of the divinely ordained discourse. This applies to other doctrines, as well: tyranny is unity without *shura*; the disengagement of freedom from unity turns it into licentiousness. Islamic liberation, grounded in *shura*, is the balance of both and is the instrument that frees people from intellectual *jahiliyya*, religious *shirk*, and political *taghut*. Again, an Islamically derived, liberating *shura* becomes, for al-Turabi, the instrument of change and of searching for the true meaning of *tawhid* and constant transcendence of human intransigence. A new discourse based on the ideology of liberating *shura* must, then, be adopted to redirect the course of both religiosity and political action. It should be treated as an essential part of a modern Islamic philosophy of transcendence, negation, and challenge. Such a philosophy of liberation can then produce a political ideology capable of ending ideologically conflicting discourses and of unifying Muslim actions.[20]

A philosophy like this, according to al-Turabi, could very well become a motivating force for developing a political discourse based not on traditional historical discourses but rather on a newly found intellectual discourse that leads to progressive reinterpretations grounded in abstract underpinnings of his liberation philosophy. Without the development of a new major interpretative discourse, people have no chance of any real revival. The West, says al-Turabi, has penetrated the Muslim world ideologically due to the absence of such a discourse and because of the regimes' coercion and ideological imposition. However, the starting point of such a transformation is to adopt liberation discourses that could liberate the Islamic *umma* from *tawaghit al-ard* (the tyrants of earth) and spark a revolt against all externally imperialistic and internally suppressive orders and discourses. These liberation discourses are capable of motivating people to reorganize their forces and reorient their powers toward unity. To al-Turabi, this cannot be done by rehashing old, ideological slogans without first developing a new and authentic set of roots, or *usul*. Only a discourse that is constructed on a basic process of innovative interpretation may lead to a theoretically and politically solid order that could make important issues such as freedom a totally religious and unifying fundamental. This might constitute the inception of a new liberation theology.[21]

To put this more concretely, al-Turabi sees that a liberation theology leads by necessity to political reconceptualization or to the formation of a new discourse on power and social, economic, and political relations. If *shura* is deconstructed or "liberated" from its historical constructions and practices, it might be reconstructed as democracy; conversely, democracy might be reconstructed as *shura*. Thus, a process of deconstruction and reconstruction makes *shura* and democracy synonymous, and even identical, and creates, in fact, a unifying discourse. For example, while democracy was associated originally with Greek mobocracy, where it was partially exercised, al-Turabi argues that the Europeans deconstructed and reconstructed it to mean direct government of the small and limited entities of Europe. However, Europe's extension of its political geography, without the immediate means to communicate, transformed democracy into indirect representative governments and parliaments. Later on, and by the end of the Middle Ages, European thought considered democracy as a rule for government.[22] The Muslim world, then, is in need of a philosophy or discourse that takes into consideration and reformulates important issues like freedom, *shura,* and democracy.

However, such a reformulation of democracy and *shura,* al-Turabi continues, has some Islamic root, for democracy in the West developed under the indirect impact of Islamic political thought and specifically under the Islamic doctrine of religious and political equality of Muslims. *Ijma'* in the history of Islam has been viewed theoretically by Muslim scholars as the source of political authority whose legitimate continuation depends on popular confirmation, or *'aqd al-bay'a* (contract of allegiance), between the people and the designated ruler. Al-Turabi further argues that Western philosophy could not have developed, without external reference and experience, the doctrine of equality of all and the need for a contract between the ruler and the ruled. The development of the Western view of contract was not historically derived but rather advocated as a means toward reducing the absolute powers of rulers and increasing the limited power of the people. The issue of freedom was originally a political doctrine that aimed at liberating the people economically and politically, but democracy developed to mean the free exchange of opinions and the interaction of free wills. Consequently, the theory of social contract in liberal democracy became the source of compromise and interdependency between the government and people. However, the uneven distribution of power and wealth led to another breed of democracy, socialism, which attempted to deconcentrate the capital held by the few and to reintroduce the essence of democracy as political equality.[23]

Third World countries have failed in developing democratic institutions due to four factors, according to al-Turabi. First, societies are still traditional and not open to change easily. Second, poor economic conditions, exploitation, and unequal distribution of wealth did not

encourage the transition to democracy. Third, military institutions
are by nature undemocratic, not to mention the long-standing cultural, military, and political imperialism that has been unconducive
to establishing a democratic atmosphere. The fourth and last reason
is related more to people's psychology, which became conditioned to
tyranny and, consequently, resulted in the absence of individual political awareness of democracy. All these factors together led to a
deep-rooted conviction that, although democracy might be a good
political ideal, real politics rested on actual power, itself dependent
on the use of force, coercion, and the monopoly of authority. Thus,
the exercise of democracy in the Third World became no more than
charades used by political regimes to give an impression of popular
legitimacy before the international audience, especially the West. But
the truth, in al-Turabi's view, is that this was no more than hero-
worship ceremonies imposed by the ruler on his people, who were in
turn mobilized so as to serve his legitimacy. In fact, such false democracy weakened real democracy, and instead of governments serving
the people, people served governments; freedom came to mean the
freedom of governments to use all means and methods to coerce people
into following unpopular views and systems.[24]

Contemporary Eastern practices, as well as Western development
of democracy, do not push al-Turabi to decry democracy. On the
contrary, they indicate to him the possibility of remodeling democracy in a modern form that could do away with the historicity and
misuse of the doctrine. He exhorts Muslims to adapt it, after redefining it in terms of Islamic terminology and after reformulating it within
the conditions of contemporary Islamic life. Mere imitation of Western democracy, without a proper consideration of the conditions of
its new environment, may lead to faulty application, be it social, philosophical, political, or ethical. It also makes democracy more of an
alien doctrine superimposed by a foreign culture and, consequently,
a sign of foreign hegemony and imposition. What is needed then,
according to al-Turabi, is the reacquisition of democracy and its Islamization so that it becomes self-induced, native, natural, and beneficial.[25]

Adapting democracy to the general conditions of Muslims and its
proper grounding in an Islamically developed new discourse seem, in
al-Turabi's opinion, to be requirements for both democracy and *shura*.
While Islam, according to al-Turabi, is open to foreign ideas and doc-

trines, or even a non-Islamic view, it works them through its own priorities. Al-Turabi uses a pre-Islamic proverb like *"Unsur akhaka zaliman au mazluman"* ("Support your brother whether he is the oppressor or the oppressed") in order to convey the openness of Islam to all possibilities of adoption and adaptation. While this proverb had a general, literal, and absolute significance, Islam, according to al-Turabi, kept it as such but made the support for the oppressor a matter of advice and reorientation toward what is just and away from what is unjust. For the same reasons and on a higher methodological level, al-Turabi reminds us that the Muslims adopted Greek logic without hesitation and have used it extensively in all fields of knowledge. Borrowing, as al-Turabi explains, does not only show liking or disliking a particular proverb or science but also reflects cultural and political power relationships. When the dominant discourse was the Islamic one, Muslims had no problem with introducing and Islamizing foreign or non-Islamic doctrines, sciences, and methods. The same applies to the development of Islamic terms. While the caliphate's literal meaning, according to al-Turabi, is a human vicegerency for conducting the general affairs of the *umma*, it developed later to indicate a particular system of government, as the experience of the rightly guided caliphate, or power, introduced into Islam the doctrine of such a system of government.

However, the nature of the relationship, or power, between the government and people changed when the seizure of power became the norm of governmental succession. Instead of signifying choice, which was the original intention of the caliphate, government came to signify political force and coercion. Similarly, while *al-bay'a* (oath of allegiance) indicated the free acceptance and contract between equals, it was transformed later, because of the arbitrary and coercive power of rulers, into no more than formal acts of submission and automatic delegation and commitment to rulers. In this case, the very essence of political government—i.e., the contract—was transformed into no more than a ceremonious act, thus rendering *al-bay'a* more or less insignificant. The response of Islamic thinkers during that period was to overlook the real and original meaning of *al-bay'a* by adopting descriptive definitions based on realities, instead of adopting corrective prescriptions that would restore its original meaning.[26] Put differently, Islamic political thought, in al-Turabi's view, has been derived mostly from submitting unreflectively to realities and to the dominant political discourse of rulers and, more specifically, to the relationships of power and its distribution. Jurists have yielded repeatedly to governing powers and developed their discourses accordingly. Political powers have always been able, directly and indirectly, to influence the religious discourse; consequently, the religious discourse has never been purely abstract or innovative but, more important, imbued and loaded with ideas dominant among the politically and militarily powerful elites.

From al-Turabi's point of view, if this power relationship is mirrored on the international level today, one finds a similar relationship between power and the dominance of a particular discourse. When Islamic civilization confronted other civilizations and Muslims lost both geopolitically and scientifically, weakness crept into their discourses. The ascendance of the discourses of the victorious marginalized Islamic discourses and made them unattractive. In other words, the dominance of a particular discourse is related to power. Because al-Turabi believes that Muslims are now on the rise and are attaining some power, a new Muslim discourse—that is, the fundamentalist—is also on the rise. Such a description makes al-Turabi confident that Muslims can again adopt and adapt foreign doctrines in order to deal with modern conditions of life. Muslims can, in particular, seize and reconceptualize significant and powerful doctrines, such as revolution, democracy, and socialism, in order to reorient and reinforce their liberation theology.[27] For al-Turabi, there is no doubt that political dominance produces dominant intellectual discourses; in turn, dominant discourses increase power and the spread of a particular civilization. When Islamic civilization was dominant, its discourses were spread universally, directly and indirectly. When the West became dominant, its discourses also became universally dominant, directly and indirectly. According to al-Turabi, Muslims should now borrow from the dominant Western culture in order to strengthen their discourse and, consequently, their power. Otherwise, their discourse may become nothing more than a mere appendage to the dominant Western discourse. But if Muslims adopt into their discourse what is valuable in the West, then there would be no need either to sacrifice their discourse and culture or to have them replaced with others. Selective borrowing from the dominant other is one of the sources that allow the rejuvenation of Islamic thinking and prevent its sinking into oblivion. Thus, al-Turabi poses the necessity of developing a new, formative discourse that uses the modern and dominant language, either through a process of original linguistic derivation or historical denudation or through arabization in order to strike a revival and strengthen Muslims' political conditions.[28]

Democracy occupies a major role in al-Turabi's discourse, because of his perception that it personifies Islam's capability of readoption and readaptation of modern doctrines. He argues that this adoptive and adaptive process makes democracy and *shura* equivalent. Muslims cannot anymore turn a blind eye to the importance of the democracy that was introduced into Muslim areas by the dominant West and its discourses. It must be now reworked into modern Islamic thought, linked to Islamic political jurisprudence, and, in particular, identified with *shura*. While it is true that *shura* has not been solidly conceptualized or practiced as democracy, al-Turabi has nevertheless tried to conceptualize it as a synonym for democracy, and he has seen no religious or cultural obstacle to doing that. Furthermore, he advocates linking it to the two fundamentals of Islam—the Qur'an and the *sunna*. In fact, *shura* as a general method of government can be read from and into the religious texts if they are read in a specific way since the religious texts exhort the community to take responsibility of its own affairs, which would include issues of rule and organization. The Islamization of democracy as *shura* needs only its linkage to *tawhid*, which makes equality and freedom into universal religious doctrines instead of secular and human doctrines. In this sense, *shura* and its concomitant doctrines actually become more compelling and concrete.[29]

Al-Turabi explains that *shura* is a doctrine that is derived from the roots of religion and its general postulates, not specifically from any particular text. Textual references to *shura* relate to one aspect of life or another. In other words, it must belong to how Muslims understand Islam. Islam has viewed the important issues of divinity, governance, and authority as the domain of God. It has also viewed all members of humankind equally; therefore, vicegerency belongs to them generally. The crisis of applying an Islamic system of *shura* in Islamic countries cannot be resolved just by adding some sort of formalities or cosmetic institutions to existing power structures but, instead, must be reworked through the spirit of Islam, where the entire community, not only an individual or a group of individuals, carries the responsibilities of government. *Shura* must be transformed into a way of life, not a limited political practice. A state that is not built on such a system does not lead its society to success; it ends up being more an instrument of social oppression and destruction. Modern national states of the Islamic world do not pay any regard to human rights or similar rights because they are founded not on freedom but on the sultanic conception of authority, which leaves no room for the community either to express its views or to develop a representative system.[30] Contemporary realities call on Muslims to feel ashamed of their conditions and to recreate a discourse that reinstitutes the Islamic state and the Muslim society—not one that merely imitates the West. The Muslims must focus on the issues of freedom and *shura*, or democracy, and direct all of this toward developing a dialogue with the West.[31]

Part of this dialogue and the new system that al-Turabi calls for is the relationship between *shura* and democracy, or, in fact, that between the Muslim world and the West. He argues that the difference between Islamic democratic *shura* and Western democracy is not merely formal but also conceptual, because the former is based on divine *hakimiyya* and, consequently, on humankind's common *istikhlaf* (vicegerency). The latter, however, is based on concepts of nature. Thus, in Islam, freedom, as well as what it entails, is both metaphysical and doctrinal; that is, freedom is a religious doctrine whose violation goes beyond mere political violation to constitute a violation of something divine. In liberalism, however, freedom is a legal and political concept but never a religious or divine one. Thus, Islamic discourse does not speak only to the interests of individuals or their fears of government. It also speaks to popular consciousness, whose strengthening serves as a guarantee against any violation of political rule that bestows on itself communal powers. In this sense, *shura* becomes a liberating religious doctrine which cannot be claimed by political authority and which must rule only contractually and in the service of the social order.[32]

To al-Turabi, the individual then becomes religiously responsible for acquiring freedom and religiously justified in fighting oppression. Al-Turabi reduces state powers to a minimum and increases the individual's to a maximum—a view unprecedented in the history of Islamic thought, which is developed to empower the community. He believes that making *shura* obligatory in determining social, economic, and political issues—as opposed to the advisory nature of elitist *shura*—leads to empowering the community in a new religious and modern form. Thus, if an *ijma'* were to be attained in such a manner, and without contradicting any Qur'anic text, it can then form normative principles. *Shura* could also take many forms: a parliament, a constitutional council, or any other instrument of representation. But there must always be an institution that could look into the decisions taken by representative bodies to ensure that they do not violate any clear-cut religious principle.[33]

It is obvious, thus far, that al-Turabi's acceptance of democracy is formal and not completely substantive, because he does not ground it in rationality or historical development alone. On the contrary, he grounds it in religion, itself, which has been assumed to be more or less incapable of furthering democratic notions. In the Middle East, it seems that such a grounding of democracy may strengthen its popularity, while its secularization may posit the state against it and the people against their governments, which pretend to adhere to secular democracy. That the Qur'anic text is the ultimate founding and justifying power of democracy makes it a solid, social, and political instrument of evaluation to be applied to both society and state, the ruler and the ruled. State machinery becomes needful of the represented and always subject to a higher law than that of the state. This is, in fact, one of the reasons why al-Turabi Islamized democracy. *Shari'a* in this context becomes a popular power, higher than the law of the state, and is developed popularly, not by the state. As such, state institutions and policies become balanced by both social institutions and will.[34]

In this fashion, the discourse of democracy is validated by the formative—indeed, the interpretive—power of the text and its reading within a specific age and time that are dominated by the West and its discourse. But this discourse on democracy is also made in view of establishing a common ground with the West which may lead to dialogue. Al-Turabi believes that it is the duty of the modern Islamic movement to open up to the whole world so as to transmit its message after a period of isolation. The Muslim world now is part of the globalized world, and in directing the Islamic discourse to the West, the Muslims who are followers of the West are also addressed. The West also has the choice between having a dialogue with the others or giving credit to the well-publicized, new confrontational doctrine, or "the clash of civilizations."[35] Al-Turabi concludes that the real conflict in the world is not a political one between East and West but, rather, a metaphysical conflict between *tawhid* and *ishrak* and between human *jahiliyya* and divine *hakimiyya*.

In al-Turabi's view, the modern Islamic movement, as the leading force of revival in Muslim societies, must prepare itself to start a fruitful dialogue with the world on all levels—economic, social, political, and above all, intellectual.[36] Muslims should deal with others in terms of their discourses and languages. Both Muslim and Western societies should transcend their history of conflict and bloodshed in order to bring the diverse parts of the world closer to one another. Al-Turabi's agenda for dialogue includes the freedom to discuss all issues of culture, civilization, politics, economics, information, society, arts, and even sports. The dialogue between the West and the Islamic movement should substantively deal with two main aspects: first, the notions of a Muslim political society and issues of false representation of people, suppression of freedoms, political oppression, and political unrest; second, the Islamic political system and issues of change in humans, society, and reality, *shura* and democracy, Islamic revivalism, and the new world order. To al-Turabi, there is now no "end of history," and the "clash of civilizations" is not the destined fate of humankind—that is, if humankind seeks liberation from its miseries and catastrophes.[37]

Conclusion

Al-Turabi's interpretive discourse on revivalism focuses essentially on the termination of the normativeness of the past, both as a history and as a system. Of course, he exempts the Qur'an and the *sunna* from such a termination, since he views them metaphysically and metahistorically as formative and constitutive Islamic fundamentals and authentic sources. As such, they enjoy an affirmative and a negative interpretive and formative function on a multitude of realities— such as the idea that *shura* is democracy or that *shura* is not what has been practiced. In fact, they have to be superimposed on internal and external events in order to make sense of, and to evaluate them, as well. Thus, al-Turabi conceives them as nonhistorical but eternal principles of Islam which must be used to create good societies and rectify evil ones. Again, he uses them to deny the existence, whether in the past or the present, of a perfect society—with the noted exemption of that of the Prophet—or a complete, collective Islamic self-awareness. But he employs them, as well, in order to push for achieving modern Muslim societies and a newly developed self-awareness, for they permit an unending process of revival based on interpretation and reinterpretation.

Al-Turabi's quest for reinterpretation rests on developing an intellectual and formative discourse that rediscovers the appropriate meanings and significance of the texts within the framework of modern life—a discourse that must reformulate the religious roots, or *usul al-din*. This discourse reformulates, in turn, a political theology loaded with political ramifications, as it is directed not at a more substantive understanding of the divine but rather at the control of the mundane and, in particular, the political. Questions relating to divine theology are bypassed in favor of those relating to political theology. To al-Turabi, the former can be realized only in terms of the latter. While obedience to God, for instance, is still an important demand, in al-Turabi's view, its most important manifestation is not mere individual religiosity but essentially holding certain political doctrines, such as those of the Islamic state and unity of the community. Again, the most important measure of divine *tawhid* manifests itself not in private conscience but in commitment and actions toward the Islamization of state and society. Deep theological commitment to Islam must involve the economic, social, and political concerns of society. Practical Islamic activism signifies the deep-rootedness of belief, while shallow and ceremonial, nonactive commitment to Islam weakens belief, if not destroying it altogether.

Al-Turabi's grounding of his democracy in a metaphysically conceived composition reifies it into an act of worship, whereas the application of *tawhid* in a democratically structured institution makes it a justification for political rule. In this way, al-Turabi transmutes the substantive *tawhid* into a form, and formalizes *shura* into a substantive principle. Therefore, the discourse is interpreted by its form. Thus, al-Turabi condenses the religious discourse into no more than a political footnote and makes creedal belief and unbelief into political belief and unbelief. Political belief depends on a sound application of divine *hakimiyya;* political unbelief results from depending on human *hakimiyya.*

In this fashion al-Turabi negates the usefulness of traditional jurisprudence and transforms a modern religious jurisprudence into an ideologically derived political discourse. In his explanation of the true essence of Islam, one cannot fail to notice how politics informs all of his doctrines, even that of the metaphysical. Because no individual can understand the real metaphysical meaning of the text, the only credible meaning becomes that resulting from politics—i.e., a consensual agreement—through *shura*. But this cannot be properly conducted without a state machinery, because the rendering of categorical and lasting interpretations of the text requires a continuous ratifying process by all Muslim generations and the continuous existence of the Islamic state.

The disintegration of state and society brings back the need for another appropriate, interpretive discourse. An eternal interpretation is an interpretive impossibility, since interpretation is conditional and tentative. In his attempt to find a proper channel for a relative interpretation of the text, al-Turabi finds the power of the Muslim society. But the Muslim society does, indeed, need an Islamic state, which becomes the symbol of collective self-awareness and the possibility of a relatively correct textual understanding. Thus, al-Turabi opens up, at least theoretically, a host of possible Islamic discourses that are in tune with realities but are nonetheless relative, conditional, and tentative.

In doing so, al-Turabi theoretically frees Muslims from the finished products of early and medieval thinking and ways of life. He exhorts Muslims to modernize Islam and Islamize modernity; *shura* becomes democracy, and democracy becomes *shura*. This forceful, conceptual correspondence, which takes place through a process of historical neutralization, brings modern Islamic and Western political thought closer together and creates the possibility of a new Islamic political discourse and a meaningful dialogue.

Conclusion

Modernism and fundamentalism, the two most obvious and influential currents in modern interpretation of Islam, focus on identity issues through linking the revival of Islam to human consciousness. While their objectives are developing and leading social and political movements that aim at attaining material, political, and spiritual progress, they have developed modern readings of Islam that lay down the basic conditions for modernizing and reforming Islamic civilization and societies. After serious reexaminations of modernity and Islam, proponents of each interpretation have found that Islam must accommodate modernity and modernity must accommodate Islam.

Fundamentalist theoreticians treat *tawhid* as an empowering doctrine that turns, in practice as opposed to theory, political government into a human occupation. While radical fundamentalists employ *tawhid* as a vehicle for dominating others, moderate fundamentalists employ it as a doctrine justifying independence and sovereignty of Muslims vis-à-vis dominant regimes and world powers. The Qur'anic discourse is employed as an empowering discourse through legitimizing popular consent; thus, power is legitimate only when it is popularly elected and exercised. If the *umma* can produce the only legitimate power, then other imposed powers are illegitimate. The fundamentalist discourse on *tawhid* is, then, a politically motivated one that is to serve as an organizing principle between dominant powers and the people. It is used to counterbalance some forms of de facto political authorities. The quest for *tawhid* is simply a quest for popular empowerment which takes a religious form, especially after the collapse of nationalist, communist, socialist, and liberal experience in most of the Islamic world.

Fundamentalist discourses on the demystification of history are also a call for empowerment, since history as represented by traditional religious, social, and political institutions not only has been used as an instrument of traditionalism but also has imposed state and religious institutions that could not any longer represent the people's interests. The quest for religious revival, through separating Islam from its history and through its modernization, is a quest for liberation from authorities that have for centuries or decades been denying any modern and meaningful development in people's lives. To the fundamentalists, because this liberation lies essentially in human nature, it is the humans who should now realize the spiritual, intellectual, political, and economic revival. Thus, the quest for liberation and revival is not strictly religious; it is mainly social and political, freeing humans from the past and empowering them in the present.

Fundamentalist textual analyses of the scripture do just that. They posit the possibility of rediscovering doctrines relating to modernity, legitimacy, and the Islamic state on mostly new and modern foundations. The process of rediscovering, for the fundamentalists, is neither absolute nor rigid; it depends on available sources, conditions, and human wills. This process is a quest for legitimacy insofar as it attempts to reargue the sources of legitimacy, which in turn leads to rearguing theories of knowledge and epistemology in a modern way. Thus, while the fundamentalists shed doubts on modern epistemology, they adopt many of its aspects and use them to challenge the constructions of medieval and classical Islamic thought. The fundamentalists adopt and adapt modern theories into the main body of modern Islamic epistemological thought. At an epistemological level, the impact of fundamentalism on Islamic traditions is at least comparable to the impact of Protestantism on Catholicism and its institutions. Because the fundamentalists view, for instance, the individual as the source of legitimate interpretation, they downplay well-established institutional rights and privileges. This view shatters medieval philosophical and juristic epistemological constructions that were, directly and indirectly, based on elitist understanding of knowledge, religion, and, therefore, politics, aiding in the creation and maintenance of unrepresentative, authoritarian, religious and political institutions.

The quest for modernity disguised as a quest for authenticity serves both as an enabling vehicle to adopt modern Western theories and as an instrument for rearguing Islamic traditions. The quest for modernity and authenticity empowers the fundamentalists to modernize without yielding to the Western modernity that is linked, in their consciousness, to colonialism and imperialism and to authenticate new doctrines without yielding to the Islamic traditionalism that is linked to deterioration and weakness. An Islamized modernity allows the fundamentalists to adopt technology, sciences, and institutions that could enhance the power of Muslims. A modernized authenticity allows the fundamentalists to distinguish themselves from what they perceive as unjust, illegitimate, and oppressive powers, locally and internationally. Thus, the new fundamentalist identity derives from a powerful text that provides moral superiority, an Islamized modernity that provides the means and ways to consolidate power, and a modernized authenticity that sets Muslims as a nation vis-à-vis other nations.

The construction of fundamentalist views of knowledge on the interaction between *fitra* and the text is a way to empower individuals to charter their destiny. *Fitra,* as the guiding light in the search for what is true and beneficial within the parameters of the Qur'anic discourse, stands opposite long-standing traditions of dictating what is true and beneficial. The Qur'an as interpreted by individual *fitras* presents possibilities for new human experiences that can selectively choose from traditional Islam and from the modern West. It has also been employed as the focal point in the process of creating a new identity.

This new identity cannot but spring from the process of historicizing long-standing authoritarian, traditional readings of Qur'anic and *sunna* texts. The historicist aspect of fundamentalist readings of traditions and texts is the quintessence of a new liberation theology that liberates, first, the text from its historical authorities and, second and more important, Muslims from their imposed and/or traditional authorities. Because the justification of a particular reading is not the text itself, it needs an exterior justification that is provided by *fitra.* But because the fitra is not reason, the exterior justification provides no more than a psychological feeling of satisfaction. A true reading, then, is a reading that goes beyond reason and rationalism and centers on a state of being. In fact, it is, in many regards, a postmodern reading that cannot be final or meaningful except to the reader, himself. Thus, a text could have, in principle, as many readings as there are *fitras,* for neither the modern aspects of the West nor the traditional readings of Islam have any normative value in the construction of what is true, according to most fundamentalists. Also, while the fundamentalists seek the inclusion of scientific knowledge into their views of Islam, it still plays a minor role in the construction of their thought and ideology. As with reason, science cannot be a final or normative source for interpretation, although it could be used as an instrument for attaining physical power and well-being. Its adoption is based on its usefulness, not on its truths or claims. Science should not interpret the text. The interpretation of the text is left to the individual, and individual readings are equal to each other. In treating a text as a reality that can have unfettered possibilities of individual understandings, fundamentalist thought displays a postmodern feature. Ultimate and final interpretative legitimacy does not exist on earth. This is why most fundamentalists sound postmodern when they reject the finality of interpretations, methodology, and ideological views such as rationalism, empiricism, positivism, and historicism as well the traditional Islamic methods of jurisprudence, theology, and linguistics. If Islam is valid for all times and places, its interpretations must be postmodern.

The fundamentalist insistence on Islamizing every social or political doctrine is also a quest for identity and for social and political legitimacy. Fundamentalists' rejection of the traditional modes of understanding—such as theology, philosophy, sufism, and jurisprudence—is not motivated by pure intellectualism. While this rejection removes a layer of intellectual authoritarianism, it eases the movement toward popular legitimacy which empowers the community to take matters into its own hands and to delegitimize the imposed elites. Most political elites embody a rupture with the past representing the original interests of colonialist and imperialist powers and the current interests of world powers. If the Qur'an and *sunna* are the source materials for a comprehensive Islamic revival, then the removal of the elites is a Qur'anically legitimate matter. The moderate fundamentalist quest for democracy through reinterpreting *shura* and *ijma'* is a quest for more representative authorities that reflect the people's choices, for if all Muslims are equal in terms of reading the text, it stands to reason that they are equally capable of charting their political destiny. Here one can see how the individual right to interpret the text becomes a political right of proper representation. One can compare the impact of this idea to Martin Luther's view on religious and individual freedom, later transformed into political freedom that ultimately made possible the development of liberal democracy in the West. Like Luther's epistemological break with Catholicism, fundamentalism represents an epistemological break with Islamic traditionalism and its institutions. While it is too early to evaluate the impact of this break on the future of Islamic thought, what is clear is that it has started to lead many Muslim thinkers to reargue the usefulness of dominant political traditions and paradigms as well as their institutions.

In this sense, the quest for an Islamic state should be seen as a quest for liberation from authoritarian states and unrepresentative authorities that have dominated the Islamic arena for a long time. While the moderate fundamentalist views of an Islamic state entertain a democratic and, at times, liberal vision of the state, state legitimacy centers on not contradicting textual Qur'anic references and on supporting popular elections and encouraging moral behavior. The emphasis on textual references by the fundamentalists is employed as an empowering and balancing principle that allows people to legitimately act in opposition to their rulers, who control the means of suppression. When the interests of the rulers and ruled are contradictory—and because the rulers can resort to sheer power to force people to yield to their interests—textual references are employed to empower revolting against the rulers. However, popular elections, made equal to *shura* and *ijma'* and, consequently, made religious duties by the fundamentalists, are the means of representing and maintaining people's interests and of lifting oppression and exploitation. This is the reason fundamentalists equate public morality, resulting from people's control of public space and leading to social and political justice, with proper political behavior and sincere belief. Proper political behavior and sincere belief become synonyms, and improper political behavior is equated with unbelief. In a sense, the political evaluation of individual behaviors dominates the Islamic public space. Theological arguments about belief and unbelief, Islamization and Westernization, and authentication and marginalization are, thus, political arguments about justice and injustice, liberation and oppression, and self-fulfillment and self-victimization.

At this stage, many fundamentalists view Islam as an ideological alternative to communism, socialism, liberalism, capitalism, and other "-isms." The distinguishing mark of an Islamic political ideology is morality. The fundamentalists view dominant world ideologies and their representative institutions as internally corrupt, externally inhuman, and globally exploitative. The morality of Islam, as discussed by the fundamentalists, is a quest for global empowerment that, at least, preserves a place for and, at best, legitimizes the role of Muslims in global politics. If the West provides the fabric of material progress through development of technology, then Islam provides its humanizing factor, morality, which leads to spreading the positive aspects of material progress to all nations. When fundamentalists divide the world into *dar al-Islam* and *dar al-harb*, they are dividing it into a perceived morally backward but materially advanced society as opposed to a potentially morally advanced but materially backward world. Bringing together Western technology and Islamic morality suggests to the fundamentalists the possibility of a universally moral and materially advanced global world order. This stands in contrast with current Western domination of technology and control over world capitals without a strong morality that takes into consideration the redistribution of wealth and the equality of nations.

To the fundamentalists, morality applies to poor and rich, alike, and a morally distributive system, for instance, must take into consideration the interests of the poor as well as those of the rich who dominate the capitalist system. Thus, while the capitalist mode of production is accepted by almost all fundamentalists, the end product of capitalist distribution of wealth, or its political economy, is mostly condemned as being unethical, unjust, and exploitative. The fundamentalists fear that the globalization of technology and the capitalist mode of distribution is leading humanity into a potentially more divided and conflict-ridden world that has no place for the technologically less advanced and the materially less fortunate.

Though religion, capitalism, and technology are the main preoccupations of fundamentalists, they should be the concern of all people, as they present themselves as the powers that are to shape our world in the twenty-first century. While capitalism is concentrating wealth in fewer hands and technology is spreading into more hands, religion—whether Islam, Christianity, or Hinduism—is spreading and intensifying to such an extent that it cannot be ignored or excluded in the formulation of new world, regional, and state policies. The basic contribution of religion could very well be its universalist character, providing inspiration and resources for the humanization of the use of technology and the distribution of capitalist wealth. Unbridled capitalism and unguided technology could very well lead to new and unprecedented conflicts that fulfill the vision of the prophets who foretell "the clash of civilizations," with "the West against the rest," and warn that "the Muslims are coming." However, an excluded religion without the necessary access to material advancement and technological development may prove to be a gravely destabilizing factor in world politics. Nonetheless, a well thought out scheme for the globalization of religion as morality, of capitalism as more production and more just distribution, and of technology as universal human development may prove all the pessimists wrong. In this context, while Islam is being fitted for the role of the new universal enemy (the green danger), it could very well provide a universal code for both a more just capitalist system and a more humanized technological development. Islam may further prove to be a humanizing force for the newly envisioned, globalized world of the next century.

An example that shows the rising role of religion in world politics and the need to tackle religious concerns is the Arab-Israeli conflict. While the need to resolve Middle Eastern conflicts—and particularly the Arab-Israeli one—came about in part from the realization of many American strategists and policy makers that the explosive nature of these conflicts might be detrimental to their interests, the United States has a vested interest in a new world order that aims at the reactivation of the world economy along the lines of its capitalist model. However, the United States' attempt to establish a new regional order in the area cannot succeed without first eliminating the basic obstacle in the Middle East—the Arab-Israeli conflict. The settlement of this crisis requires that Arabs and Israelis enter into a dialogue that would eventually lead to a peaceful resolution of the conflict as well as subsequent normalization of relations. However, it seems that the new enemy to be vanquished has become Islamic fundamentalism, along with the radical regimes of Iran, Libya, Iraq, and the Sudan, which are capable of developing weapons of mass destruction and which have individual, regional ambitions that do not conform to the requirements of capitalism. In response to this perceived obstacle, the United States has made Israel an advanced post for both logistical support and storage of arms in order to intervene in the Persian Gulf by preventing nuclear proliferation and limiting the use of ballistic and conventional armaments.

The main opposition to the ongoing peace process is portrayed by the West, Israel, and many others as being orchestrated by Iran, the Sudan, and other Arab Islamic movements. Israel and some Arab countries, such as Egypt, position the Islamic movements and the Islamic states of Iran and the Sudan as the frontline of an elaborate scheme to topple the existing regimes that are theoretically capable of reaching peace agreements with Israel and, consequently, of forming the needed regional order. Thus, the Islamic threat is being represented as the new enemy of U.S. interests in the Middle East as well as those of Israel and of moderate Arab states. Israel has transformed its fights with Muslim fundamentalists in Palestine and southern Lebanon into a war with the Islamic movements in the world. It has projected an image of itself as a state, like any other in the area, that is confronting the fundamentalist threat; consequently, its fights with Hamas, for example, are portrayed not as struggles with a disenfranchised people but rather as battles directed at weakening the internal, fundamentalist Palestinian organizations and preventing the establishment of a radical Palestinian state.

Although the Palestinians and Israel have mutually recognized each other in different ways, the future of the Arab-Israeli conflict seems to be shifting focus from the traditional lines of disagreement between Arabs and Israelis to another level. Although this level has long existed—as exemplified in the conflicts between Hamas and the PLO and between the Israeli Labor and Likud parties—the foreseeable future is going to be plagued with radical Islamic and Jewish fundamentalists struggling against the recognition of each other under the guise of historical and religious identity. In this way, the Palestinians and the Israelis have genuinely become part of the troubled Middle East, where they are likely to suffer like any other state in the area, such as Egypt or Algeria, by having their legitimacy questioned by religiously oriented individuals and movements. Claims and counter-claims are postulated, leading to the internalization of what has been largely an external problem, which has helped the cohesion of both the Israeli and Palestinian societies. Thus, no wonder that civil war, civil strife, and uprising against the Palestinian and Israeli establishments cannot be discounted. It seems that all countries of the area are going to share one concern among many—fundamentalism.

When the historic "Gaza and Jericho First" agreement was signed in September 1993 at the White House in Washington, D.C.—in the presence of PLO chairman Yasir Arafat, Israeli premier Yitzhak Rabin, and President Bill Clinton—uproar and discontent were registered by all radical groups, Israeli and Palestinian. The main objections raised were religiously based: the giving up of greater Israel, or the Promised Land, or Palestine, the eternal religiously endowed land. Of course, the first Muslim groups to object were the fundamentalist organizations such as Hamas and al-Jihad al-Islami.

While breakthrough steps have been taken at the formal level, which serve the interests of the United States, Israel, and the concerned Arab parties as well as other Arab states, and while similar steps with Syria and Lebanon for the completion of the peace process are expected in the future, major obstacles remain and are likely to intensify. Although formal peace is commended, it is still insufficient for regional cooperation in the long run. What is needed immediately after or during the completion of the peace process is to take into consideration the deeper issues, whose resolution might put the peoples of the area into a genuine popular peace and, thus, cooperation. The normalization of relations strictly between Israel and other Arab regimes is not conducive in the long run to the region's security or to the well-being of its people. Opposition is expected to intensify against both Israel and the Arab regimes, spearheaded by fundamentalist movements. While the regimes are capable of destroying the fundamentalists' infrastructure, they cannot liquidate their bases or dismiss their grievances, which happen to be the grievances of the broader Jewish and Islamic movements, of the nationalist movements, and, above all, of the people themselves.

That the Islamic movements are on the rise and likely to be more so after peace treaties are signed with the concerned parties has to be given priority in resolving the roots of cultural animosity. That there are terrorism and violence is a matter of fact, but not every opposition by the fundamentalists is a terrorist act. In other words, the ultimate solution to the people's grievances cannot be merely of a security nature; it has to address and resolve the underlying causes. The Islamicity of East Jerusalem serves as the ideological focus of the current and future opposition, as the status of occupied East Jerusalem goes beyond that of an ordinary occupied territory to the status of religious aggression; it is a holy land for Muslims—and of course for the Jews and Christians. The repeated refrain of Prime Minister Rabin and others, that united Jerusalem was the eternal capital of Israel, seemed offensive and insensitive to the feelings and identities of Muslims and even Christians. Although Rabin was catering to Jewish fundamentalist factions, at the same time he underlined the religiosity of the conflict.

In the opinion of Hamas, the Palestinian National Authority represents neither all nor even the majority of Palestinians, especially since the Oslo meeting, after which it became organically linked to Israel and is, as a matter of fact, serving Israeli interests. Violent acts such as the bus bombings in Jerusalem and Tel Aviv in 1996 force all parties concerned into reevaluating their positions vis-à-vis Hamas. What makes the language of Hamas appealing to most Palestinians is that so far they have not benefited either economically or politically from the peace treaty. The Palestinian authority seems to be more of a security buffer between Israel and the Palestinians, and Hamas's extension of its activities into Israel proper weakens such an authority. Again, the political language of Hamas has been religiously developed. In an interview, Bassam Jarrar, a leading thinker of Hamas, clearly stated that, although Hamas rejected the September 1993 Israeli-Palestinian Declaration of Principles, it would not use force to abort it. Hamas, he added, was ready to take part in election of municipalities and associations but not of the Palestinian authority. Also, Hamas did not plan to participate in self rule, because to do so would legitimize the peace process and the terms of the Oslo agreement.[1]

The Islamization of the conflict with Israel transforms it into a twofold religious duty: first, the elimination of the state of Israel; second, the establishment of an Islamic state. Today's fundamentalist ideologies present themselves as the alternative to nationalist and secular ideologies. And since the late 1980s, Hamas, the military wing of the Muslim Brotherhood, has come to portray the Arab-Israeli conflict as a struggle between the forces of Judaism and those of Islam, with the former being regarded as the source of evil and the symbol of Western civilization.The Islamic movement has entered into an open struggle with the PLO, resulting in bloody confrontations. Both Hamas and al-Jihad al-Islami have launched many military operations against the Israeli army, of which the most famous is the one that led to the 1992 deportation of more than four hundred people affiliated with the Islamic movements. Moreover, Hamas has declined to join the Palestinian National Council and has declared—in its Covenant (*al-Mithaq*) of 1988—its rejection of United Nations Resolution 242 and the recognition of Israel. It has also developed its security apparatuses significantly and has refused to join the unified leadership of the *intifadah*. At times, it has even fought the PLO, especially after the Gulf War, because of Hamas's resistance to peace negotiations. The PLO's attempts to contain Hamas failed, since the latter had put forward difficult conditions for joining the National Council.

It seems that Hamas is going to be a force to reckon with, whether in Palestinian internal politics or as regards Israel. Hamas is, first of all, the main Sunni fundamentalist movement in the Gaza Strip and the West Bank. It is deeply rooted in the famous Muslim Brotherhood, which is known as an international umbrella for many sorts of fundamentalist movements that call for the reinstitution of Islam as a universal ideology and for the application of Islamic divine law as the law of the land. Hamas has become the military wing of the Muslim Brotherhood since the inception of the *intifadah*. The ideology of Hamas is, therefore, based on religious principles, which have transformed the Arab-Israeli conflict into a religious war between Islam and Judaism. *Al-Jihad al-Islami* in Palestine also represents an identity challenge to both Israel and the PLO. According to *al-Jihad* leader As'ad al-Tamimi, author of *The Liquidation of Israel: A Qur'anic Duty*, *al-Jihad* does not recognize the establishment of a Jewish state in Palestine, since the struggle between the Islamic movement and Israel is everlasting and has a religious background.[2] Consequently, there is no possible compromise to settle the conflict in a way that will satisfy the two parties. The Jews must, therefore, go back to wherever they came from. Furthermore, and as a challenge to the PLO, *al-Jihad* has rejected the National Council resolutions and compromises and demanded withdrawal from the peace process.

It is very clear that the ongoing peace negotiations are taking place in a strategically changing environment, for Iran has been exerting extensive efforts in order to get recognition as a great regional power in the Middle East, in general, and in the Gulf, in particular. It has been financing, directly or through the Sudan, many fundamentalist movements—such as Hamas in Palestine, the Islamic Salvation Front in Algeria, *al-Nahda* in Tunisia, and, more important, Hizbullah in

Lebanon—in order to establish itself on the Arab agenda and to pre-empt setting up a new regional order that might stand against its interests in the area. Therefore, Iran regards its relations with Islamic fundamentalist movements and states as the strategic bedrock for future resistance to negotiations and accords that do not serve its interests, and as a reminder to Arab states that Iran cannot be iso-lated from any regional plan and is capable of using its fundamental-ist credentials.

Hizbullah in Lebanon is functioning in accordance with local, regional, and international formulas. Like Hamas, it sees in the aggravation of the Arab-Israeli conflict an opportunity to hinder the negotiations. As is well known, Hizbullah represents the Iranian dimension that can be used to remind the negotiators that Iran is around and must not be neglected. Lebanon is one of the the the few countries in the Arab world where Iran can have some influence. Thus Hizbullah, for instance, in a speech by its deputy general secretary, Sheikh Na'im Qasim, criticized Yasir Arafat for granting Israel concessions and claimed that it was the correct per-formance of the confrontation forces that prevented the realization of the Israeli scheme. He described the peace negotiations as necessary to affirm, for the Americans and "its Arabs" as well as for Israel, Arafat's leadership over the Palestinians. Also, maintained Qasim, the peace ne-gotiations served as a vehicle to ending the Palestinian identity by estab-lishing a formula that would provide self rule for some Palestinians on a small part of their land. He accused Arafat of preparing the ground for an internal Palestinian civil war that would erupt in that part of the land. From this angle, Qasim believed that the deportation of some fun-damentalist leaders and the promise to return some of the PLO people were part of the same agenda.[3]

The general secretary of Hizbullah, Hasan Nasrallah, reaffirmed, at the end of Hizbullah's third annual conference in 1993, the con-tinuation of the party policies concerning the substantive positions that were upheld by the conference, including the support and devel-opment of the Islamic resistance in southern Lebanon and the Beka' Valley. Resistance was the chosen alternative to the negotiations, which Hizbullah felt would not lead to the restoration of the Islamic and Arab rights. He considered the rejection of the negotiations and peace accords, in addition to not recognizing Israel, as incontestable ac-tions and linked the foreign policy orientation of the party with Iran's structure of authority. Relations with Iran have been seen as strategic, and the Palestinian resistance has been considered as concomitant to the Islamic resistance in Lebanon.

The Islamic resistance in Lebanon has viewed the peace talks as futile and, thus, has increased its armed resistance. Furthermore, Hizbullah has been organizing some marches against the Lebanese-Israeli peace talks, such as that commemorating the abortion of the May 17 Peace Accord. Sheikh Muhammad Hussein Fadlallah, the spiritual leader of Hizbullah, has already decried the peace talks and described them as illegal, since they give peace and legitimacy to Israel and to its use of force in the occupation of land. He added that "the issue [peace and recognition of Israel] is not related to the decision of individuals or of governments but it is the decision of the Muslim nation. And anyone who misuses its decision, the nation will take sooner or later its decision about him."[4] On the substantive level, Hizbullah considers that Israel is a foreign and occupying entity of the area and the holy places and a challenge to Muslim identity. It therefore views fighting Israel as a religious duty. This is why, in my opinion, an ultimate, popular resolution of the status of East Jerusalem takes away the religiosity of the conflict and opens the possibility of real normalization between the Arabs and the Israelis. Egypt is a good example of the future of Arab regimes that are going to be accused of giving up the holy land. Iran and numerous fundamentalist movements have already been using the religious nature of Palestine and mobilizing the people accordingly. Again, Egypt's mounting internal problems with the fundamentalists and its unsuccessful normalization of relations with Israel serve as the future model. But this is an unstable situation for all the parties concerned, especially given the possibility of a fundamentalist takeover in one of the states in the Arab world. While a satisfactory and real resolution to the ambiguity of the status of East Jerusalem disarms the opposition, Arabs' acceptance of such a resolution is a must for the longevity and genuineness of peace among the peoples of the area. Those strategists, especially the Americans and Israelis, who think that the Muslims and Arabs are just going to accept the Muslim and Christian holy places as tourist attractions would be making a serious political and cultural error. In other words, the religious values of all the peoples of the area, not only of one people, should be taken into consideration or else there are going to be built-in dangers in any possible future for the area.

The other important issue that must be dealt with seriously is the economic status of the concerned parties—Israel, Egypt, Jordan, Syria, Lebanon, and Palestine. These states are plagued more or less, and in one way or another, with poverty, inflation, unemployment, and exploitation. Many Palestinians or Egyptians, for instance, may turn to Islamic fundamentalism because of the corruption of their political elites, exploitation of the nouveau riche, nepotism, favoritism, and the like. The fundamentalist groups have been raising the issue of social justice, which as a popular demand is likely to accelerate, given the dire needs of the people. Thus, the economic pressures that Israel puts on the Palestinian Authority—by cutting off the Territories from Israel and not allowing seventy-five thousand Palestinian workers to enter Israel and work, in retaliation for violent acts—support the interest of the fundamentalists and not the other way around, since a real stake in the economy reduces the membership of the fundamentalists and makes people more likely to cooperate and preserve the system.

Liberalism and pluralistic democracy should be also encouraged and implemented. Jordan may serve as a good example of a successful liberalization process. Opposition in the Arab world, thus far, has had nothing to lose, economically and politically, which indeed makes the opposition more clandestine and outspoken without a need to tune its views to the realities of the world. But an institutionalized opposition becomes more responsible, more realistic, for it has to deal with the real issues of economy and politics.

While the three steps mentioned above seem of great magnitude and require much work, they are necessary for the well-being of the area, the United States, and the world. The status of Jerusalem, its economy and politics, and the need for all parties concerned to tackle them skillfully must be the future concern of politicians, policy makers, and political scientists. However, because the Islamic fundamentalist movements have long been positioned to react to state policies, the contexts of their politics do help in either their inclusion or their exclusion and, therefore, their compromise or rejection, respectively. Hizbullah, for instance, has exhibited within the Lebanese context the ability to reformulate its ideological views and policies as it reacted to the policies of inclusion of the Lebanese state. While the parliamentary elections of 1992 in Lebanon radicalized further the already radical Christian opposition, they have had a different impact on Hizbullah and other Islamic fundamentalist groups—whose deputies constituted the largest parliamentary bloc, consisting of twelve members. While the ease of their victory was due partly to Christian boycotts in certain areas like Beirut, their popularity was mainly due to the services that they have been offering, to their reputation for integrity, and to good organization. Their victory also reflected the replacement of traditional political leaders with party-oriented choices. Furthermore, most traditional leadership, such as speaker Kamil al-As'ad, lost. By playing the electoral game, Hizbullah turned from op-position from outside the system to opposition from within, thus both taking into consideration changes within Lebanon and preparing itself for the major changes in the area at large.

Most fundamentalist organizations in Lebanon have been able to ac-commodate themselves to the country's new formula of inter-sectarian coexistence, forged in the Ta'if Accord of 1990. While the fundamental-ist movements are violently repressed in Syria, they have already started in Lebanon a process of compromise by accepting the legitimacy of the Lebanese Republic. For instance, al-Jama'a al-Islamiyya decided to par-ticipate in the 1992 parliamentary elections, seeking to replicate the ex-amples of the Jordanian and Algerian models.

Iran has supported the Ta'if Accord to resolve the Lebanese civil war, and Ali Akbar Muhtashimi, one of the Iranian founders of Hizbullah, was removed from the Iranian government earlier in 1989. The Iranian "radical wing," most of whom had very strong ties to Hizbullah, lost in the Iranian elections of 1992, and the Revolution-ary Guards' foreign role was ended. Still, Iran maintains strong rela-tions with Hizbullah, but major financial cuts have been taken and the political cover has been reduced. In 1991 and 1992, the Iranian foreign minister "accepted" the expansion of the Lebanese authority over the Lebanese territories. The liquidation of the radicals from the Iranian government was reflected by a similar change in the lead-ership of Hizbullah in Lebanon. The Lebanese elections of 1992 pro-duced the practical effect of that change by bringing it into postwar politics and in tune with the peace process with Israel. Hizbullah's acceptance of the American-Syrian security arrangements after the Israeli bombardment of the South, and its new political behavior to-ward secular and Christian political parties and openness to dialogue, are two main examples.

It seems that the current leadership of Hizbullah, under Nasrallah, is preparing itself to face the consequences of the peace process along with the internal debates about avoiding paying the cost of regional settlements. Since its entrance into the parliament, its discourse has undergone massive changes, such as dropping its slogan of the illegitimacy of the Lebanese system and becoming part of it. It has proven its capability to adapt to the quickly moving events in the region—like accepting Syrian-Israeli peace talks. While its entrance into the parliament did not preclude its special relations with Iran, it is now more in line with Syrian orientations on regional issues. Its relations to Syria seem to be the main principle around which its relations to the Lebanese system are built, and consequently its liquidation seems unlikely, since it is one of the factors that the Syrians use to control the Lebanese system.

While the radical wing in the Party—like former general secretary Sobhi al-Tufayli, who is now on the run—is opposed to Syrian orientations, especially on the issue of peace with Israel, the majority is not anymore. While most of the Party officially seems to follow the doctrine of the governance of juriconsult in Iran, Muhammad Hussein Fadl Allah seems to be challenging the religious authority of Iran and positing himself as one, if not the, highest religious authority in the world of *Shi'ism*. But a total break has not taken place yet, and it is more likely that the Party will be more Lebanonized with the progress of the peace process. Hizbullah is distancing itself now from terrorism, and its general secretary Nasrallah now accepts dismantling its military organization if the Israelis withdraw from the South, whereas before the peace talks Hizbullah considered as its goal the destruction of Israel. Again, it has accepted the Syrian strategic view on the Arab-Israeli conflict, and its leadership is preparing the economic and social conditions for absorbing its military organization in its civilian organizations. Furthermore, its political leadership has opened up to other Lebanese political powers and toward the Maronite church in an attempt to show its new accommodating attitude.

A properly constructed peace in the area will make Hizbullah and other fundamentalist movements shift their focus from radical confrontational policies with Israel and Arab regimes to normal opposition of an economic and political nature. In brief, a liberal and democratic context that takes the outstanding religious-identity issues into consideration would go a long way to softening political transition, facilitating the empowerment of people, and legitimizing political rule in a modern environment.

Notes

Introduction

1. See, for instance, "The March of Islamism," 30; "The Deadly Party of God: Hizbullah Threatens the West," 28; "Khomeini Strikes Back," 25; "Blocking the Goal," 47; and "Will Islamic Fundamentalists Spread?" 57. See also the interview with Hasan al-Turabi, the Sudanese leader of the Islamic Front, in House Committee, *Implication for U.S. Policy.*

2. Recent books on Islamic fundamentalism, many of them reflecting journalistic concerns, include: Hiro, *Holy Wars;* Mortimer, *Faith and Power;* Sivan, *Radical Islam: Medieval Theology and Modern Politics;* Hussain, *Political Perspectives on the Muslim World;* Roff, *Islam and the Political Economy of Meaning;* Warburg and Kumpferschmidt, *Islam, Nationalism and Radicalism;* Munson, *Islam and Revolution in the Middle East;* al-Sayyid Marsot, *Protest Movements and Religious Undercurrents;* Taylor, *The Islamic Question in Middle East Politics;* Watt, *Islamic Fundamentalism and Modernity;* Lawrence, *Defenders of God;* Barry, *Islamic Fundamentalism in Egyptian Politics;* and Choueiri, *Islamic Fundamentalism.*

3. This topic is discussed again, but more extensively, in chapter three. See the debates between John Voll and John Esposito, on the one hand, and Patrick Clawson, Joshua Muravichik, Barry Rubin, and Robert Satloff, on the other, in *Middle East Quarterly* 1, no. 3. See also Kepel, *The Revenge of God.*

4. Sisk, *Islam and Democracy,* vii.

5. See the articles in *New Perspective Quarterly* 2 (Spring 1994), no. 2, 20–37.

6. "Media Mongols at the Gate of Baghdad," 10.

7. "The Islamic-Confucian Connection," 19. See also "The Clash of Civilizations," 22–49. For similar attitudes, see "Will Democracy Survive in Egypt?" 149; and "The Arab World Where Troubles for the U.S. Never End," 24. Also see Miller, "Challenge of Radical Islam," 43–55. In the same vein, see Lewis, "Islam and Liberal Democracy," 89–98.

8. "Inclusion Can Deflate Islamic Populism," 50. For studies that deal with similar issues and on the relationships among political elites, Islamists, and the West, see Salame, "Islam and the West," 22–37. See also Eickelman, "Changing Interpretations," 13–30.

9. Zartman, "Democracy and Islam," 191.

10. Esposito and Piscatori, "Democratization and Islam," 434. Along the same line of argument, see Kramer, "Islamist Democracy," 2–8.

11. On the hot issue of the term "fundamentalism," see al-Azm, "Islamic Fundamentalism Reconsidered," pt. 1, 93–131, pt. 2, 73–98. See also Marty and Appleby, *Accounting for Fundamentalisms, Fundamentalisms and Society,* and *Fundamentalisms and the State.*

Chapter 1. Two Discourses on Modern Islamic Political Thought

1. See Halpern, *Politics of Change;* Sharabi, "Islam and Modernism," 26–36; and Khadduri, "From Religious to National Law," 37–51. See also Dessouki, ed., *Islamic Resurgence;* and Curtis, ed., *Religion and Politics.*

2. Armajani, *Middle East,* 287–88.

3. See Qutb, *Hadha al-Din,* 20–22, 24–26. See also Qutb, *Al-Mustaqbal,* 13.

4. Qutb, *Al-'Adala,* 24–29.

5. On the *fitra* and its importance, see Qutb, *Khasa'is,* 4, 51, 83, 114, 127, 133, 134, 135, 137, 146–47, 166–67, 206, 207, 210; and idem, *Hadha al-Din,* 11. In *Khasa'is* (116–18, 140, 164–65), Qutb uses numerous Qur'anic verses to support his position—for instance, 2:164; 3:2–6, 191; 4:82; 6:12–19; 13:8–16; 33:62; 55:82; and, especially, 30:30. See also idem, *Al-Mustaqbal,* 11–13, 57–61.

6. Qutb, *Al-Mustaqbal,* 17–18.

7. Al-Mawdudi, *Mafahim Islamiyya,* 10–12, 28–29; and idem, *Nizam,* 6–7.

8. Shari'ati, *Marxism,* 80.

9. Al-Afghani, *Al-'Urwa,* 60–61; and see idem, *Al-A'mal,* 9–13, 16–17.

10. Qutb, *Al-Mustaqbal,* 12–14; and idem, *Khasa'is,* 212–15. The Qur'anic verses that Qutb quotes in *Khasa'is* (36–39, 230) include 12:40; 42:21; 5:47; 4:65; 9; 10:18; and 39:3–4.

11. Qutb, *Al-Mustaqbal,* 15–17.

12. Al-Mawdudi, *Nahnu,* 146–48, 150, 174.

13. Al-Banna, *Majmu'at Rasa'il al-Imam,* 429–31, 471–74.

14. 'Abduh, *Risalat,* 19–20, 31, 46–51.

15. Ibid., 111–13.

16. Iqbal, *Reconstruction,* 2, 9, 22.

17. Al-Mawdudi, *Minhaj,* 28–34; idem, *Nahnu,* 267–70; and idem, *Nizam,* 21–22.

18. Iqbal, *Reconstruction,* 145–55.

19. Shari'ati, *Sociology of Islam,* 83.

20. Ibid., 63.

21. Iqbal, *Reconstruction,* 4, 14–15, 42, 54–57, 196.

22. 'Abduh, *Risalat,* 18–19, 28–32, 46–47, 59, 69–70, 108, 112–32.

23. Al-Afghani, *A'mal,* 440–41.

24. Al-Mawdudi, *Nahnu,* 13–18.

25. Iqbal, *Reconstruction*, 8, 63–64, 70.

26. On the the role of history for the authenticity of the Holy Qur'an, see as-Said, *Recited Koran*, 19–60, 121–25. Also, on the importance of historical accuracy for understanding the *shari'a*, see Hodgson, *Venture of Islam*, 315–58.

27. See 'Abduh, *Risalat*, 17–51. The traditional structure of his arguments, like his description of God's actions, is noticeable. For a brief essay on, and references to, al-Ghazali's understanding of science and logic as not being contrary to religion, see Marmura, "Ghazali's Attitude," 100–109. Also, for more details, see al-Ghazali, *Tahafut*, 74, 77–78, 83–87, 89–124; and on the division of philosophy, idem, *Al-Munqidh*, 47–57. On 'Abduh's reluctance to involve himself in controversies, see his treatment of the Muslim philosophers, wherein he explains their differences from the main orthodoxy without commending or censuring them (*Risalah*, 28–32).

28. Al-Mawdudi, *Nahnu*, 47–51, 23–25.

29. Qutb, *Mar'rakat*, 60; also see 49.

30. Qutb, *Hadha al-Din*, 16–19; idem, *Ma'alim*, 49–114 *passim*; idem, *Fi Zilal*, 34; idem, *Fiqh al-Da'wa*, 60–61; idem, *Al-'Adala*, 105; and idem, *Tafsir Surat*, 51.

31. Al-Mawdudi, *Mafahim Islamiyya*, 24–25.

32. See Iqbal, *Reconstruction*, 157. Al-Afghani, for instance, accepted the rule of the Ottoman Caliph 'Abd al-Hamid and argued for the modernization of the Muslim *umma* through a spiritual and political regeneration of Muslims and by adopting Western institutions.

33. Qutb, *Ma'alim*, 26; also see 101; idem, *Al-Ra'simaliyya*, 70. See also idem, *Al-'Adala*, 250. In *Al-'Adala* (258 and 249–50), Qutb quotes the following verses: 3:139–40; 4:59, 65, 74, 144; and 8:60.

34. Qutb, *Fi al-Tarikh*, 24–25.

35. Qutb, *Ma'alim*, 68.

36. Ibid., 67–71. Also, Qutb quotes in *Al-'Adala* (67) the following verses to support his argument: 3:64; 12:40; and 43:84.

37. See 'Amara, *Muslimun Thuwwar*, 154; also, the whole chapter on al-Afghani. See also idem, *Al-Islam*, 234–38; and idem, *A'mal*, 333.

38. For instance, see al-Mawdudi, *Al-Jihad*, 25–28.

39. Dessouki, "Islamic Organization," 113.

40. On al-Afghani, see, for instance, "Al-Kharitat" in al-Afghani, "Political Writings," 9, 10, 11–13. On the fundamentalists, see, for instance, Asad, *Islam at a Crossroad*, 3; the quotation is from al-Mawdudi, *Nahnu*, 79.

41. For example, al-Mawdudi, *Minhaj*, 5–6; idem, *Nahnu*, 193–94.

42. Qutb, *Ma'alim*, 22; idem, *Khasa'is*, 15–31.

43. Naff, "Muslim Theory of History," 28.

44. Humphreys, "Islam and Political Values," 108.

45. On traditional understanding of the Qur'an and the *sunna*, see Peters, *Allah's Commonwealth*, 41–134; Gibb, *Mohammadanism*, 24–35, 36–48; and Gibb, *Studies*, 186–207.

46. On the reasons for modern Islamic revival and its beginning, see Gibb, *Mohammadanism*, 111–31. On modern concepts of the Islamic state, see Enayat, *Modern Islamic Political Thought*, 69–110. On the lack of leadership and existence of absolutism, see Cragg, *Contemporary Counsels*, 181–93.

47. Qutb, 58, 63–69, 72.

48. On differences between the Shi'ite and Sunnite attitudes toward governments, see Lambton, *State and Government*, 246–63; Peters, *Allah's Commonwealth*, 544–634; and Enayat, *Modern Islamic Political Thought*, 18–51.

49. Enayat, *Modern Islamic Political Thought*, 207–9, 230–32.

50. Al-Mawdudi, *Nizam*, 54; also see 50–53.

Chapter 2. Fundamentalist Discourses on Epistemology and Political Philosophy

1. See Qutb, *Fi al-Tarikh*, 26; and al-Banna, *Majmu'at Rasa'il al-Shahid*, Dar al-Qalam, 246 and, on the insufficiency of reason, 473. Also, compare with the reformist Shariati, *Sociology of Islam*, 49.

2. Al-Banna, *Majmu'at Rasa'il al-Shahid*, Dar al-Qalam, 246–48.

3. Al-Banna, *Majmu'at Rasa'il al-Shahid*, Dar al-Qalam, 9; Qutb, *Hadha al-Din*, 6–7. On reason and metaphysics, see al-Banna, *Majmu'at Rasa'il al-Shahid*, Dar al-Qalam, 345–436; on God and His qualities, see idem, *Majmu'at Rasa'il al-Shahid*, Dar al-Qalam, 471; and on reason and God's knowledge, see idem, *Majmu'at Rasa'il al-Shahid*, Dar al-Qalam, 445–49. On imposing limitations on metaphysics, see al-Nadawi, *Madha Khasira*, 149; and Qutb, *Ma'alim*, 25–54.

4. Al-Nadawi, *Madha Khasir*, 147–50.

5. See al-Mudarrisi, *Al-Islam*, 70–71; al-Banna, *Majmu'at Rasa'il al-Shahid*, Dar al-Qalam, 179–80, 307; al-Nadawi, *Madha Khasir*, 215–16, 272–73; Qutb, *Hadha al-Din*, 22–23; and al-Mawdudi, *Understanding Islam*, 15–16.

6. Al-Nadawi, *Madha Khasir*, 150–70.

7. Qutb, *Khasa'is*, 52; al-Nadawi, *Madha Khasir*, 132; al-Banna, *Majmu'at Rasa'il, al-Shahid*, Dar al-Qalam 11, 65–66, 169–170; al-Mudarrisi, *Al-Islam*, 11–12, 16–17; and al-Khumayni, *Al-Hukuma*, 67–88.

8. Qutb, *Khasa'is*, 52–54.

9. Al-Banna, *Majmu'at Rasa'il al-Shahid*, Dar al-Qalam, 117, 205, 219–20, 431–33, 473–75; Qutb, *Khasa'is*, 53, 66–67; idem, *Ma'alim*, 11–12, 14–17, 43, 126–27; idem, *Al-'Adala*, 69, 140, 142–43, 146–47, 267–70; al-Khumayni, *Al-Hukuma*, 59–63, 65–66; and al-Mawdudi, *Understanding*, 30–31, 36–37.

10. Al-Banna, *Majmu'at Rasa'il al-Shahid*, Dar al-Qalam, 179–80.

11. Al-Khumayni, *Al-Hukuma*, 52, 62–68.

12. See al-Khumayni, *Al-Hukuma*, 132–34; Qutb, *Ma'alim*, 30, 38–40, 52; idem, *Khasa'is*, 9–10, 53; idem, *Al-'Adala*, 19, 167–69; al-Nadawi, *Madha Khasir*, 149; al-Mawdudi, *Understanding*, 30–31; and al-Banna, *Majmu'at Rasa'il al-Shahid*, Dar al-Qalam, 81–82, 125.

13. Al-Banna, *Majmu'at Rasa'il*, 78–81.

14. Al-Banna, *Majmu'at Rasa'il al-Shahid*, Dar al-Qalam, 84, 217–18, 223–25, 247, 250, 263–64; al-Khumayni, *Al-Hukuma*, 57–59; al-Nadawi, *Madha Khasir*, 217–18, 223–25, 263–64; Qutb, *Ma'alim*, 25, 42, 48; and idem, *Al-'Adala*, 30, 196, 285.

15. Al-Nadawi, *Madha Khasir*, 214–17.

16. Qutb, *Ma'alim*, 41–44.

17. Al-Banna, *Majmu'at Rasa'il al-Shahid*, Dar al-Qalam, 117, 148, 169–70, 219–20, 272–77; al-Nadawi, *Madha Khasir*, 263–64, 275–76; al-Mudarrisi, *Al-Islam*, 69–70; Qutb, *Al-Mustaqbal*, 10; and al-Mawdudi, *Revivalist Movements*, 34–35.

18. Al-Mudarrisi, *Al-Islam*, 48–51.

19. Al-Nadawi, *Madha Khasir*, 258–59.

20. Al-Banna, *Majmu'at Rasa'il al-Shahid*, Dar al-Qalam, 100–101, 168–69; Qutb, *Al-Mustaqbal*, 29; idem, *Khasa'is*, 25, 51, 53, 66–67, 80; idem, *Ma'alim*, 42, 140; Yasin, *Muqaddima*, 158–59.

21. Al-Banna, *Majmu'at Rasa'il al-Shahid*, Dar al-Qalam, 179–80, 269–71.

22. Al-Banna, *Majmu'at Rasa'il al-Shahid*, Dar al-Qalam, 82–83; Qutb, *Khasa'is*, 150; idem, *Ma'alim*, 293–94; al-Nadawi, *Madha Khasir*, 275–77, 293–94; and al-Khumayni, *Al-Hukuma*, 85.

23. Qutb, *Khasa'is*, 148–50; idem, *Ma'alim*, 275–77.

24. Al-Nadawi, *Madha Khasir*, 135, 156–61; Qutb, *Khasa'is*, 10.

25. Al-Nadawi, *Madha Khasir*, 136.

26. Qutb, *Al-'Adala*, 42; idem, *Khasa'is*, 10–11. On corrupting Islam, see al-Nadawi, *Madha Khasir*, 136.

27. Qutb, *Khasa'is*, 12–14.

28. Al-Banna, *Majmu'at Rasa'il al-Shahid*, Dar al-Qalam, 148, 169–70, 272–77; Qutb, *Al-Mustaqbal*, 12–14; and al-Mawdudi, *Understanding*, 30–31.

29. Al-Banna, *Majmu'at Rasa'il al-Shahid*, Dar al-Qalam, 147–58.

30. Ibid., 248. See also al-Nadawi, *Madha Khasir*, 214; al-Mawdudi, *Revivalist*, 36–43; idem, *Understanding*, 15–86; idem, *Nizam*, 267–70; Qutb, *Al-Mustaqbal*, 15–18, 33–34; and idem, *Ma'alim*, 38, 54, 57, 92–95.

31. Qutb, *Ma'alim*, 37–44.

32. Al-Banna, *Majmu'at Rasa'il al-Shahid*, Dar al-Qalam, 121–29, 223–24. Also see Qutb, *Khasa'is*, 16; idem, *Ma'alim*, 26–27, 30, 67; idem, *Al-'Adala*, 69; and idem, *Al-Mustaqbal*, 1, 2–14, 25.

33. Al-Banna, *Majmu'at Rasa'il al-Shahid*, Dar al-Qalam, 223–27.

34. Al-Mudarrisi, *Al-Islam*, 9, 49–52; Qutb, *Al-Islam wa Mushkilat*, 65–66, 124.

35. Al-Banna, *Majmu'at Rasa'il al-Shahid*, Dar al-Qalam, 168, 331–32. Also see al-Nadawi, *Madha Khasir*, 258–59; and Qutb, *Al-Islam wa Mushkilat*, 7–8.

36. Al-Nadawi, *Madha Khasir*, 259–62.

37. Al-Banna, *Majmu'at Rasa'il al-Shahid*, Dar al-Qalam, 337–55. See also al-Mudarrisi, *Al-Islam*, 52, 56–64.

38. Al-Mudarrisi, *Al-Islam*, 59–61.

39. Yasin, *Muqaddima*, 8, 158, 165; Qutb, *Al-Islam wa Mushkilat*, 195; and al-Banna, *Majmuʿat Rasaʾil al-Shahid*, Dar al-Qalam, 343–47.

40. Al-Nadawi, *Madha Khasir*, 260–63.

41. Qutb, *Nahwa*, 13–15; idem, *Al-Islam wa Mushkilat*, 28, 124, 195; and idem, *Al-Islam wa al-Raʾsimaliyya*, 116.

42. Yasin, *Muqaddima*, 141; al-Mudarrisi, *Al-Islam*, 47–48; and Qutb, *Nahwa*, 69.

43. Al-Mudarrisi, *Al-Islam*, 44–47.

44. Al-Nadawi, *Madha Khasir*, 92–94; Qutb, *Nahwa*, 5–13, 92–94; al-Banna, *Majmuʿat Rasaʾil al-Shahid*, Dar al-Qalam, 347.

45. Al-Khumayni, *Al-Hukuma*, 8.

46. Al-Nadawi, *Madha Khasir*, 88–93.

47. Qutb, *Nahwa*, 17. See also al-Banna, *Majmuʿat Rasaʾil al-Shahid*, Dar al-Qalam, 76, 101; al-Khumayni, *Al-Hukuma*, 10, 27–28; and al-Nadawi, *Madha Khasir*, 270–71.

48. Al-Khumayni, *Al-Hukuma*, 8–12.

49. Al-Banna, *Majmuʿat Rasaʾil al-Shahid*, Dar al-Qalam, 318–19; al-Nadawi, *Madha Khasir*, 262–64, 268–69; and Yasin, *Muqaddima*, 103.

50. Al-Banna, *Majmuʿat Rasaʾil al-Shahid*, Dar al-Qalam, 314–17.

51. On *hakimiyya*, see al-Nadawi, *Madha Khasir*, 268–269; Qutb, *Nahwa*, 150–59; idem, *Khasaʾis*, 3–4; al-Mawdudi, *Understanding*, 4, 113; and *Islamic Way of Life*, 7, 21–22; idem, *Nahnu*, 267–70; and al-Khumayni, *Al-Hukuma*, 41–44.

52. Al-Mawdudi, *Islamic Way of Life*, 16–17.

53. See al-Mawdudi, *A Short History*, 22–27; idem, *Understanding*, 93; Qutb, *Al-Mustaqbal*, 12–14; idem, *Khasaʾis*, 212–15; idem, *Al-Islam wa Mushkilat*, 196; al-Banna, *Majmuʿat Rasaʾil al-Shahid*, Dar al-Qalam, 63, 169, 309, 332–33; and al-Khumayni, *Al-Hukuma*, 122–23.

54. Qutb, *Al-Mustaqbal*, 14–17.

55. See, for instance, ʿAmara, *Muslimun Thuwwar*, 154.

56. On *al-jihad*, see Ibn Taymiyya, *Al-Siyasa*, 128–35; al-Mawardi, *Al-Ahkam*, 84–97; and Ibn Khaldun, *Al-Muqaddima*, chap. 37. See also Yasin, *Al-Muqaddima*, 104–5, 151, 155; and Qutb, *Al-Salam*, 25.

57. Qutb, *Maʿalim*, 161–65.

58. Qutb, *Al-Salam*, 21–23; see also idem, *Maʿalim*, 162–63; idem, *Nahwa*, 62; idem, *Hadha al-Din*, 32–33; al-Banna, *Majmuʿat Rasaʾil al-Shahid*, Dar al-Qalam, 54–55, 174–75, 347–48; and Yasin, *Muqaddima*, 167.

59. Al-Banna, *Majmuʿat Rasaʾil al-Shahid*, Dar al-Qalam, 54.

60. Qutb, *Al-Salam*, 170–71; idem, *Maʿalim*, 26; al-Mawdudi, *A Short History*, 22–25; al-Nadawi, *Madha Khasir*, 268–69; and al-Khumayni, *Al-Hukuma*, 32–35.

61. Al-Khumayni, *Al-Hukuma*, 33–34.

62. Al-Nadawi, *Madha Khasir,* 130–31; Qutb, *Maʿalim,* 100–131, 277; al-Khumayni, *Al-Hukuma,* 31–32; and Qutb, *Al-Salam,* 3.

63. Al-Nadawi, *Madha Khasir,* 131–32.

64. Qutb, *Maʿalim,* 20–22, 69–77, 159, 162–63; idem, *Fi al-Tarikh,* 23–24; idem, *Fiqh al-Daʿwa,* 15–31; idem, *Hadha al-Din,* 87–88; idem, *Al-ʿAdala,* 76–78; and al-Banna, *Majmuʿat Rasaʾil al-Shahid,* Dar al-Qalam, 140.

65. Qutb, *Maʿalim,* 28.

66. Al-Banna, *Rasaʾil al-Shahid,* Dar al-Qalam, 59. See also Qutb, *Al-Salam,* 108–36.

67. Al-Banna, *Majmuʿat Rasaʾil al-Shahid,* Dar al-Qalam, 143–44.

68. Al-Nadawi, *Madha Khasir,* 267–68; Qutb, *Al-Salam,* 5; idem, *Nahwa,* 114, 124–25; and al-Mawdudi, *Islamic Way of Life,* 23.

69. Al-Nadawi, *Madha Khasir,* 268–69.

70. Al-Mawdudi, *Islamic Way of Life,* 21–22.

71. Qutb, *Al-Salam,* 36–39, 44–45.

72. Al-Banna, *Al-Salam,* 21–24, 43–44.

73. Ibid., 68–78, 102–5, 114–15.

74. Yasin, *Muqaddima,* 29, 76, 186–90; and Qutb, *Al-Salam,* 29.

75. See Qutb, *Al-Salam,* 12–15, 19–20, 168, 173; al-Nadawi, *Madha Khasir,* 296–97; and Yasin, *Muqaddima,* 173–74.

Chapter 3. Fundamentalist Discourses on Politics

1. On democracy and pluralism in the Arab world, see *Al-Hayat,* 4 August 1993, 19, 25; *Al-Hayat,* 25 September 1993, 14, 17. The series ran 2–6 August. See also *Qadaya al-Isbuʿ* 15 (10–17 September 1993), 1–2. For fundamentalists interested in the same issue, see al-Ghannushi, *Al-Hurriyyat,* and al-Huwaidi, *Al-Islam wa al-Dimocratiyya.*

In 1990, the Beirut Center for the Studies of Arab Unity convened a conference in Cairo to discuss democracy in the Arab world. The London-based, widely read Arabic newspaper, *Al-Hayat,* serialized in August 1993 a five-day debate on civil society, pluralism, and democracy in Egypt and the Arab world.

2. "Will Democracy Survive," 149; "Arab World," 24; "Clash of Civilizations," 22–49.

3. Sisk, *Islam and Democracy,* vii.

4. *New Perspective Quarterly,* 20–37.

5. Ibid., 3. The editor is Nathan Gardels.

6. "Media Mongols," 10.

7. "Islamic-Confucian Connection," 19. See also "Clash of Civilizations," 22–49. For similar attitudes, see "Will Democracy Survive," 149; and "Arab World," 24.

8. Ibid., 21.

9. Miller, "Challenge," 54–55; also see the complete article, 43–55. In the

same vein, see Lewis, "Islam and Liberal Democracy," 89–98. This article is used by Miller to support her argument.

10. "One Man, One Vote," 49.

11. Ibid.

12. Norton, "Inclusion Can Deflate Islamic Populism," 50.

13. Ibid., 51. For studies that deal with similar issues and on the relationships between political elites, Islamists, and the West, see Salame, "Islam and the West," 22–37. See also Eickelman, "Changing Interpretations," 13–30.

14. Zartman, "Democracy and Islam," 191.

15. Esposito and Piscatori, "Democratization and Islam," 434. Along the same line of argument, see Kramer, "Islamist Democracy," 2–8.

16. Gudrun Kramer, "Liberalization and Democracy," 25; also see 22–24.

17. Al-Hayat, 24 April 1993, 19. Some of the books that have been resurrected include *Freedom of Thought* by Salame Musa, *Islam and the Fundamentals of Government* by ʿAli ʿAbd al-Raziq, *The Future of Culture in Egypt* by Taha Hussein, *The Liberation of Woman* by Qasim Amin, and *The Nature of Tyranny* by ʿAbd al-Rahaman al-Kawakibi. There are also many others, including briefs for modernist political thinkers such as ʿAbduh and al-Afghani. On the war of ideas and political control, see Flores, "Secularism," 35–38.

18. Al-Safir, 2 April 1993, 8.

19. Al-Hayat, 3 June 1993, 8. See also Flores, "Secularism," 32–33; and *Al-Diyar*, 22 July 1994, 14.

20. For details on this issue, see *Al-Safir*, 10 June 1993, 1, and 16 June 1993, 1, 10. On the views of the mufti of Egypt on violence, see *Al-Wasat*, 11 November 1993, 20–21.

21. Al-Safir, 10 July 1993, 10. His books include *Al-Imam al-Shafiʿi and the Foundation of Moderate Ideology* and *The Concept of Text: A Study in Qurʾanic Sciences*.

22. Al-Safir, 10 July 1993, 10. On the latest figures, see *Al-Wasat*, 25 July 1994, 4–5. All sentences are not given by the regular courts; fifty-six of the fifty-eight death sentences are taken by martial courts, the other two by the higher courts of national security (emergency court).

23. Al-Safir, 3 April 1993, 10. ʿAwwa, *Fi al-Nizam*, 85–113.

24. Al-Hayat, 4 February 1994, 7. See also the five long and diversified articles and dialogues that *Al-Hayat* has serialized in 2–5 August 1993 under the title "Civil Society in Egypt and the Arab World." On interest in democracy in the Arab world and the resistance of the governments to such a society, see, for instance, *Al-Hayat*, 4 August 1993, 19, and 25 September 1993, 14, 17.

25. Al-Shuʿla, March 1993, 38, 39–40.

26. Al-Hayat, 3 August 1993, 19. See also *Al-Hayat*, 3 February 1994, 17. On the democratic changes that have been taking place in the Arab world and North Africa, see Anderson, "Liberalism in Northern Africa," 145–46, 148, 174–75. See also, on the state of democracy in the Arab world, Khashan, "Quag-

mire," 17–33. Consult also Esposito, "Political Islam," 19–24. Al-Jawjari's views are contained in his book *Al-Hizb al-Islami*.

27. *Qira'at Siyasiyya* 3, no. 2, 197–98. *Qadaya Dawliyya* published the Manifesto in its March 1993 issue.

28. Sa'id, *Hasan al-Banna*, 93–94, 99–100, 112–16. Al-Sa'id's leftist account is not favorable, but still the facts mentioned in it, minus the author's analysis, serve to show that the Brotherhood has not officially sanctioned or employed violence. On the active involvement of al-Banna and his organization in civil society, and their cooperation with other civil segments, see, for instance, al-Hussaini, *Moslem Brethren*, Mitchell, *The Society of the Muslim Brothers*, and Adams, *Islam and Modernism*. See also the views of 'Umar al-Tilmisani in Ahmad, *Al-Nabiy al-Musallah*, 199–200. On al-Banna's ideology, see Moussalli, "Hasan al-Banna's Islamist Discourse," 161–74.

29. Sa'id, *Hasan al-Banna*, 101–7, 112, 117, 122–24.

30. Ibid., 129, 132–39, 169–79.

31. Al-Banna, *Rasa'il al-Imam*, 48, 56–60; al-Banna, *Majmu'at Rasa'il al-Shahid*, 4th ed., 14, 169, 309, 331–22, 335–37; al-Banna, *Kalimat Khalida*, 45.

32. Munson, *Islam and Revolution*, 78–79. See also Hiro, *Rise of Islamic Fundamentalism*, 69–72.

33. Al-Banna, *Din wa-Siyasa*, 40–45; al-Banna, *Majmu'at Rasa'il al-Shahid*, 4th ed., 161–65. On al-Banna's biography, see, for instance, Shaikh, *Memoirs of Hasan al-Banna Shaheed*, and Sa'id, *Hasan al-Banna*.

34. Al-Banna, *Majmu'at Rasa'il*, 165; idem, *Majmu'at Rasa'il al-Imam*, 304, 343–47; and idem, *Din wa-Siyasa*, 57–59.

35. Al-Banna, *Majmu'at Rasa'il al-Shahid*, 4th ed., 160–61, 317–18; idem, *Al-Imam Yatahaddath*, 99; and idem, *Majmu'at Rasa'il al-Imam*, 99, 332–37.

36. Al-Banna, *Majmu'at Rasa'il al-Shahid*, 4th ed., 95–96, 165–67, 317, 320–23, 325, 328–30; idem, *Minbar al-Jum'a*, 78–79, 136; and idem, *Al-Da'wa*, 9. On the centrality of this demand, the Islamic state, in the fundamentalist thought, see Lawrence, *Defenders of God*, 187–226.

37. Al-Banna, *Majmu'at Rasa'il al-Shahid*, 4th ed., 96–97, 161–63, 167–69; and idem, *Rasa'il al-Imam*, 53.

38. Al-Banna, *Nazarat*, 194; idem, *Minbar al-Jum'a*, 24–25, 63, 72, 347; idem, *Majmu'at Rasa'il al-Shahid*, 4th ed., 317; idem, *Majmu'at Rasa'il al-Imam*, 63, 72, 101, 104, 317; idem, *Rasa'il al-Imam*, 53–55; and idem, *Al-Imam al-shahid Yatahaddath*, 15–17.

39. Al-Banna, *Al-Salam*, 27–29. On his acceptance of pluralism, see 'Ata, "Al-Haraka al-Islamiyya," 115–16; on al-Banna's own declaration of accepting equal rights and pluralism, see al-Banna, *Al-Salam*, 37 and passim. For similar views in Jordan, see al-Nabahani, *Al-Takatul*, 23–57; and idem, *Nizam*, 56–59.

40. Al-Nabahani, *Al-Takatul*, 23–25.

41. Ibid., 24–57.

42. Al-Nabahani, *Nizam*, 56–59.

43. Barghouty, "Al-Islam bayna al-Sulta," 237–38. On an update of the current status of Islamic parties in Jordan, see "'Itijahat al-Harakah," *Al-Safir,* 20 August 1993, 13; and "Tanzimat al-Harakat," *Al-Hayat,* 14 August 1993, Tayyarat sec., 3. On the importance of justice as a political doctrine in Islamic political thought, see Butterworth, *Political Islam,* 26–37.

44. Shafiq, "Awlawiyyat," 64–65.

45. Hawwa, *Al-Madkhal,* 13–18. On the Muslim Brotherhood's participation in elections in Syria, see al-Janhani, "Al-Sahwa al-Islamiyya," 105–20.

46. Hawwa, *Al-Madkhal,* 282.

47. Al-'Awwa, *Al-Hayat,* 3 August 1993, 19. See also idem, "Al-Ta'addudiyya," 134–36.

48. Al-'Awwa, *Al-Hayat,* 19. On the Islamic movement in Egypt, see Khalafallah, "Al-Sahwa al-Islamiyya," 37 and passim. See also al-Din, "Al-Din wa al-Ahzab," 180 and passim.

49. Al-'Awwa, "Al-Ta'addudiyya," 129–32 and passim.

50. Ibid., 133–34. For a summary of the historical acceptance of pluralism by the scholars, such as Ibn Taymiyya, and authoritative exegesis of the Qur'an, such as *Tafsir al-Jilalain,* see 136–52. On an independent source for the views of the scholars who accepted the people's choice as the legitimate means of government, see al-Jassas, *Abu Bakr al-Jassas, Dirash fi Fikratihi,* 29–41; on those who rejected it, such as the majority of *Shi'ites,* see 75–86. On the relationship between actual politics and the development of religion and *ijtihad,* see Isma'il, *Sociolojia,* 138–39.

51. Al-'Awwa, *Fi al-Nizam al-Siyasi,* 77; and idem, "Al-Ta'addudiyya," 136–37, 152–53.

52. Cantouri and Lowrie, "Islam, Democracy," 52–54.

53. Al-Turabi, *Tajdid Usul al-Fiqh,* 10–16; and idem, *Qadaya al-Huriyya,* 17–18.

54. Al-Turabi, *Tajdid al-Fikr,* 20, 73, 132–33; idem, "Awlawiyyat," 21–26, 69–72, 81–82, 136–38, 167–69, 198–99.

55. Al-Turabi, *Qadaya,* 25–27, 31–33; idem, *Tajdid al-Fikr,* 68–80; and idem, "Awlawiyyat," 16. On the differences between *shura* and democracy, see Sami', *Azmat al-Hurriyya,* 49–61.

56. Al-Turabi, *Qadaya,* 51–57; and idem, *Tajdid al-Fikr,* 45, 66–68, 75, 93–97, 162–63.

57. On al-Turabi's definition of religion and the need for revolution, see al-Turabi, *Tajdid al-Fikr,* 106–19, 200–203; on the general bonds and the Islamic ones that make the establishment of society worthwhile, see al-Turabi, *Al-Iman wa Atharuhu,* 181–261; on the social connotations and their fulfillment, see ibid., 112–21; on the role of science in society, see ibid., 269–301; and on the importance of the unity of society for general interests, see ibid., 325–29.

58. Al-Turabi, *Usul al-Fiqh,* 27–29.

59. Al-Turabi, *Al-Itijah al-Islami,* 6–13, 42–44. On the essential conditions and requirements for the independence of women, see ibid., 45–49.

60. Al-Turabi, *Tajdid al-Fikr*, 108–9, 164–65, 133–39, 160–63.

61. Al-Turabi, *Usul al-Fiqh*, 18–25, 32–35.

62. Ibid., 36–37, 42–45; idem, *Tajdid al-Fikr*, 26–31, 36–49, 54–63, 76–77, 148–49, 143–72.

63. Al-Turabi, *Tajdid al-Fikr*, 68–71; for a discussion of the forms of *shura*, see idem, *Qadaya*, 72–77, 80–81.

64. Turabi, *Qadaya*, 10–19, 22–28.

65. Ibid., 20–21, 29–30.

66. Ibid., 34–37, 44–47.

67. Al-Turabi, *Al-Salat*, 124–33, 138–47, 156–58.

68. Al-Ghannushi, *Bayrut al-Masa'*, 15; and idem, "Mustaqbal al-Tayyar," 23–32. For a general discussion of al-Ghannushi and *Al-Harakat*, see 'Ata, "Qadiyat al-Ta'addudiyya," 116–17.

69. Al-Ghannushi and al-Turabi, *Al-Harakah al-Islamiyya wa al-Tahdith*, 34–35. See also al-Hirmasi, "Al-Islam al-Ihtijaji fi Tunis," 273–86.

70. Al-Ghannushi, "Hiwar," 14–15, 35–37; and idem, "Al-Islam wa al-Gharb," 36–37. On his and other fundamentalists' acceptance of democracy, see also Esposito and Piscatori, "Democratization and Islam," 426–34, 437–38. On his political life, see al-Ghannushi, "Hiwar," 5; and al-Zugul, "Al-Istratijia," 346–48. See also, on the possibilities of liberalization, Kramer, "Liberalization and Democracy," 22–25.

71. Rashid al-Ghannushi, "Al-Islam wa al-Gharb," 37.

72. Al-Hamidi, "Awlawiyyat Muhimma," 19–21; the quotation is from 14–15.

73. See the "Program of the Islamic Salvation Front" (*"Al-Barnamaj al-Siyasi li Jabhat al-Inqadh al-Islamiyya"*), in *Minbar al-Sharq*, no. 1, March 1993. On the Front and democracy, see Esposito and Piscatori, "Democratization," 437–38. Also see, on the possibilities of civil society in Islam, "Bahth 'an Mujtama'," 225–37.

74. Moussalli, *Radical Islamic Fundamentalism*, 19–24 and passim.

75. Ibid., 24–30. See also Qutb, *Nahwa*, 11–12; idem, *Al-Mustaqbal*, 71–90; and idem, *Al-Islam wa Mushkilat*, 77–78, 83–87.

76. Moussalli, *Radical Islamic Fundamentalism*, 31–39. See Mitchell, *The Society of the Muslim Brothers*, 103, 187–89. Hasan, *Milestones*, 7–13, 30–31; Hussain, *Islamic Movements*, 7–11, 91.

77. Qutb, *Hadha al-Din*, 32, 123; and idem, *Ma'rakat al-Islam*, 49, 60.

78. On the necessity of the choice of people, see Qutb, *Ma'alim fi al-Tariq*, 50, 71–77; and idem, *Al-'Adala*, 73, 107–8, 206–7; idem, *Ma'rakat al-Islam*, 67, 75, 85; idem, *Fiqh*, 61.

79. Qutb, *Al-'Adala*, 102–5, 167; idem, *Fiqh*, 84; idem, *Ra'simaliyya*, 60.

80. Qutb, *Nahwa*, 46–52.

81. Qutb, *Al-'Adala*, 37, 107–8, 111, 157–69; idem, *Fi Zilal*, vol. 1, part 3, 329; idem, *Ma'alim*, 58–96, 72, 132; idem, *Ra'simaliyya*, 66–70; idem, *Tafsir*, 84; and idem, *Nahwa*, 46–69.

82. Qutb, *Al-ʿAdala*, 66–68, 111; and idem, *Al-Salam*, 102–18.

83. Qutb, *Fi al-Tarikh*, 23–36, 76; idem, *Al-ʿAdala*, 35, 59, 73–80, 86, 113, 119; and, idem, *Fi Zilal*, vol. 2, 689. On his view on women and family structure, see Qutb, *Fi Zilal*, vol. 1, pt. 1, 235, pt. 2, 234, pt. 4, 587; idem, *Al-ʿAdala*, 60–65.

84. Qutb, *Hadha al-Din*, 11, 91; idem, *Maʿalim*, 64–67, 162–63; idem, *Al-ʿAdala*, 107, 198; idem, *Nahwa*, 62, 92–99, 102–20, 123, 134, and idem, *Al-Salam*, 161–65.

85. Qutb, *Maʿalim*, 11–15, 22; idem, *Al-ʿAdala*, 197; idem, *Hadha al-Din*, 11, 29–30, 65–57; idem, *Fiqh*, 15–32, 88–89. See also Qutb, *Al-Salam*, 118–20; idem, *Nahwa*, 137–43; and idem, *Al-Islam wa Mushkilat*, 189–93. On the proper political system according to Qutb, see Qutb, *Al-Salam*, 122–43.

86. Qutb, *Al-Islam wa Mushkilat*, 96–107; and idem, *Nahwa*, 150–52 and passim. On the characteristics of the two parties and the West, see Qutb, *Hadha al-Din*, 84–87; idem, *Al-Islam wa Mushkilat*, 7–9; idem, *Al-Raʾsimaliyya*, 58; and idem, *Maʿalim*, 59, 89.

87. On these issues and his life, see Barakat, *Sayyid Qutb*, 19; Khalidi, *Sayyid Qutb*, 147–49; Qutb, "Limadha Aʿdamuni?" 6–9; and Moussalli, *Radical Islamic Fundamentalism*, chap. 1.

88. On the prison experience, see Rifʿat al-Sayyid, "Al-Islam al-Siyasi," 15 and passim. See also Moussalli, *Radical Islamic Fundamentalism*, 34–36. For a first-hand and sympathetic account of the torture that Shukri, Qutb, and others were subjected to as well as of the movement, itself, see Mahfuz, *Alladhina Zulimu*, 7–141. On Shukri Mustafa's thought as put forward at his trial, see Ahmad, "Al-Nas al-Kamil," in *Al-Nabiy al-Musallah: Al-Rafidun*, 53–57.

89. Sirriyya, "Risalat al-Iman," *Al-Rafidun*, 31–32.

90. Ibid., 42–44, 48; and Mahfuz, *Alladhina Zulimu*, 83, 120–23, 222, 233, 242.

91. Al-Zumar, "Minhaj Jamʿat al-Jihad al-Islami," *Al-Rafidun*, 113–21; and Mahfuz, *Alladhina Zulimu*, 226, 254, 267–68, 271, 273.

92. "Mawqif al-Haraka al-Islamiyya Min al-ʿAmal al-Hizbi," *Al-Rafidun*, 150, 160–64; ʿAta, "Al-Haraka al-Islamiyya," 118–20. See also Saʿid, "Al-Islam al-Siyasi," 30–31; "Safahat min Mithaq al-ʿAmal al-Hizbi," *Al-Rafidun*, 165, 169, 173–74. On the organization itself, see Ahmad, *Al-Nabiy al-Musallah*, 185–86.

93. ʿUmar ʿAbd al-Rahman, "Wathiqat Iʿlan al-Harb," *Al Thaʾirun*, 187–89. For a description of how this organization views each political party and the political system in Egypt, see 193–97.

94. "Wathiqat Muhakamat al-Nizam al-Misri," 273–75, and also see 290–91, where the diverse kinds of rulers are specified. On similar views see Kamil Habib, "Wathiqat al-Ihyaʾ al-Islami," in *Al-Thaʾirun*, 199–229. On Tanzim al-Jihad and its numerous splits and offshoots, see Mahfuz, *Alladhina Zulimu*, 213–83.

95. *Al-Safir,* 25 September 1993, 10; and *Al-Diyar,* 25 September 1993, 14.
96. Sadowski, "New Orientalism," 19.

Chapter 4. The Discourse of Hasan al-Banna

1. For biographical information, see Moussalli, "Hasan al-Banna's Discourse." See also al-Banna, *Memoirs of Hasan al-Banna Shaheed;* Qarqar, *Dawr al-Haraka;* Sa'id, *Hasan al-Banna;* and Shaikh, *Hasan al-Banna Shahid.* See also Harris, *Nationalism and Revolution,* chaps. 4–5.

2. Numerous studies have attempted to focus on his political arguments. Older references include al-Husaini, *Moslem Brethren;* Heyworth-Dunne, *Religious and Political Trends;* Harris, *Nationalism and Revolution;* Adams, *Islam and Modernism in Egypt;* and Mitchell, *The Society of the Muslim Brothers.* Recent references to him occur throughout the literature on modern Islamic thought and fundamentalism; see, for instance, al-Sayyid Marsot, *Protest Movements,* 1–9; Lapidus, *Contemporary Islamic Movements,* 23–29; Taheri, *Holy Terror,* 37–49; Munson, *Islam and Revolution,* 29–37; Warburg, Introduction, 4–9, 24–27, 46–47, A. Gamma, 143–47, and Olivier Carré, 262–80, in Warburg and Kumpferschmidt, *Islam, Nationalism, and Radicalism;* Hussain, *Political Perspectives,* 117–21, 174–77; Mortimer, *Faith and Power,* 250–57; and Hiro, *Rise of Islamic Fundamentalism,* 60–69.

3. Al-Banna, *Nazarat,* 178–79.

4. Al-Banna, *Al-Imam al-Shahid Yatahaddath,* 65–66.

5. Ibid., 66–67, 38–39.

6. Al-Banna, *Majmu'at Rasa'il al-Shahid,* 4th ed., 317–28.

7. Ibid., 157–59, 119–21. On the four main objectives, see al-Banna, *Al-Imam al-Shahid Yatahaddath,* 71–83.

8. Al-Banna, *Nazarat,* 112–15.

9. Ibid., 192–94. See also al-Banna, *Din wa Siyasa,* 23–29.

10. Al-Banna, *Al-Salam,* 14–15.

11. Al-Banna, *Din wa Siyasa,* 62–62

12. Al-Banna, *Majmu'at Rasa'il al-Shahid,* 4th ed., 379–81.

13. Ibid., 357–59, 382–90.

14. Ibid., 71–73.

15. Al-Banna, *Majmu'at Rasa'il al-Shahid,* 4th ed., 33–36.

16. Ibid., 25–27.

17. Ibid., 317; and idem, *Din wa Siyasa,* 37–45.

18. Al-Banna, *Rasa'il al-Imam,* 70–71.

19. Ibid.; and idem, *Majmu'at Rasa'il al-Shahid,* 4th ed., 95–96.

20. Al-Banna, *Majmu'at Rasa'il al-Shahid,* 4th ed., 276–85. The translations of Qur'anic verses are taken from *The Glorious Qur'an,* translated by Abdallah Yusuf Ali.

21. Al-Banna, *Nazarat,* 194.

22. This is a collection of Friday sermons published in *Al-Ikhwan al-Muslimun* newspaper (hereafter cited as *Minbar*). See also al-Banna, *Majmu'at Rasa'il al-Shahid*, 4th ed., 63, 72, 347.

23. Al-Banna, *Majmu'at Rasa'il al-Shahid*, 4th ed., 317.

24. Al-Banna, *Rasa'il al-Imam*, 53–55, 101, 104.

25. Al-Banna, *Al-Imam al-Shahid Yatahaddath*, 15–17.

26. Al-Banna, *Rasa'il al-Imam*, 55.

27. Al-Banna, *Minbar*, 24–45.

28. Al-Banna, *Majmu'at Rasa'il al-Shahid*, 4th ed., 95–96. See also al-Banna, *Minbar*, 138–39; and idem, *Rasa'il al-Imam*, 59.

29. Al-Banna, *Majmu'at Rasa'il al-Imam*, 36–37, 317.

30. Al-Banna, *Rasa'il al-Imam*, 56.

31. Al-Banna, *Majmu'at Rasa'il al-Shahid*, 4th ed., 317; idem, *Majmu'at Rasa'il al-Imam*, 347.

32. Al-Banna, *Majmu't Rasa'il al-Shahid*, 4th ed., 317; idem, *Majmu'at Rasa'il al-Imam*, 54.

33. Al-Banna, *Al-Imam al-Shahid Yatahaddath*, 99–100.

34. Al-Banna, *Din wa-Siyasa*, 37–39.

35. Ibid., 40–41. See also *Sura* 5:44, 45, 47, where the Qur'an describes those who do not rule by what God has revealed as unbelievers, unjust, and infidels.

36. Al-Banna, *Din wa-Siyasa*, 40–45.

37. Al-Banna, *Majmu'at Rasa'il al-Shahid*, 4th ed., 61–62.

38. Ibid., 165.

39. Al-Banna, *Al-Imam al-Shahid Yatahaddath*, 95.

40. Al-Banna, *Majmu'at Rasa'il al-Imam*, 304.

41. Al-Banna, *Din wa-Siyasa*, 57–59.

42. Al-Banna, *Nazarat*, 126–28.

43. Al-Banna, *Rasa'il al-Imam*, 59–61; idem, *Majmu'at Rasa'il al-Imam*, 343–47.

44. Al-Banna, *Majmu'at Rasa'il al-Shahid*, 4th ed., 48; idem, *Majmu'at Rasa'il al-Imam*, 14, 169, 309, 331–32.

45. Al-Banna, *Kalimat Khalida*, 45.

46. Ibid., 45–46.

47. Al-Banna, *Rasa'il al-Imam*, 56–58; idem, *Majmu'at Rasa'il al-Imam*, 355–57.

48. Al-Banna, *Rasa'il al-Imam*, 58–60.

49. Ibid., 318–19.

50. Al-Banna, *Majmu'at Rasa'il al-Shahid*, 4th ed., 160–61; idem, *Al-Imam Yatahaddath*, 99. See also Qur'an 5:48–50.

51. Al-Banna, *Majmu'at Rasa'il al-Shahid*, 4th ed., 317–18; idem, *Majmu'at Rasa'il al-Imam*, 332–37, 63.

52. Al-Banna, *Majmu'at Rasa'il al-Shahid*, 4th ed., 318–19.

53. Ibid., 320–23.

54. Al-Banna, *Minbar*, 78–79. See also al-Ikhwan's journal, *Al-Da'wa*, 9.

55. Al-Banna, *Minbar*, 79, 136; idem, *Al-Da'wa*, 9.

56. Al-Banna, *Majmu'at Rasa'il al-Shahid*, 4th ed., 95–96, 317.

57. Ibid., 325, 328–30.

58. Ibid., 165–67.

59. Al-Banna, *Majmu'at Rasa'il al-Shahid*, 4th ed., 166–67.

60. Ibid., 167–69.

61. Al-Banna, *Rasa'il al-Imam*, 53; *Majmu'at Rasa'il al-Shahid*, 4th ed., 96–97, 161–62.

62. Al-Banna, *Majmu'at Rasa'il al-Shahid*, 4th ed., 162–63.

63. Ibid., 163. See verses 3:110, 2:143, 63:8, and 8:60.

64. Al-Banna, *Majmu'at Rasa'il al-Shahid*, 4th ed., 304–7. See also idem, *Majmu'at Rasa'il al-Imam*, 53.

Chapter 5. The Discourse of Sayyid Qutb

1. Qutb, *Ma'alim fi al-Tariq*, 134–44. For a fuller analysis of Qutb's life and thought, see Moussalli, *Radical Islamic Fundamentalism*.

2. Hasan, *Milestones*, 4. See also al-Balihi, *Sayyid Qutb*, 42.

3. Khalidi, *Nazariyyat*, 64–66. On the intellectual life in Egypt in the first half of this century, see, for instance, Vatikiotis, *Modern History of Egypt*, chap. 10. See Khalidi, *Qutb*, 94, and Khalidi, *Nazariyyat*, 134; Hasan, *Milestones*, 4 and passim; and al-Balihi, *Sayyid Qutb*, 43–49. See also Hilal, *Al-Siyasa*, 200–208.

4. Khalidi, *Qutb*, 125, and Khalidi, *Nazariyyat*, 137–38.

5. Ibid., 138–94. See Qutb, "Limadha A'damuni," 3–4. Khalidi, *Qutb*, 138, 144; al-Balihi, *Sayyid Qutb*, 48–49; and see al-Husaini, *Moslem Brethren*, 23; and Mitchell, *Society of Muslim Brotherhood*, 188.

6. Hasan, *Milestones*, 8–11 and passim; also see Vatikiotis, *Modern History*, 326; Qutb, "Limadha A'damuni," 4. Hussain, *Islamic Movements*, 9; and Hasan, *Milestones*, 8. Barakat, *Khulasat*, 19; and Khalidi, *Nazariyyat*, 149.

7. *Chronology of Arab Politics*, 296. For more details, see also Hasan, *Milestones*, 12; and Hussain, *Islamic Movements*, 10.

8. Qutb, *Fi al-Tarikh*, 22.

9. Qutb, *Khasa'is*, 3–4.

10. Qutb, *Khasa'is*, 228, and see 211–22.

11. Qutb, *Al-Mustaqbal*, 12–14; and idem, *Khasa'is*, 212–15 .

12. Qutb, *Al-Mustaqbal*, 15–17.

13. Qutb, *Khasa'is*, 16.

14. Ibid., 45, and see 46–49.

15. Ibid., 50, and see, 45–49.

16. Qutb, *Khasa'is*, 9–11. On philosophy, see Mahdi, *Al-Farabi Philosophy*, 13–15, 32–33, 44–48, and compare with the references to Plato, 35, 45, 48. For al-Farabi's preference for philosophy over religion, see 44–48. See also al-Farabi, *Virtuous City*, pt. 1 and passim. Also, see al-Farabi, *Rasa'il al-Farabi*, 2. See al-Ghazali, *Tahafut al-Falasifa*, 4–7.

For a rebuttal of al-Ghazali's attacks on the philosophers, see Averroes, *Tahafut al-Tahafut*. For a secondary source, see Butterworth, "Elites"; and on Averroes' political philosophy, see idem, "New Light," 118–27. On philosophy and the Qur'an, see Anawati, "Philosophy," 350–58.

17. Qutb, *Khasa'is*, 50, 85–88.

18. Ibid., 89–90.

19. Ibid., 24–25. See also Qutb, *Al-Mustaqbal*, 11 and 58; idem, *Hadha al-Din*, 11.

20. Qutb, *Khasa'is*, 98–107.

21. Qutb, *Al-Mustaqbal*, 16–26; and idem, *Khasa'is*, 107–9.

22. Ibid., 134, 140–41.

23. Qutb, *Khasa'is*, 10–14, 139.

24. On science, see Qutb, *Ma'alim*, 25, 140; and idem, *Khasa'is*, 140. On *fitra*, see Qutb, *Al-'Adala*, 30–33; idem, *Hadha al-Din*, 24; and idem, *Khasa'is*, 25, 50–53. On philosophy, see Qutb, *Al-Mustaqbal*, 29; and idem, *Khasa'is*, 66–67.

25. Qutb, *Khasa'is*, 170–71.

26. Ibid., 192–210. Qutb, *Al-Mustaqbal*, 3; and see idem, *Fi al-Tarikh*, 16–20.

27. Qutb, *Hadha al-Din*, 33, and see 32 and passim.

28. Qutb, *Ma'rakat*, 49, 60.

29. Qutb, *Hadha al-Din*, 19, and see 16–18; and idem, *Ma'alim*, 49, 114, and passim. Qutb, *In the Shades*, 34; and see idem, *Fiqh*, 60–61. See also idem, *Al-'Adala*, 105; and idem, *Tafsir*, 51.

30. Qutb, *Al-'Adala*, 107.

31. Ibid., 206–7.

32. Qutb, *Ma'alim*, 58, 63–69, 72.

33. Qutb, *Hadha al-Din*, 39–42; and see idem, *Ra'simaliyya*, 66; and idem, *Tafsir*, 84. On *shura*, its history, and definition, see 'Amara, *Islam wa Falsafat*, 57–72. See also Qutb, *Ra'simaliyya*, 72; idem, *Riba*, 84; and idem, *Al-'Adala*, 37, 108.

34. Qutb, *Hadha al-Din*, 85.

35. Ibid., 87. Also see Qutb, *Ra'simaliyya*, 58; idem, *Ma'alim*, 59, 89; and idem, *Mushkilat*, 7–9. Also see Qutb, *Nahwa*, 13.

36. Qutb, *Ra'simaliyya*, 25. On socialism and Marxism, see *Mushkilat*, 6 and passim; and see idem, *Nahwa*, 33–38, 86–87, 88–89.

37. Qutb, *Al-'Adala*, 33, and also see 39, 73–77, 82. And see idem, *Fi Zilal*, vol. 2, pt. 5, 689.

38. Qutb, *Al-'Adala*, 41–42, 45–46, 82–83; and idem, *Ra'simaliyya*, 52.

39. Qutb, *Al-'Adala*, 47, and see 115–16. See also idem, *Ra'simaliyya*, 34–36, 55.

40. Qutb, *Al-'Adala*, 55.

41. Qutb, *Ra'simaliyya*, 47, 84.

42. Qutb, *Fi al-Tarikh*, 32–35, 76. See also idem, *Al-'Adala*, 73–77, 119.

43. Qutb, *Ra'simaliyya*, 59. See also idem, *Fi Zilal*, vol. 2, pt. 5, 689; idem, *Al-'Adala*, 35, 113; and idem, *Fi al-Tarikh*, 36.

44. Qutb, *Al-'Adala*, 59.

45. Ibid., 69–70, 124; and idem, *Ra'simaliyya*, 40.

46. Qutb, *Al-'Adala*, 123, and see 131, 184. On the theoretical prescriptions of the Qur'an on economics and on historical development of economy, see Rodinson, *Islam and Capitalism*.

47. Qutb, *Al-'Adala*, 142; see also Qutb, *Fi al-Tarikh*, 32.

48. Qutb, *Ra'simaliyya*, 44, and see also 46–47; and idem, *Al-'Adala*, 157–58.

49. Qutb, *Ma'alim*, 26, 101; and idem, *Ra'simaliyya*, 70. See also idem, *Al-'Adala*, 250.

50. Qutb, *Fi al-Tarikh*, 24–25.

51. Qutb, *Ra'simaliyya*, 28.

52. Qutb, *Fi al-Tarikh*, 23–24.

53. Qutb, *Ma'alim*, 68.

54. Ibid., 69–71. Also, see Qutb, *Ma'alim*, 67 and passim.

55. Qutb, *Hadha al-Din*, 87–88; and idem, *Ma'alim*, 159.

56. Qutb, *Ma'alim*, 64.

57. Ibid., 65, 66, 72, 81–91. For instance, see Rida's opinion in Badawi, *Reformers of Egypt*, 114. Contrast with Qutb in *Ma'alim*, 75–83.

58. Qutb, *Ma'alim*, 64–65, 66; and see idem, *Hadha al-Din*, 11, 91.

59. Qutb, *Ma'alim*, 162–63. See also idem, *Nahwa*, 62.

Chapter 6. The Discourse of Hasan al-Turabi

1. Esposito, "Sudan," 192–201; and Choueiri, *Islamic Fundamentalism*, 78. On al-Turabi's political life and the history of Islamic movements in the Sudan, see Voll and Voll, *The Sudan,:* 68; Fluehr-Lobban, Lobban, and Voll, *Historical Dictionary*, 149; and Gurdon, *Sudan at the Crossroads*, 68.

2. References can be found about his importance, but no major English study on his thought is available so far. See, for instance, Esposito, *Islam: The Straight Path*, 184–85, 189. See also Moussalli, "Hasan al-Turabi's Islamist Discourse," 52–63.

3. U.S. House Committee, *Hearing on the Implication for U.S. Policy.*

4. Al-Turabi, *Tajdid al-Fikr*, 9–10, 156.

5. Ibid., 12, 64–65.

6. Ibid., 20, 73.

7. Ibid., 76–79, 132–33; al-Turabi, "Awlawiyyat," 21–22.

8. Ibid., 25–26, 69–70, 81–82, 136–38.

9. Ibid., 27–82.

10. Ibid., 167–69, 198–99.

11. Al-Turabi, *Qadaya al-Huriyya*, 1–10.
12. Al-Turabi, *Qadaya*, 12, 14, 16, 18; and idem, "Awlawiyyat," 104–5.
13. Al-Turabi, *Qadaya*, 19–20; and idem, *Tajdid*, 72–75.
14. Al-Turabi, *Qadaya*, 20–21; and idem, *Tajdid*, 58–64.
15. Al-Turabi, *Qadaya*, 21–23; and idem, *Tajdid*, 88–91, 100, 153–55, 160–61, 178, 179.
16. Al-Turabi, *Qadaya*, 23–25.
17. Ibid., 25–26; and idem, *Tajdid*, 79–80.
18. Al-Turabi, *Qadaya*, 26–27.
19. Ibid., 26–29; and idem, *Tajdid*, 68–70.
20. Al-Turabi, *Qadaya*, 31–33; idem, *Tajdid*, 70–72; and idem, "Awwaliyyat," 16.
21. Al-Turabi, *Qadaya*, 34–35, 37–38.
22. Ibid., 41–43; and idem, *Tajdid*, 59–60, 65, 146, 174–75, 192.
23. Al-Turabi, *Qadaya*, 44–46.
24. Ibid., 46–47.
25. Ibid., 47–48.
26. Ibid., 48–9; and idem, *Tajdid*, 174–75.
27. Al-Turabi, *Qadaya*, 49–51.
28. Ibid., 51–53.
29. Ibid., 53–54.
30. Al-Turabi, "'Utruhat," 89–90.
31. Ibid., 90–91.
32. Al-Turabi, *Qadaya*, 56–57.
33. Al-Turabi, *Tajdid*, 29.
34. Ibid., 45, 66–68, 75, 93, 94, 97, 162–63.
35. Al-Turabi, "'Utruhat," 75–76.
36. Ibid., 77–80.
37. Ibid., 91–98.

Conclusion

1. Jarrar, interview.
2. *Sh'un al-Awsat*, 59–60, 65–67.
3. *Al-Safir*, 22 August 1994, p. 11.
4. Ibid., 10 May 1993, p. 6.

Bibliography

Aanuri, Tariq. "Justice Is the Strife." *New Perspectives Quarterly* 2, no. 2 (1994): 23–34.

Abaza, Mona. "The Discourse of Islamic Fundamentalism in the Middle East and Southeast Asia: A Critical Perspective." *Institute Southeast Asian Studies* (Singapore) 6 (1991): 203–39.

'Abbas, Ahmad. *Al-Ikhwan al-Muslim fi Rif Misr.* Cairo: Dar al-Tawziʿ wa al-Nashir, 1987.

'Abd al-Halim, Mahmud. *Al-Ikhwan al-Muslimin, Ahdath Sanaʾat al-Tarikh: Raʾy min al-Dakhil.* Alexandria, Egypt: Dar al-Daʿwa, 1979.

'Abd Allah, Ismaʿil Sabri. *Al-Harakat al-Islamiyya al-Muʿasira fi al-ʿAlam al-ʿArabi.* Beirut: Markaz Dirasat al-Wihda al-ʿArabiyya, 1987.

'Abd al-Rahman, 'Umar. "Wathiqat Iʿlan al-Harb ʿala Majlis al-Shaʿb." In *Al-Nabiy al-Musallah: Al-Thaʾirun,* edited by Rifʿat Sayyid Ahmad. London: Riad el-Rayyes Books, 1991, pp. 187–98.

'Abd al-Raziq, Ahmad Muhammad Jad. *Falsafat al-Mashruʿ al-Hadari: Bayna al-Ihyaʾ al-Islami wa al-Tahdith al-Gharbi.* 2 vols. Herndon, Va.: International Institute of Islamic Thought, 1995.

'Abd al-Samiʿ, 'Umr. *Al-Islamiyyun: Hiwarat Hawla al-Mustaqbal.* Cairo: Maktabat al-Turath al-Islami, 1992.

'Abduh, Muhammad. *Risalat al-Tawhid.* 2d ed. Beirut: Al-Muʾassasa al-ʿArabiyya li al-Dirasat wa al-Nashr, 1981.

Abdullah, Ahsan. *Pan-Islamism.* Leicester, England: Islamic Foundation, 1992.

Abedin, Syed Z. "Islamic Fundamentalism, Islamic Ummah and the World Conference on Muslim Minorities." *Journal Institute of Muslim Minority Affairs* 12 (1991): 1–21.

Abraham, Antoine J. *Khoumani and Islamic Fundamentalism: Contributions of Islamic Sciences to Modern Civilization.* 2nd ed. N.p.: Cloverdale Library, 1989.

Abu Ghunaymah, Zayid. *Al-Haraka al-Islamiyya wa Qadiyyat Filistiyn.* Amman: Dar al-Furqan, 1985.

Abu Khalil, Asʿad. "The Incoherence of Islamic Fundamentalism: Arab Islamic Thought at the End of the Twentieth Century." *Middle East Journal* 48 (1994): 677–94.

———. "A Viable Partnership: Islam, Democracy, and the Arab World." *Harvard International Review* 15, no. 2 (Winter 1992–1993): 22–23, 65.

Abul-Fadl, Mona. *Introducing Islam from Within.* Leicester, England: Islamic Foundation, 1991.

Abu-Lughod, I. "Retreat from the Secular Path? Islamic Dilemmas of Arab Politics." *Review of Politics* 28, no. 4 (1966): 447–76.

Abu Rabiʿ, Ibrahim. *Intellectual Origins of Islamic Resurgence in the Modern Arab World.* Albany: State University of New York Press, 1996.

———. "Islamic Resurgence and the 'Problematic of Tradition' in the Modern Arab World: The Contemporary Academic Debate." *Islamic Studies* (Islamabad) 34, no. 2 (1995): 43–46.

———. "A Note on Some Recent Western Writing on Islamic Resurgence." *Al-Tawhid* 11, nos. iii–iv (1994): 233–46.

Abu Rabiʿ, Ibrahim, ed. *Islamic Resurgence: Challenges, Directions, and Future Perspectives. A Round Table with Ahmad Kurshad.* Tampa, Fla.: World and Islam Studies Enterprise, 1994.

AbuSulayman, ʿAbdul Hamid. *The Islamic Theory of International Relations: New Directions for Islamic Methodology and Thought.* Herndon, Va.: International Institute of Islamic Thought, 1987.

Adams, Charles. *Islam and Modernism in Egypt.* New York: Russell and Russell, 1986.

Addi, Lahouari. "Islamist Utopia and Democracy." *ANNALS, Journal of the American Association of Political Science,* 542, no. 92 (November 1992): 120–30.

Adelowo, Dada. "The Concept of Tauhid in Islam: A Theological Review." *Islamic Quarterly* 35, no. 1 (1991): 23–36.

Al-Afghani, Jamal al-Din. "Political Writings." Pt. 2 of *Al-Aʿmal al-Kamila.* Edited and introduced by Muhammad ʿAmara. Beirut: Al-Muʾassasa al-ʿArabiyya li al-Dirasat wa al-Nashr, 1980.

———. *Al-ʿUrwa al-Wuthqa.* Cairo: Dar al-ʿArab, 1957.

Afshary, Reza. "An Essay on Islamic Cultural Relativism in the Discourse of Human Rights." *Human Rights Quarterly* 16 (1994): 235–76.

Ahady, Anwar-ul-Haq. "The Decline of Islamic Fundamentalism." *Journal of Asian and African Studies* 27, nos. 3–4 (1992): 229–43.

Ahmad, Rifʿat Sayyid. *Al-Bawwaba al-Sawdaʾ: Al-Tarikh al-Sirri li Muʿtaqal.* Cairo: al-Zahraʾ li al-Iʿlam al-ʿArabi, 1986.

———. *Al-Din wa al-Dawla wa al-Thawra.* Cairo: Dar al-Hilal, 1985.

———. *Al-Nabiy al-Musallah: Al-Rafidun.* London: Riad el-Rayyes Books, 1991.

———. *Al-Nabiy al-Musallah: Al-Thaʾirun.* London: Riad el-Rayyes Books, 1991.

———. *Tanzimat al-Ghadab al-Islami fi al-Sabʿinat.* Cairo: Maktabat Madbuli, 1989.

Ahmad Khalafallah, Muhammad. *Al-Qurʾan wa al-Dawla.* Cairo: Maktabat al-Anglo al-Misriyya, 1973.

Ahmed, Akbar S. "Media Mongols at the Gate of Baghdad." *New Perspectives Quarterly* 10, no. 3 (1993): 10–18.

———. *Postmodernism and Islam: Predicament and Promise.* New York: Routledge, 1992.

Ahrari, M. E. "Islam as a Source of Conflict and Change in the Middle East." *Security Dialogue* 25, no. 2 (1994): 177–92.

Ajami, Fouad. *The Arab Predicament: Arab Political Thought and Practice since 1967.* Cambridge: Cambridge University Press, 1981.

Akhtar, Karm B., and Ahmad H. Sakr. *Islamic Fundamentalism.* Cedar Rapids, Iowa: Igram Press, 1982.

'Ali, Haydar Ibrahim. *Al-Tayyarat al-Islamiyya wa Qadiyyat al-Ta'addudiyya.* Beirut: Center for the Studies of Arab Unity, 1996.

Allen, Richard. *Imperialism and Nationalism in the Fertile Crescent: Sources and Prospects of the Arab-Israeli Conflict.* London: Oxford University Press, 1975.

'Amara, Muhammad. *Abu al-A'la al-Mawdudi wa al-Sahwa al-Islamiyya.* Beirut: Dar wa al-Wahda, 1986.

———. *Al-A'mal al-Kamilah: Jamal al-Din al-Afghani.* Beirut: Al-Mu'assasa al-'Arabiyya li al-Dirasat wa al-Nashr, 1980.

———. *Al-Islam wa Falsafat al-Hukum.* Beirut: Al-Mu'assasa al-'Arabiyya li al-Dirasat wa al-Nashr, 1981.

———. *Al-Islam wa al-Hurub al-Diniyya.* Cairo: Dar al-Thaqafa al-Jadida, 1996.

———. *Al-Khilafa wa Nash'at al-Ahzab al-Siyasiyya.* Beirut: Al-Mu'assasa al-'Arabiyya li al-Dirasat wa al-Nashr, 1977.

———. *Muslimun Thuwwar.* Beirut: Al-Mu'assasa al-'Arabiyya li al-Dirasat wa al-Nashr, 1981.

Amuzegar, Jahangir. "The Truth and Illusion of Islamic Fundamentalism." *SAIS Review* 13 (1993): 127–39.

Anawati, Georges. "Philosophy, Theology, and Mysticism." In *The Legacy of Islam,* edited by Joseph Schacht, 350–58. Oxford: Oxford University Press, 1974.

Anderson, Gerald. "Challenge of Islam for Christian Missions." *International Bulletin of Missionary Research* 17 (1993): 160–73.

Anderson, Lisa. "Liberalism in Northern Africa." *Current History* 89 (1990): 145–48.

———. "Liberalism, Islam, and the Arab State." *Dissent* 41 (1994): 439–44.

———. "Obligation and Accountability: Islamic Politics in North Africa." *Daedalus* 120 (1991): 93–112.

———. "Remaking the Middle East: The Prospects for Democracy and Stability." *Ithacas and International Affairs* 6 (1992): 163–78.

———. "The State in the Middle East and North Africa." *Comparative Politics* 20, no. 1 (1987): 1–18.

Anderson, Sean, and Stephen Sloan. *Historical Dictionary of Terrorism.* Metuchen, N.J.: Scarecrow Press, 1995.

Antoun, Richard, and Mary Elaine Hegland, eds. *Religious Resurgence: Contemporary Cases in Islam, Christianity, and Judaism.* Syracuse: Syracuse University Press, 1987.

Appleby, R. Scott. *Spokesmen for the Despised: Fundamentalist Leaders of the Middle East.* Chicago: University of Chicago Press, 1996.

"Arab World Where Troubles for the U.S. Never End, The." *U.S. News and World Report* 96 (6 February 1984): 24.

Arjomand, Said Amir. *The Shadow of God and the Hidden Imam.* Chicago: University of Chicago Press, 1984.

———, ed. *Authority and Political Culture in Shi'ism.* Albany: State University of New York Press, 1988.

Armajani, Yahya. *Middle East: Past and Present.* Englewood Cliffs, N.J.: Prentice Hall, 1970.

Asad, Muhammad. *Islam at a Crossroad.* Lahore: Arafat Publications, 1963.

'Ata, 'Abd al-Khabir Mahmud. "Al-Haraka al-Islamiyya wa Qadiyat al-Ta'addudiyya." *Al-Majalla al-'Arabiyya li al-'Ulum al-Siyasiyya* 5 and 6 (1992): 103–28.

Avinery, Shlomo. "The Return to Islam." *Dissent* 40 (1993): 410–12.

Al-'Awwa, Muhammad. *Fi al-Nizam al-Siyasi al-Islami li al-Dawla al-Islamiyya.* Cairo: Dar al-Shuruq, 1989.

———. "Al-Ta'addudiyya min Manzur Islami." *Minbar Al-Hiwar* 6 (1991): 129–38.

Ayalon, Ami, ed. *Middle East Contemporary Survey.* Boulder, Colo.: Westview Press, 1989.

Ayoob, Mohammad. *The Politics of Islamic Reassertion.* New York: St. Martin's Press, 1981.

Ayubi, Nazih. *Over-Stating the Arab State: Politics and Society in the Middle East.* London: I. B. Tauris, 1995.

———. *Political Islam: Religion and Politics in the Arab World.* New York: Routledge, 1991.

Al-Azm, Sadik. "Islamic Fundamentalism Reconsidered: A Critical Outline of Problems, Ideas and Approaches." Parts 1 and 2. *South Asia Bulletin* 13, nos. 1 and 2 (1993): 93–131; 14, no. 1 (1994): 73–98.

———. *Naqd al-Fikr al-Dini.* 6th ed. Beirut: Dar al-Tali'a, 1988.

Al-Azmeh, Aziz. *Islam and Modernity.* London: Verso, 1993.

Al-Azmi, Tarik Hamid. "Religion, Identity, and State in Modern Islam." *Muslim World* 84, nos. 3–4 (1994): 334–41.

Azzam, Maha. "The Gulf Crisis: Perceptions in the Muslim World." *International Affairs* 67 (1991): 473–85.

Babeair, Abdulwahab Saleh. "Contemporary Islamic Revivalism: A Movement or a Moment?" *Islamic Quarterly* 37, no. 1 (1993): 5–23.

Badawi, M. A. Zaki. *The Reformers of Egypt.* London: Croom Helm, 1967.

Al-Balihi, Ibrahim Ibn 'Abd al-Rahman. *Sayyid Qutb wa-Turathuhu al-Adabi wa-al-Fikri.* Riyad: n.p., 1972.

Bangura, Yusuf. *The Search for Identity: Ethnicity, Religion, and Political Violence.* Geneva: United Nations Research Institute for Social Development, 1994.

Al-Banna, Hasan. *Din wa-Siyasa.* Beirut: Maktabat Huttin, 1970.

———. *Al-Imam al-Shahid Yatahaddath ila Shabab al-ʿAlam al-Islami.* Beirut: Dar al-Qalam, 1974.

———. *Kalimat Khalida.* Beirut: n.p., 1972.

———. *Majmuʿat Rasaʾil al-Shahid Hasan al-Banna.* Beirut: Dar al-Qalam, 1984.

———. *Majmuʿat Rasaʾil al-Shahid Hasan al-Banna.* 4th ed. Beirut: Al-Muʾassasa al-Islamiyya, 1984.

———. *Majmuʿat Rasaʾil al-Imam al-Shahid Hasan al-Banna.* Cairo: Dar al-Qalam, n.d.

———. *Memoirs of Hasan al-Banna Shaheed.* Translated by M. N. Shaikh. Karachi: International Islamic Publishers, 1981.

———. *Minbar al-Jumʿa.* Alexandria, Egypt: Dar al-Daʿwa, 1978.

———. *Nazarat fi Islah al-Nafs wa al-Mujtamaʿ.* Cairo: Maktabat al-Iʿtizam, 1969.

———. *Rasaʾil al-Shahid Hasan al-Banna.* Beirut: Dar al-Qurʾan al-Karim, 1984.

———. *Al-Salam fi al-Islam.* 2d ed. Beirut: Manshurat al-ʿAsr al-Hadith, 1971.

Barakat, Halim. *Al-Mujtamaʿ al-ʿArabi al-Muʿasir.* 3d ed. Beirut: Center for the Studies of Arab Unity, 1986.

Barakat, Muhammad T. *Sayyid Qutb: Khulasat Hayatih, Minhajuhuh fi al-Haraka wa al-Naqd al-Muwajjah ilayh.* Beirut: Dar al-Daʿwa, n.d.

Barghouty, Iyad. "Al-Islam bayna al-Sulta wa al-Muʿarada." In *Qadaya Fikriyya: Al-Islam al-Siyasi, al-Usus al-Fikriyya wa al-Ahdaf al-ʿAmalliyya.* Cairo: Dar al-Thaqafa al-Jadida, 1989, 234–41.

———. "Al-Barnamaj al-Siyasi li Jabhat al-Inqadh." *Minbar al-Hiwar* no. 1 (March 1993): 206–13.

Barry, Rubin. *Islamic Fundamentalism in Egyptian Politics.* New York: St. Martin's Press, 1990.

"Bayan min al-Ikhwan al-Muslimin Hawla Mawjat al-ʿUnf wa al-Irhab. *Qiraʾat Siyasiyya* 3, no. 2 (1993): 197–98.

Beeley, B. "Global Options: Islamic Alternatives." In *A Global World? Re-Ordering Political Space,* edited by J. Anderson et al. Oxford: Oxford University Press, 1995.

Binder, Leonard. *The Ideological Revolution in the Middle East.* New York: John Wiley and Sons, 1964.

———. *Islamic Liberalism: A Critique of Development Ideologies.* Chicago: University of Chicago Press, 1988.

Bizri, Dalal. *Akhawat al-Zill wa al-Yaqin. Islamiyyat bayna al-Hadatha wa al-Taqlid.* Beirut: Dar al-Nahar li al-Nashr, 1996.

"Blocking the Goal." *Economist* 310, no. 7594 (1989): 47.

Brumberg, Daniel. "Islamic Fundamentalism, Democracy, and the Gulf War." In *Islamic Fundamentalisms and the Gulf Crisis,* edited by James Piscatori, 155–85. Chicago: American Academy of Arts and Sciences, 1991.

Bulliet, Richard W. "The Israeli-PLO Accord: The Future of the Islamic Movement." *Foreign Affairs* 72 (1993): 38–44.

Burgat, Francois, and William Dowell. *The Islamic Movement in North Africa.* Austin: University of Texas Press, 1993.

Burke, Edmond. *Struggle for Survival in the Modern Middle East.* London: I. B. Tauris, 1994.

Burrows, Bernard. *Footnotes in the Sand: The Gulf in Transition.* London: Michael Russell, 1991.

Busool, Assad N. *Islamic Fundamentalism.* American Islamic Education, 1993.

Butterworth, Charles. "Political Islam." *Annals of the American Academy of Political and Social Sciences* 524 (1992): 26–37.

———. "State and Authority in Arabic Political Thought." In *The Foundations of the Arab State,* edited by Ghassan Salame, 91–111. London: Croom Helm, 1987.

Cantouri, Louis J. "Democratization in the Middle East." *American-Arab Affairs* 36 (1991): 1–51.

Cantouri, Louis, and Arthur Lowrie. "Islam, Democracy, the State and the West: Summary of a Lecture and Roundtable Discussion with Hasan al-Turabi." *Middle East Policy* 1, no. 3 (1992): 52–54.

Carré, Olivier. *Les Frères Musulmans: Egypte et Syrie, 1928–1982.* Paris: Callimard, Dulliard, 1983.

Charfi, Farida Faouzia. "When Galileo Meets Allah." *New Perspectives Quarterly* 2 (1994): 30–32.

Charnayl, Jean Paul. *Islamic Culture and Socio-Economic Change.* Leiden: Brill, 1971.

Chelkowski, Peter, and Robert J. Pranger. *Ideology and Power in the Middle East: Studies in Honor of George Lenczowski.* Durham, N.C.: Duke University Press, 1988.

Choudhury, Golam W. *Islam and the Modern Muslim World.* London: Scorpion, 1993.

Choueiri, Youssef M. "Theoretical Paradigms of Islamic Movements." *Political Studies* 41, no. 1 (1993): 108–16.

———. *Islamic Fundamentalism.* Boston: Twayne/G. K. Hall, 1990.

Clawson, Patrick. "Liberty's the Thing, Not Democracy." *Middle East Quarterly* 1, no. 3 (1994): 12–13.

Cleveland, W. L. *A History of the Middle East.* Boulder, Colo.: Westview Press, 1994.

Cole, Juan R. I., and Nikki R. Keddie, eds. *Shi'ism and Social Protest.* New Haven: Yale University Press, 1986.

Cragg, Kenneth. *Contemporary Counsels in Islam.* Edinburgh: Edinburgh University Press, 1956.

Curtis, Michael, ed. *Religion and Politics in the Middle East.* Boulder, Colo.: Westview Press, 1981.

Dallal, Ahmad. "The Origins and Objectives of Islamic Revivalist Thought, 1750–1850." *Journal of the American Oriental Society* 113 (1993): 341–59.

Al-Da'wa 7 (1979).

"Deadly Party of God, The: Hizbullah Threatens the West." *Maclean's* 102, no. 33 (1989): 28.

Deegan, H. "Democratization in the Middle East." In *The Middle East in the New World Order,* edited by Haifa A. Jawad. Basingstoke, England; New York: St. Martin's Press, 1994.

Dekmejian, Hrair. "The Arab Anatomy of Islamic Revival: Legitimacy Crisis, Ethnic Conflict and the Search for Islamic Alternatives." *Middle East Journal* 34 (1980): 1–12.

———. *Islam in Revolution: Fundamentalism in the Arab World.* 2nd ed. Syracuse: Syracuse University Press, 1995.

Dessouki, Ali E. Hillal. "The Impact of Islamism on the Arab System." In *The Islamist Dilemma: The Political Role of Islamist Movements in the Contemporary Arab World,* edited by Laura Guazzone, 247–64. Reading, England: Ithaca Press, 1995.

———. "Islamic Organization." In *Islam and Power,* edited by A. Dessouki. Baltimore: Johns Hopkins University Press, 1981.

———, ed. *Islamic Resurgence in the Arab World.* New York: Praeger, 1982.

Al-Din, Rislan Sharaf. "Al-Din wa al-Ahzab al-Siyasiyya al-Diniyya." *Al-Din fi al-Mujtama' al-'Arabi.* Beirut: Center for the Studies of Arab Unity, 1990.

Al-Diyar. 25 September 1993–22 July 1994.

Djerejian, Edward. "One Man, One Vote, One Time." *New Perspectives Quarterly* 10, no. 3 (1993): 49.

Donohue, John, and John L. Esposito, eds. *Islam in Transition: Muslim Perspectives.* New York: Oxford University Press, 1982.

Dunn, Michael C. "Islamic Activists in the West: A New Issue Produces Backlashes." *Middle East Policy* 3 (1994): 137–45.

Durrani, K. S. *Impact of Islamic Fundamentalism.* Bangalore, India: ISPCK, Delhi, 1993.

East, R., and T. Joseph. *Political Parties of Africa and the Middle East: A Reference Guide.* Harlow, n.p.: Longman, 1993.

Ehteshami, Anoushiravan. *Islamic Fundamentalism.* Boulder, Colo.: Westview Press, 1996.

Eickelman, Dale. "Changing Interpretations of Islamic Movements." In *Islam and the Political Economy of Meaning,* edited by William R. Roff, 13–30. London: Croom Helm, 1987.

———. "Islamic Liberalism Strikes Back." *Middle East Studies Association Bulletin* 27, no. 2 (1993): 163–68.

Enayat, Hamid. *Modern Islamic Political Thought.* Austin: University of Texas Press, 1982.

Encyclopedia of Islam, The. New ed. Edited by M. Th. Houtsma, A. J. Wensinck, et al., 1911–38. Leiden, Netherlands: E. J. Brill, 1960.

Encyclopedia of Islam, The, edited by Bernard Lewis, V. L. Menage et al. Leiden, Netherlands: E. J. Brill, 1971.

Entelis, John P. *Comparative Politics of North Africa: Algeria, Morocco and Tunisia.* Syracuse: Syracuse University Press, 1980.

El-Erian, Mohamad A. *Jamjoom: A Profile of Islam, Past, Present, and Future. A Resource Book of Islam and the Muslim World.* Melbourne: Islamic Publications, 1990.

Esack, Farid. *Qur'an, Liberation, and Pluralism: An Islamic Perspective of Interreligious Solidarity against Oppression.* Oxford, England: Oneworld Publications, 1996.

Esposito, John L. *Islam and Development: Religion and Sociopolitical Change.* Syracuse: Syracuse University Press, 1980.

———. *Islam and Politics.* 3d ed. Syracuse: Syracuse University Press, 1991.

———. *Islam: The Straight Path.* Expanded ed. New York: Oxford University Press, 1994.

———. "Islamic Movements, Democratization, and U.S. Foreign Policy." In *Riding the Tiger: The Middle East Challenge after the Cold War,* edited by Phebe Marr and William Lewis, 187–209. Boulder, Colo.: Westview Press, 1993.

———. *The Islamic Threat: Myth or Reality?* New York: Oxford University Press, 1992.

———. *The Oxford Encyclopedia of the Modern Islamic World.* New York: Oxford University Press, 1995.

———. "The Persian Gulf War, Islamic Movements and the New World Order." *Iranian Journal of International Affairs* 5, no. 2 (1993): 340–65.

———. "Political Islam: Beyond the Green Menace." *Current History* 93 (1994): 19–24.

———. "Sudan." In *The Politics of Islamic Revivalism: Diversity and Unity,* edited by Shireen Hunter, 192–201. Bloomington: Indiana University Press, 1988.

———, ed. *Voices of Resurgent Islam.* New York: Oxford University Press, 1983.

Esposito, John L., and James P. Piscatori. "Democratization and Islam." *Middle East Journal* 45 (1991): 427–40.

Esposito, John, and John Voll. *Islam and Democracy.* Oxford: Oxford University Press, 1996.

Falk, Richard. "In Search of a New World Model: The Emerging World Order after the Cold War." *Current History* 92 (1993): 145–49.

Al-Farabi, Abu Nasr. *Al-Farabi Philosophy of Plato and Aristotle.* Intro. and trans. by Husin Mahdi. Ithaca, N.Y.: Cornell University Press, 1969.

———. *Rasa'il al-Farabi.* Hyderabad: Matba'at Majlis Da'irat al-Ma'arif al-'Uthmaniyya, 1926.

———. *Virtuous City.* Cairo: Maktabat Subh, n.d.

Farah, Caesar. "Political Dimensions of Islamic Fundamentalism." *Digest of Middle East Studies* 5 (1996): 1–14.

Al-Fasi, Allal. *Durus fi al-Haraka al-Salafiyyah*. Dayda, Morocco: Manshurat 'Uyun, 1986.

Filali-Ansari, A. "Islam and Liberal Democracy: The Challenge of Seculariza-tion." *Journal of Democracy* 7, no. 2 (1996): 76–80.

Flores, Alexander. "Secularism, Integralism and Political Islam." *Middle East Report* 183 (1993): 32–38.

Fluehr-Lobban, Carolyn, Richard Lobban, and John O. Voll. *Historical Dictio-nary of the Sudan*. Metuchen, N.J.: Scarecrow Press, 1992.

Fuller, Graham E. *Islamic Fundamentalism in the Northern Tier Countries: An Integrative View*. Boulder, Colo.: Westview Press, 1991.

Fuller, Graham, and Iran Lesser. *A Sense of Siege: The Geopolitics of Islam and the West*. Boulder, Colo.: Westview Press, 1995.

Gause, F. Gregory. "Sovereignty, Statecraft and Stability in the Middle East." *Journal of International Affairs* 45, no. 2 (1992): 441–69.

Gellner, Ernest. *Culture, Identity and Politics*. Cambridge: Cambridge Univer-sity Press, 1988.

Gerami, Shahim. *Women and Fundamentalism*. Oxford, England: Garland Pub-lishers, 1996.

Ghadbian, Najib. *Democratization and Islamist Challenge in the Arab World*. Boulder, Colo.: Westview Press, 1997.

Ghalun, Burhan. *Al-Dawla wa al-Din: Naqd al-Siyasa*. Beirut: Al-Mu'assasa al-'Arabiyya li al-Dirasat wa al-Nashr, 1991.

Al-Ghannushi, Rashid. "Hiwar." *Qira'at Siyasiyya* 1, no. 4 (1991): 14–37.

———. *Al-Hurriyyat al-'Amma fi al-Dawla al-Islamiyya*. Beirut: Markaz Dirasat al-Wahda al-'Arabiyya, 1993.

———. "Al-Islam wa al-Gharb." *Al-Ghadir* 10–11 (December 1990).

———. "Ma'alim fi Istratijiyya al-Da'wa al-Islamiyya." *Al-Hiwar* 19 (1990).

———. *Mahawir Islamiyya*. Cairo: Matabi' al-Zahra', 1989.

———. "Mustaqbal al-Haraka al-Islamiyya." *Al-Huda* [Fez] 23 (1991).

———. "Mustaqbal al-Tayyar al-Islami." *Minbar al-Sharq* 1 (1992): 23–32.

———. "Tahlil li al-'Anasir al-Mukawwina li al-Zahira al-Islamiyya fi Tunis." In *Al-Harakat al-Islamiyya fi al-Watan al-'Arabi*, edited by I. S. 'Abd Allah and others. Beirut: Markaz Dirasat al-Wahda al-'Arabiyya, 1987.

Al-Ghannushi, Rashid, and Hasan al-Turabi. *Al-Harakah al-Islamiyya wa al-Tahdith*. n.p., 1981.

Al-Ghazali. *Al-Munqidh min al-Dalal*. Cairo: Maktabat al-Jundi, 1973.

———. *Tahafut al-Falasifah*. Cairo: Dar al-Ma'arif, 1957.

Gibb, Hamilton A. R. *Modern Trends in Islam*. Chicago: University of Chicago Press, 1947.

———. *Mohammadanism*. Oxford: Oxford University Press, 1976.

———. *Studies on the Civilization of Islam*. Princeton, N.J.: Princeton Univer-sity Press, 1982.

———. *Whither Islam? A Survey of Modern Movements in the Moslem World.* New York: AMS Press, 1973.

Gilsenan, Michael. *Recognizing Islam: Religion and Society in the Modern Middle East.* London: I. B. Tauris, 1994.

Glasse, Cyril. *The Concise Encyclopedia of Islam.* London: Stacey International, 1989.

Green, Jerrold D. "Islam, Religiopolitics, and Social Change." *Comparative Studies in Society and History* 27 (1985): 312–22.

Guazzone, Laura, ed. *The Islamist Dilemma: The Political Role of Islamist Movements in the Contemporary Arab World.* Reading, England: Ithaca Press, 1995.

Guolo, R. *Il partito di dio: l'Islam radicale contro l'Occidente.* Milan: Guerini e Associati, 1994.

Gurdon, Charles. *Sudan at the Crossroads.* Cambridgeshire, England: Menas Press, 1994.

Habib, Kamal al-Sa'id. "Wathiqat al-Ihya' al-Islami." In *Al-Nabiy al-Musallah: Al-Tha'irun,* edited by Rif'at Sayyid Ahmad, 199–243. London: Riad el-Rayyes Books, 1991.

Hadar, Leon T. "What Green Peril." *Foreign Affairs* 72 (1993): 27–42.

Haddad, Yvonne Y. *Contemporary Islam and the Challenge of History.* Albany: State University of New York Press, 1982.

———. "Islamists and the 'Problem of Israel': The 1967 Awakening." *Middle East Journal* 46, no. 2 (1992): 266–85.

———. "The Qur'anic Justification for an Islamic Revolution: The View of Sayyid Qutb." *Middle East Journal* 37, no. 1 (1983): 14–29.

Haddad, Yvonne Y., Byron Haynes, and Ellison Finfly, eds. *The Contemporary Islamic Revival: A Critical Survey and Bibliography.* Westport, Conn.: Greenwood, 1991.

———, eds. *The Islamic Impact.* Syracuse: Syracuse University Press, 1984.

Haider, Gulzar. "An 'Islamic Future' without a Name: Islam and the Future." *Futures* 23 (1991): 311–16.

Halliday, Fred. *Islam and the Myth of Confrontation: Religion and Politics of the Middle East.* London: I. B. Tauris, 1995.

Halliday, Fred, and Hamza Alavi. *State and Ideology in the Middle East and Pakistan.* New York: Monthly Review Press, 1988.

Halpern, Manfred. *The Politics of Change in the Middle East and North Africa.* 4th ed. Princeton, N.J.: Princeton University Press, 1970.

Hamad, Wadood. "The Dialectics of Revolutionary Islamic Thought and Action." *Arab Review* 2, no. 3 (1994): 35–41.

Hamadani, Abbas. "Islamic Fundamentalism." *Mediterranean Quarterly* 4, no. 4 (1993): 38–47.

Hamdi, M. E. "Islam and Liberal Democracy: The Limits of the Western Model." *Journal of Democracy* 7, no. 2 (1996): 81–85.

Al-Hamidi, Muhammad al-Hashimi. "Awlawiyyat Muhimma fi Daftar al-Harakat

al-Islamiyya: Nahwa Mithaq Islami li al-'Adl wa al-Shura wa Huquq al-Insan."
Al-Mustaqbal al-Islami 2 (1991): 19–21.

Hammuda, Husayn M. *Asrar Harakat al-Dubbat al-Ahrar wa al-Ikhwan al-Muslimun.* Cairo: Al-Zahra' li al-I'lam al-'Arabi, 1985.

Hanafi, Hasan. *Al-Yamin wa al-Yasar fi al-Fikr al-Dini.* Cairo: Dar al-Thaqafa al-Jadida, 1996.

Al-Harakat al-Islamiyya fi Muwajahat al-Taswiya. Beirut: Center for Strategic Studies, 1995.

Harik, Iliya. "Rethinking Civil Society: Pluralism in the Arab World." *Journal of Democracy* 5, no. 3 (1994): 43–56.

Harris, Christina P. *Nationalism and Revolution in Egypt: The Role of the Muslim Brotherhood.* Westport, Conn.: Hyperion Press, 1981.

Hasan, Badrul. *Milestones.* Karachi: International Islamic Publishers, 1981.

Hawwa, Sa'id. *Al-Madkhal ila Da'wat al-Ikhwan al-Muslimin bi-Munasabat Khamsin 'Aman 'ala Ta'sisiha.* 2d ed. Amman: Dar al-Arqam, 1979.

Al-Hayat. 24 April 1993–4 February 1994.

Herichow, A., and J. B. Simonson, eds. *Islam in a Changing World: Europe and the Middle East.* Surrey, England: Curzon Press, 1997.

Hermassi, Mohamed Abdelbaki. "Islam, Democracy, and the Challenge of Political Change." In *Democracy in the Middle East: Defining the Challenge,* edited by Yehuda Mirsky and Matt Abres, 41–52. Washington, D.C.: 1993.

———. *Society and State in the Arab Maghreb.* Beirut: Center for the Studies of Arab Unity, 1987.

Heyworth-Dunne, James. *Religious and Political Trends in Modern Egypt.* Washington, D.C.: n.p., 1950.

Al-Hibri, Azizah Y. *Islamic Constitutionalism and the Concept of Democracy.* New York: American Muslim Foundation, 1992.

Hilal, 'Ali al-Din Hilal. *Al-Siyasa wa al-Hukm fi Misr: 1923–52.* Cairo: Maktabat Nahdat al-Sharq, 1977.

Al-Hirmasi, 'Abd al-Baqi. "Al-Islam al-Ihtijaji fi Tunis." In *Al-Harakat al-Islamiyya al-Mu'asira,* 273–86. Beirut: Center for the Studies of Arab Unity, 1987.

Hiro, Dilip. *Holy Wars: The Rise of Islamic Fundamentalism.* New York: Routledge, 1989.

———. *Inside the Middle East.* London: Routledge and Kegan Paul, 1981.

———. *Islamic Fundamentalism.* London: Paladin Grafton Books, 1988.

Hodgson, Marshall. *Venture of Islam.* Vol. 1. Chicago: University of Chicago Press, 1961.

Hottinger, A. "How Dangerous Is Islamism?" *Swiss Review of World Affairs* 1 (1994): 10–12.

Hourani, Albert. *History of the Arab Peoples.* Cambridge, Mass.: Harvard University Press, 1990.

Hourani, George. *Essays on Islamic Philosophy and Science.* New York: State University of New York Press, 1975.

Hovsepian, Nubar. "Competing Identities in the Arab World." *Journal of International Affairs* 49 (1995): 1–24.

Hudson, Michael. "After the Gulf War: Prospects for Democratization in the Arab World." *Middle East Journal* 45, no. 3 (1991): 407–26.

———. *Arab Politics.* New Haven: Yale University Press, 1977.

———. "Arab Regimes and Democratization: Responses to the Challenge of Political Islam." In *The Islamist Dilemma: The Political Role of Islamist Movements in the Contemporary Arab World,* edited by Laura Guazzone, 217–45. Reading, England: Ithaca Press, 1995.

Huergensmeyer, M. *The New Cold War? Religious Nationalism Confronts the Secular State.* Berkeley: University of California Press, 1994.

Humphreys, Richard. "Islam and Political Values in Saudi Arabia, Eqypt, and Syria." In *Islam and Power,* edited by Ali E. Hillal Dessouki, 108. Baltimore: Johns Hopkins University Press, 1981.

Hunter, Shireen T. "The Rise of Islamist Movements and the Western Response: Clash of Civilizations or Clash of Interests?" In *The Islamist Dilemma: The Political Role of Islamist Movements in the Contemporary Arab World,* edited by Laura Guazzone, 317–50. Reading, England: Ithaca Press, 1995.

———, ed. *The Politics of Islamic Revivalism: Diversity and Unity.* Bloomington: Indiana University Press, 1988.

Huntington, Samuel. "The Clash of Civilizations." *Foreign Affairs* 72, no. 3 (1993): 22–49.

———. "The Islamic-Confucian Connection." *New Perspectives Quarterly* 10, no. 3 (1993): 19.

Husain, Mir Zohair. *Global Islamic Politics.* New York: HarperCollins, 1995.

Al-Husaini, Ishaq Musa. *Moslem Brethren.* Beirut: Khayat's College Book, 1956.

Hussain, Asaf. *Islamic Movements in Egypt, Pakistan, and Iran: An Annotated Bibliography.* New York: Mansell, 1983.

———. *Political Perspectives on the Muslim World.* New York: St. Martin's Press, 1984.

Huwaidi, Fahmi. *Al-Islam wa al-Dimuqratiyya.* Cairo: Markaz al-Ahram li al-Tarjama wa al-Nashr, 1993.

———. "Al-Islam wa al-Dimuqratiyya." *Al-Mustaqbal al-'Arabi* 166 (1992): 5–37.

———. *Al-Qur'an wa al-Sultan. Humum Islamiyya Mu'asira.* Cairo: Dar al-Shuruq, 1982.

———. "Al-Sahwa al-Islamiyya wa al-Muwatana wa al-Musawat." *Al-Hiwar* 7 (1987): 53–70.

Hyman, Anthony. "Islamic Bogeymen." *World Today* 46 (1990): 160–61.

———. "The Muslim Fundamentalism." *Conflict Studies* 174 (1985): 1–27.

Ibrahim, Anwar. "The Ummah and Tomorrow's World." *Futures* 23 (1991): 302–10.

Ibrahim, Saad Eddin. "Islamic Activism: A Rejoinder." *Security Dialogue* 25, no. 2 (1994): 193–98.

'Ilwani, Taha. *Islah al-Fikr al-Islami.* Herndon, Va.: International Institute of Islamic Thought, 1991.

'Imad, 'Abd al-Ghani. *Hakimiyyat Allah wa Sultan al-Faqih.* Beirut: Dar al-Tali'a, 1997.

Iqbal, Muhammad. *The Reconstruction of Religious Thought in Islam.* Lahore: Ashraf, 1960.

Isma'il, Mahumd. *Sociologia al-Fikr al-Islami.* Cairo: Maktabat Madbuli, 1988.

Isma'il, Sabri. *Al-Harakat al-Islamiyya al-Mu'asira fi al-Watan al-'Arabi.* Beirut: Markaz Dirasat al-Wahda al-'Arabiyya, 1987.

Israeli, Raphael. *Fundamentalist Islam and Israel: Essays in Interpretation.* Lanham, Md.: University Press of America, 1993.

'Izzat, Hiba Ra'uf. *Al-Mar'a wa al-'Amal al-Siyasi: Ru'ya Islamiyya.* Herndon, Va.: International Institute of Islamic Thought, 1995.

Jabir, Husayn. *Al-Tariq ila Jama'at al-Muslimin.* Al-Mansura, Egypt: Dar Al-Wafa, 1987.

Ja'far, Hashim Ahmad 'Awad. *Al-Ab'ad al-Siyasiyya li Mafhum al-Hakimiyya: Ru'ya Ma'rifiyya.* Herndon, Va.: International Institute of Islamic Thought, 1996.

Jalabi, Khalis. *Fi al-Naqd al-Dhati: Darura al-Naqd al-Dhati li al-Haraka al-Islamiyya.* Beirut: Mu'assasat al-Risala, 1985.

Al-Janhani, Al-Habib. "Al-Sahwa al-Islamiyya fi Bilad al-Sham: Mithal Surya." In *Al-Harakat al-Islamiyya al-Mu'asira fi al-Watan al-'Arabi.* 2nd ed. Beirut: Center for the Studies of Arab Unity, 1989.

Jansen, Johannes J. G. *The Dual Nature of Islamic Fundamentalism.* Ithaca, N.Y.: Cornell University Press, 1997.

———. *The Neglected Duty: The Creed of Sadat's Assassins and Islamic Resurgence in the Middle East.* New York: Macmillan, 1986.

Jarrar, Bassam. "The Islamist Movement and the Palestinian Authority." Interview by Graham Usher. *Middle East Report* (July–August 1994): 28–29.

Al-Jassas, Abu Bakr. *Abu Bakr al-Jassas, Dirash fi Fikratihi: Bab al-Ijtihad,* edited by Zuhayr Kibi. Beirut: Dar al-Muntakhab, 1993.

Jawad, Haifaa. "Pan-Islamism in the Middle East: Prospects and Future." *Islamic Quarterly* 37, no. 3 (1993): 207–22.

Al-Jawjari, Adil. *Al-Hizb al-Islami.* Cairo: Arabic Center for Journalism and Publications, 1993.

Jelloun, Tahar Ben. "Laughing at God in North Africa." *New Perspectives Quarterly* 2, no. 2 (1994): 26–29.

Kabuli, Niaz Faizi. *Democracy According to Islam.* Pittsburgh: Dorrance, 1994.

Kaplan, Lawrence, ed. *Fundamentalism in Comparative Perspective.* Amherst: University of Massachusetts Press, 1992.

Karabell, Zachary. "The Wrong Threat: The United States and Islamic Fundamentalism." *World Policy Journal* 12 (1995): 37–48.

Keddie, Nikki R. *An Islamic Response to Imperialism: Political and Religious Writings of Sayyid Jamal al-Din "al-Afghani."* Berkeley: University of California Press, 1968.

———. "Pan-Islam as Protonationalism." *Journal of Modern History* 41, no. 1 (1969): 17–28.

Kedourie, Elie. *Afghani and Abduh.* London: Frank Cass, 1966.

Kelidar, Abbas. "States without Foundations. The Political Evolution of State and Society in the Arab East." *Journal of Contemporary History* 28, no. 2 (1993): 315–38.

Kepel, Gilles. *Muslim Extremism in Egypt: The Prophet and the Pharaoh.* Berkeley: University of California Press, 1984.

———. *The Revenge of God: The Resurgence of Islam, Christianity, and Judaism in the Modern World.* University Park: Penn State University Press, 1994.

Kerr, David A. "The Challenge of Islamic Fundamentalism for Christians." *International Bulletin of Missionary Research* 17 (1993): 169–73.

Kerr, Malcolm. *Islamic Reform: The Political and Legal Theories of Muhammad 'Abduh and Rashid Rida.* Berkeley: University of California Press, 1966.

Khadduri, Majid. "From Religious to National Law." In *Modernization and the Arab World,* edited by J. H. Thompson and R. J. Reischauer, 37–51. Princeton, N.J.: Van Nostrand, 1966.

———. *Political Trends in the Arab World.* Baltimore: Johns Hopkins University Press, 1970.

Khalafallah, Ahmad. *Al-Fikr al-Tarbawi lada Jama'at al-Ikhwan al-Muslimin.* Cairo: Maktabat Wahba, 1984.

Khalafallah, Muhammad. "Al-Sahwa al-Islamiyya." *Al-Harakat al-Islamiyya fi al-Watan al 'Arabi,* 35–38. Beirut: Center for the Studies of Arab Unity, 1987.

Al-Khalidi, Mahmud. *Al-Dimuqratiyya al-Gharbiyya fi Daw' al-Shari'a al-Islamiyya.* Amman: Maktabat al-Risala al-Haditha, 1986.

Khalidi, Salah 'Abd al-Fattah. *Nazariyyat al-Taswir al-Fanni 'inda Sayyid Qutb.* Amman: Dar al-Furqan, 1983.

Khashan, Hilal. "The Quagmire of Arab Democracy." *ASQ* 1, no. 1 (1992): 17–33.

"Khomeini Strikes Back." *Maclean's* 102, no. 15 (1989): 25.

Al-Khumayni, Ayatollah. *Al-Hukuma al Islamiyya.* Kuwait: n.p., n.d.

Khuri, Fuad. *Imams and Emirs: State, Religion and Sects in Islam.* London: Saqi Books, 1990.

Koloctronis, Jamilah. *Islamic Jihad: An Historical Perspective.* American Trust Publications, 1990.

Korbani, A. G. *The Political Dictionary of Modern Middle East.* Lanham, Md.: University Press of America, 1995.

Kramer, Gudrun. "Cross-Links and Double Talk? Islamist Movements in the

Political Process." In *The Islamist Dilemma: The Political Role of Islamist Movements in the Contemporary Arab World*, edited by Laura Guazzone, 39–67. Reading, England: Ithaca Press, 1995.

———. "Islamist Notions of Democracy." *Middle East Report* 23, no. 183 (1993): 2–8.

———. "Liberalization and Democracy in the Arab World." *Middle East Report* 22, no. 172 (1992): 22–25, 35.

Kramer, Martin. *Arab Awakening and Islamic Revival*. New Brunswick, N.J.: Rutgers University Press, 1996.

———. *Islam Assembled: The Advent of the Muslim Congresses*. New York: Columbia University Press, 1986.

———. "Islam in the New World Order." *Middle East Contemporary Survey, 1991* 15 (1993): 172–205.

———. "Islam versus Democracy." *Commentary* 95 (1993): 35–42.

———. *Political Islam*. Beverly Hills, Calif.: Sage Publications, 1980.

———, ed. *Shi'ism, Resistance, and Revolution*. Boulder, Colo.: Westview Press, 1987.

Kucukcan, Talip. "The Nature of Islamic Resurgence in Near and Middle Eastern Muslim Societies." *Hamdard Islamicus* 14 (1991): 65–104.

Kurdi, Rajih 'Abd al-Hamid. *Al-Ittijah al-Salafi: Bayna al-Asala wa al-Mu'asara*. Amman: Dar 'Ammar, 1989.

Laffin, John. *Holy War, Islam Fights*. London: Grafton, 1988.

Lambton, Ann. *State and Government in Medieval Islam*. Oxford: Oxford University Press, 1981.

Lamchaichi, Abderrahim. *Islam: islamisme et modernité*. Paris: l'Harmattan, 1994.

Landau, Jacob M. *The Politics of Pan-Islamism: Ideology and Organization*. Oxford: Oxford University Press, 1992.

Lapidus, Ira. *Contemporary Islamic Movements in Historical Perspective*. Berkeley: University of California Press, 1983.

Lawrence, Bruce. *Defenders of God: The Fundamentalist Revolt against the Modern Age*. San Francisco: Harper and Row, 1989.

———. *Religious Fundamentalism*. Durham, N.C.: Duke University Press, 1993.

Leach, Hugh. "Observing Islam from Within and Without." *Asian Affairs* 21 (1991).

Lee, Robert D. *Overcoming Tradition and Modernity: The Search for Islamic Authenticity*. Boulder, Colo.: Westview Press, 1997.

Leiden, Karl, ed. *The Conflict of Traditionalism and Modernism in the Muslim Middle East*. Austin: University of Texas Press, 1969.

Lemu, Aisha B. Laxity. *Moderation and Extremism in Islam*. London: International Institute of Islamic Thought, 1993.

Lewis, Bernard. "Islam and Liberal Democracy." *Atlantic Monthly* 271 (1993): 89–98.

————. *Islam and the West.* New York: Oxford University Press, 1993.

————. *The Political Language of Islam.* Chicago: University of Chicago Press, 1988.

————. "The Roots of Muslim Rage: Why So Many Muslims Deeply Resent the West, and Why Bitterness Will Not Be Easily Mollified." *Atlantic Monthly* 266 (1990): 47–57.

————. *The Shaping of the Modern Middle East.* New York: Oxford University Press, 1994.

Lowrie, Arthur L. "The Campaign against Islam and American Foreign Policy." *Middle East Policy* 4 (1995): 210–19.

MacEain, Denis. *Islam in the Modern World.* London: Croom Helm, 1983.

Maddy-Weitzman, Bruce, and Efraim Inbar, eds. *Religious Radicalism in the Greater Middle East.* London: Frank Cass, 1977.

Mahdi, Husin, trans. *Al-Farabi Philosophy of Plato and Aristotle,* by Abu Nasr al-Farabi. Ithaca, N.Y.: Cornell University Press, 1969.

Mahfouz, Naguib. "Against Cultural Terrorism." *New Perspectives Quarterly* 2, no. 2 (1994): 34–37.

Mahfuz, Muhammad. *Alladhina Zulimu.* London: Riad el-Rayyes Books, Ltd., 1988.

Makiya, Kanan. "From Beirut to Sarajevo: Can Tolerance Be Born of Cruelty?" *New Perspectives Quarterly* 2, no. 2 (1994): 20–26.

Mallat, Chibli. "On Islam and the Democracy." In *Islam and Public Law: Classical and Contemporary Studies,* edited by Chibli Mallaf. London: Graham and Trotman, 1993.

Maqsood, Ruqaiyyah Waris. *Islam: A Dictionary.* Cheltenham, England: Thornes, Ltd., 1996.

"March of Islamism, The." *World Press Review* 36, no. 7 (1989): 30.

Mardini, Zuhayr. *Al-Ladudan: Al-Wafd wa al-Ikhwan.* Beirut: Dar Iqra', 1984.

Marmura, Michael. "Ghazali's Attitude to the Secular Sciences and Logic." In *Essays on Islamic Philosophy and Science,* edited by George Hourani, 470. Albany: State University of New York Press, 1975.

Marr, Phebe. "The Islamic Revival: Security Issues." *Mediterranean Quarterly* 3 (1992).

Marr, Phebe, and William Lewis, eds. *Riding the Tiger: The Middle East Challenge for the Cold War.* Boulder, Colo.: Westview Press, 1993.

Marshall, P. "Bookwatch: Islamic Activism in the Middle East." *International Socialism* 60 (1993): 157–71.

Marty, Martin E. and R. Scott Appleby, eds. *Accounting for Fundamentalisms: The Dynamic Character of Movements.* Chicago: University of Chicago Press, 1994.

————. *Fundamentalisms and Society: Reclaiming the Sciences, the Family, and Education.* Chicago: University of Chicago Press, 1993.

————. *Fundamentalisms and the State: Remaking Polities, Economies, and Militancy.* Chicago: University of Chicago Press, 1993.

―――. *Fundamentalisms Observed.* Chicago: University of Chicago Press, 1991.

Al-Mawardi. *Al-Ahkam al-Sultaniyya.* Beirut: Dar al-Kitab al-Lubnani al-'Arabi, 1990.

Al-Mawdudi, Abul al-A'la. *The Islamic Way of Life.* Lahore: Markazi Maktaba Jama'at-i-Islami, n.d.

―――. *Al-Jihad fi-Sabilillah.* Beirut: Mu'assasat al-Risala, 1983.

―――. *Jihad in Islam.* Beirut: Holy Koran Publishing House, 1980.

―――. *Mafahim Islamiyya.* Kuwait: Dar al-Qalam, 1977.

―――. *Minhaj al-Inqilab al-Islami.* 3d ed. Beirut: Mu'assasat al-Risala, 1981.

―――. *Nahnu wa al-Hadara al-Gharbiyya.* Beirut: Mu'assasat al-Risala, 1983.

―――. *Nizam al-Hayat fi al-Islam.* Beirut: Mu'assasat al-Risala, 1983.

―――. *The Process of Islamic Revolution.* Lahore: Islamic Publications, 1977.

―――. *A Short History of Revivalist Movements in Islam.* Lahore: Islamic Publications Limited, 1963.

―――. *Towards Understanding Islam.* 8th ed. Lahore: Islamic Publications Limited, 1960.

"Mawqif al-Haraka min al-'Amal al-Hizbi." In *Al-Nabiy al-Musallah: Al-Rafidun,* edited by Rif'at Sayyid Ahmad, 150–64. London: Riad el-Rayyes Books, 1990.

Mayer, Ann E. *Islam and Human Rights: Tradition and Politics.* Boulder, Colo.: Westview Press, 1991.

Mazrui, Ali A. "Islam at War and Communism in Retreat: What Is the Connection?" In *The Gulf War and the New World Order: International Relations of the Middle East,* edited by Tareq Y. Ismael and J. S. Ismael, 502–20. Gainesville: University Press of Florida, 1994.

Menashri, David, ed. *The Iranian Revolution and the Muslim World.* Boulder, Colo.: Westview Press, 1990.

Mernissi, Fatima. *Islam and Democracy: Fear of the Modern World.* New York: Addison-Wesley, 1993.

Miller, Judith. "The Challenge of Radical Islam." *Foreign Affairs* 72, no. 2 (1993): 43–55.

Mitchell, Richard. *The Society of the Muslim Brothers.* London: Oxford University Press, 1964.

Mohaddessin, Mohammad. *Islamic Fundamentalism: The New Global Threat.* N.p.: Seven Locks Press, 1993.

Mohamed, Yasien. "Islamization: A Revivalist Response to Modernity." *Muslim Education Quarterly* 10, no. 2 (1993): 12–23.

Monshipour, Mahmood, and C. G. Kugla. "Islam, Democracy and Human Rights: The Continuing Debate in the West." *Middle East Policy* 2, no. 2 (1994): 22–39.

Moore, Clement Henry. "Political Parties." In *Polity and Society in Contemporary North Africa,* edited by I. William Zartmann and William Mark Habeeb, 42–67. Boulder, Colo.: Westview Press, 1993.

―――. *Politics in North Africa: Algeria, Morocco, and Tunisia.* Boston: Little, Brown, 1970.

Mortimer, Edward. *Faith and Power: The Politics of Islam*. London: Faber and Faber, 1982.

Moten, Abdul Rashid. *Political Science: An Islamic Perspective*. Hampshire, England: Macmillan, 1996.

Mottahedeh, Roy. *The Mantle of the Prophet: Religion and Politics in Iran*. New York: Pantheon, 1988.

Moussalli, Ahmad S. "Discourses on Human Rights and Pluralistic Democracy." In *Islam in a Changing World: Europe and the Middle East*, edited by A. Herichow and J. B. Simonson, 45–90. Surrey, England: Curzon Press, 1997.

———. "Hasan al-Banna's Islamist Discourse on Constitutional Rule and Islamic State." *Journal of Islamic Studies* 4, no. 2 (1993): 161–74.

———. "Hasan al-Turabi's Islamist Discourse on Democracy and *Shura*." *Middle Eastern Studies* 30, no. 1 (1994): 52–63.

———. *Historical Dictionary of Islamic Fundamentalist Movements in the Arab World, Iran, and Turkey*. Metuchen, N.J.: Scarecrow Press, 1999.

———. "Islamism and Modernity or Modernization of Islam." In *The Future of Cosmopolitanism in the Middle East*, edited by R. Meijer, 1–18. Amsterdam: Cultural Foundation, University of Amsterdam, 1997.

———. "Islamist Perspectives of Regime Political Response: The Case of Lebanon and Palestine." *Arab Studies Quarterly* (Summer 1996): 55–65.

———. "Modern Islamic Fundamentalist Discourses on Civil Society, Pluralism and Democracy." In *Civil Society in the Middle East*, edited by Augustus Richard Norton, 79–119. Leiden: E. J. Brill, 1995.

———. "Modern Islamic Fundamentalist Discourses on Civil Society, Pluralism and Democracy." In *Toward Civil Society in the Middle East*, edited by Jillian Schwedler. Boulder, Colo.: Lynne Rienner, 1995, 35–36.

———. *Radical Islamic Fundamentalism: The Ideological and Political Discourse of Sayyid Qutb*. Beirut: American University of Beirut, 1992. Reprint 1995.

———. "Sayyid Qutb's View of Knowledge." *American Journal of Islamic Social Sciences* 7, no. 3 (1990): 315–34.

———. *Al-Usuliyya al-Islamiyya wa al-Nizam al-'Alami*. Beirut: Center for Strategic Studies, 1992.

———, ed. *Myths and Realities of Islamic Fundamentalism: Theoretical Aspects and Case Studies*. Reading, England: Ithaca Press, 1998.

Al-Mudarrisi, Hadi. *Al-Islam wa al-Idiolojiyyat al-Munawi'a ila Ayn*. Beirut: Mu'assasat al-Balagh, 1987.

Muhammad, Muhsin. *Man Qatala Hasan al-Banna*. Cairo: Dar al-Shuruq, 1987.

Munson, Henry, Jr. *Islam and Revolution in the Middle East*. New Haven: Yale University Press, 1988.

Muravichik, Joshua. "Blaming America First." *Middle East Quarterly* 1, no. 3 (1994): 14–15.

Musa, Kaval. "Politique et theologie: L'impact sur les mouvements islamistes." *Les Cahiers de l'Orient* 34 (1994): 9–32.

Mustapha, Shukri. "Al-Nas al-Kamil." In *Al-Nabiy al-Musallah: Al Rufudun*, edited by Rif'at Sayyid Ahmad, 53–110. London: Riad el-Rayyes Books, 1990.

Mutahhari, Mohammad S. *Jihad: The Holy of Islam and Its Legitimacy in the Qur'an.* Tehran: Islamic Propagation Organization, 1985.

Mutalib, H. "Islamic Resurgence and the Twenty-First Century: Redefining the Old Agendas in a New Age." *American Journal of Islamic Social Sciences* 13, no. 1 (1996): 88–99.

Al-Mutalib, Hussein, and Taj ul-Islam Hashmi. *Islam, Muslims, and the Modern State: Case Studies of Muslims in Thirteen Countries.* New York: St. Martin's Press, 1994.

Al-Nabahani, Taqiy al-Din. *Nizam al-Hukm.* Jerusalem: Matba'at al-Thiryan, 1952.

———. *Al-Takatul al-Hizbi.* 2d ed. Jerusalem: n.p., 1953.

Nacos, B. L. *Terrorism and the Media: From the Iran Hostage Crisis to the World Trade Center Bombing.* New York: Columbia University Press, 1994.

Al-Nadawi, Abu al-Hasan. *Madha Khasira al-'Alam bi-Inhitat al-Muslimin.* 8th ed. Beirut: Dar al-Kitab al-Lubnani, 1984.

Nadvi, Syed Habib ul Huque. *Islamic Fundamentalism: A Theology of Liberation and Renaissance.* South Africa/Westville: Academia, Arabic-Persian-Urdu Department, University of Durban, 1995.

Naff, Thomas. "Towards a Muslim Theory of History." In *Islam and Power,* edited by A. Dessouki, 24–36. Baltimore: Johns Hopkins University Press, 1981.

Nafi, Basheer. "Contemporary Islamic Political Forces: Traditional or Modern." *Arab Review* 3, no. 1 (1994): 29–33.

Nasr, Seyyed Hossein. *Ideals and Realities of Islam.* London: Unwin Hyman, 1988.

———. *Traditional Islam in the Modern World.* London: KPI, 1987.

Nasr, Seyyed Hossein, Hamid Dabashi, and Seyyed Vali Reza Nasr, eds. *Expectation of the Millennium: Shi'ism in History.* Albany: State University of New York Press, 1989.

———. *Shi'ism: Doctrines, Thought, and Spirituality.* Albany: State University of New York Press, 1988.

Nasr, Seyyed Vali Reza. *Mawdudi and the Making of Islamic Revivalism.* Oxford: Oxford University Press, 1996.

———. "Religious Modernism in the Arab World, India and Iran: The Perils and Prospects of a Discourse." *Muslim World* 83, no. 1 (1993): 20–47.

Nettler, Ronald, and Suha Taji-Farouki, eds. *Muslim-Jewish Encounters: Intellectual Traditions and Modern Politics.* Reading, England: Harwood, 1997.

Niblock, Tim, and Emma Murphy. *Economic and Political Liberalism in the Middle East.* London: British Academic Press, 1993.

Nielsen, J. S. "Will Religious Fundamentalism Become Increasingly Violent?" *International Journal on Group Rights* 2 (1994): 197–209.

Nielsen, Niels C. *Fundamentalism, Mythos, and World Religions.* Albany: State University of New York Press, 1993.

Nisrin, Taslima. "On Islamic Fundamentalism." *Humanist* 56 (1996): 24–27.

Norton, Augustus Richard. "Breaking through the Wall of Fear in the Arab World." *Current History* 91 (1992): 37–41.

———. "The Challenge of Inclusion in the Middle East." *Current History* 94 (1995): 1–6.

———. *Civil Society in the Middle East.* Leiden: E. J. Brill, 1995.

———. "The Future of Civil Society in the Middle East." *Middle East Journal* 47 (1993): 205–16.

———. "Inclusion Can Deflate Islamic Populism." *New Perspectives Quarterly* 10, no. 3 (1994): 50.

O'Ballance, Edgar. *Islamic Fundamentalist Terrorism, 1979–95: The Iranian Connection.* New York: New York University Press, 1996.

Ogutco, Mehmet. "Islam and the West: Can Turkey Bridge the Gap?" *Futures* 26 (1994): 811–29.

Paris, Jonathan S. "When to Worry in the Middle East." *Orbis* 37 (1993): 545–53.

Peretz, Don. *Islam: Legacy of the Past, Challenge of the Future.* New York: New Horizon Press, 1984.

Peters, F. E. *Allah's Commonwealth.* New York: Simon and Schuster, 1973.

Peters, Rudolph. *Jihad in Classical and Modern Islam.* Princeton, N.J.: Princeton University Press, 1995.

Pietersee, J. N. "Fundamentalism Discourse: Enemy Images." *Women against Fundamentalism Journal* 1, no. 5 (1994): 2–6.

Pipes, Daniel. "Islam's Intramural Struggle." *National Interest* 35 (1994): 84–86.

Piscatori, James. "Accounting for Islamic Fundamentalisms." In *Accounting for Fundamentalisms: The Dynamic Character of Movements,* edited by Martin E. Marty and R. Scott Appleby, 361–73. Chicago: University of Chicago Press, 1994.

———. *In the Path of God: Islam and Political Power.* New York: Basic Books, 1983.

———. *Islam in a World of Nation-States.* Cambridge: Cambridge University Press, 1986.

———. *Islam in the Political Process.* New York: Cambridge University Press, 1983.

———, ed. *Islamic Fundamentalisms and the Gulf Crisis.* Chicago: American Academy of Arts and Sciences, 1991.

Porteous, Tom. "The Islamisation of Modernity." *Middle East* 220 (1993): 19–22.

Qadaya Dawliyya. March 1993.

Qadaya al-Isbuʿ. 10–17 September 1993.

Al-Qaradawi, Yusuf. *Al-Hall al-Islami Farida wa Darura.* Cairo: Maktabat Wahba, 1977.

———. *Al-Sahwa al-Islamiyya bayna al-Juhud wa al-Tatarruf.* Qatar: Matbaʿat al-Dawha al-Haditha, 1982.

Qarqar, Muhammad. *Dawr al-Haraka al-Islamiyya fi Tasfiyyat al-Iqtaʿ.* Kuwait: Dar al-Buhuth al-ʿIlmiyya, 1980.

Qutb, Sayyid. *Al-ʿAdala al-Ijtimaʿiyya fi al-Islam.* 10th ed. Cairo: Dar al-Shuruq, 1980.

————. *Fi al-Tarikh: Fikra wa-Minhaj.* Cairo: Dar al-Shuruq, 1974.

————. *Fiqh al-Daʿwa.* Beirut: Muʾassasat al-Risala, 1970.

————. *Fi Zilal al-Qurʾan.* Beirut: Dar al-Shuruq, n.d.

————. *Hadha al-Din.* 4th ed. Cairo: Maktabat Wahba, n.d.

————. *In the Shades of the Qurʾan.* London: MWH, 1979.

————. *Al-Islam wa-Mushkilat al-Hadara.* 8th ed. Beirut: Dar al-Shuruq, 1983.

————. *Khasaʾis al-Tasawwur al-Islami wa Muqawwimatuh.* Vol. 1. Cairo: Issa al-Halabi, n.d.

————. "Limadha Aʿdamuni." In *Al-Muslimun,* 34–35. Saudi Arabia: 1985.

————. *Maʿalim fi al-Tariq.* 7th ed. Beirut: Dar al-Shuruq, 1980.

————. *Marʿrakat al-Islam wa al-Raʾsimaliyya.* 4th ed. Beirut: Dar al-Shuruq, 1975.

————. *Al-Mustaqbal li-Hadha al-Din.* 2d ed. Cairo: Maktabat Wahba, 1965.

————. *Nahwa Mujtamaʿ Islami.* 6th ed. Beirut: Dar al-Shuruq, 1983.

————. *Al-Salam al-ʿAlami wa al-Islam.* 7th ed. Beirut: Dar al-Shuruq, 1983.

————. *Tafsir Ayat al-Riba.* Beirut: Dar al-Shuruq, 1970.

————. *Tafsir Surat al-Shura.* Beirut: Dar al-Shuruq, n.d.

Rahman, Fazlur. *Islam and Modernity: The Transformation of an Intellectual Tradition.* Chicago: University of Chicago Press, 1982.

Ramadan, Abd al-Aziz. *Al-Ikhwan al-Muslimin wa al-Tanzim al-Sirri.* Cairo: Maktabat Roz al-Yusuf, 1982

Ramazani, R. K. "Shiʿism in the Persian Gulf." In *Shiʿism and Social Protest,* edited by Juan R. I. Cole and Nikki R. Keddie, 30–53. New Haven: Yale University Press, 1986.

Rapoport, David C. "Comparing Militant Fundamentalist Movements and Groups." In *Fundamentalisms and the State: Remaking Polities, Economies, and Militance,* edited by Martin E. Marty and R. Scott Appleby, 429–61. Chicago: University of Chicago Press, 1993.

Regan, D. "Islamic Resurgence: Characteristics, Causes, Consequences, and Implications." *Journal of Political and Military Sociology* 21, no. 2 (1993): 259–66.

Richards, Alan, and John Waterbury. *A Political Economy of the Middle East.* Boulder, Colo.: Westview Press, 1990.

Rizq, Jabir. *Al-Dawla wa al-Siyasa fi Fikr Hasan al-Banna.* Al-Mansura, Egypt: Dar al-Wafa, 1985.

Roberson, B. A. "Islam and Europe: An Enigma of a Myth?" *Middle East Journal* 48 (1994): 288–308.

Rodinson, Maxim. *Islam and Capitalism.* Austin: University of Texas Press, 1981.

Roff, William R. ed. *Islam and the Political Economy of Meaning: Comparative*

Studies of Muslim Discourse. London: Croom Helm; Berkeley: University of California Press, 1987.

Rondot, Pierre. *The Militant Radical Current in the Muslim Community.* Brussels: Pro Mundi Vita, 1982

Roy, Olivier. *The Failure of Political Islam.* London: I. B. Tauris, 1994.

Rubin, Barry. *Islamic Fundamentalism in Egyptian Politics.* New York: St. Martin's Press, 1990.

———. "Words, Words, Words." *Middle East Quarterly* 1, no. 3 (1994): 16–17.

Ruedy, John, ed. *Islamism and Secularism in North Africa.* New York: St. Martin's Press, 1994.

Sachedina, Abdulaziz A. *Islamic Messianism: The Idea of the Mahdi in Twelver Shi'ism.* Albany: State University of New York Press, 1981.

Sadowski, Yahya. "The New Orientalism and the Democracy Debate." *Middle East Report* 183 (1993): 14–21, 40.

"Safahat min Mithaq al-'Amal al-Hizbi." In *Al-Nabiy al-Musallah: Al-Rafidun,* edited by Rif'at Sayyid Ahmad, 165–78. London: Riad el-Rayyes Books, 1991.

Safi, Louay. *The Challenge of Modernity: The Quest for Authenticity in the Arab World.* Lanham, Md.: University Press of America, 1994.

Said, Abdul Aziz. "Islamic Fundamentalism and the West." *Mediterranean Quarterly* 3 (1992): 21–36.

Sa'id, Rif'at. *Hasan al-Banna, Mu'assis Harakat al-Ikhwan al-Muslimin.* Beirut: Dar al-Tali'a, 1980.

———. "Al-Islam al-Siyasi." In *Qadaya Fikriyya: al-Islam al-Siyasi: Al-Usus al-Fikriyya Wa al-Ahdaf,* 15–33. Cairo: Dar al-Thagafa al-Jadida, 1989.

As-Said, Labib. *The Recited Koran.* Translated by Bernard Weiss, M. A. Rauf, and Morroe Berger. Princeton, N.J.: Darwin Press, 1975.

Saif, Walid. "Human Rights and Islamic Revivalism." *Islam and Christian-Muslim Relations* 5, no. 1 (1994): 57–65.

Salame, Ghassan. "Islam and the West." *Foreign Policy* 90 (Spring 1993): 22–37.

———, ed. *Democracy without Democrats? The Renewal of Politics in the Muslim World.* London: I. B. Tauris, 1994.

Sami', Salih Hasan. *Azmat al-Hurriyya al-Siyasiyya fi al-Watan al-'Arabi.* Cairo: Al-Zahra' li al-I'lam al-'Arabi, 1988.

Saqr, A. *Islamic Fundamentalism.* Chicago: Kazi Publications, 1987.

Sara, Fayiz. *Al-Haraka al-Islamiyya fi al-Magrib al-'Arabi.* Beirut: Markaz al-Dirasat al-Istratijiyya, 1995.

Satloff, Robert B. "One Democracy." *Middle East Quarterly* 1, no. 3 (1994): 18–19.

———, ed. *The Politics of Change in Saudi Arabia.* Boulder, Colo.: Westview, 1993.

Al-Sayyid Marsot, Afaf Lutfi. *Protest Movements and Religious Undercurrents in Egypt: Past and Present.* Washington, D.C.: Georgetown University/Center for Contemporary Arab Studies, 1989.

Al-Sayyid Ridwan. *Siyasat al-Islam al-Mu'asir.* Beirut: Dar al-Kitab al-'Arabi, 1997.

Schliefer, S. Abdullah. "Jihad: Modernist Apologies, Modern Apologetics." *Islamic Quarterly* 28, no. 1 (1984): 25–46.

Schmid, E. "Turkey: Rising Power of Islamic Fundamentalism." *Women against Fundamentalism Journal* 1, no. 6 (1994): 57–67.

Schwedler, J., ed. *Toward Civil Society in the Middle East? A Primer.* London: Lynne Rienner, 1996.

Seddon, David. "Riot and Rebellion in North Africa." In *Power and Stability in the Middle East,* edited by Berch Berberoglu. London: Zed Books, 1989.

Semaan, Wanis A. "The Double-Edged Challenge of Islamic Fundamentalism." *Mission Studies* 11, no. 2 (1994): 173–80.

Shafiq, Munir. "Awlawiyyat Amam al-Ijtihad wa al-Tajdid." In *Al-Ijtihad wa Tajdid fi al-Fikr al-Islami al-Mu'asir.* Malta: Center for the Studies of the Muslim World, 1991.

———. *Al-Fikr al-Islami al-Mu'asir wa al-Tahaddiyat.* Beirut: Al-Nashir, 1991.

———. *Al-Islam fi Ma'rakat al-Hadara.* Beirut: Al-Nashir, 1991.

———. *Al-Islam wa Muwajahat al-Dawla al-Haditha.* 3d ed. Beirut: Al-Nashir, 1992.

———. *Al-Nizam al-Dawli al-Jadid wa Khiyar al-Muwajaha.* Beirut: Al-Nashir, 1992.

Shaikh, M. N. *Hasan al-Banna Shahid: A Brief Life Sketch.* Karachi: International Islamic Publishers, 1981.

———, trans. *Memoirs of Hasan al-Banna Shaheed.* Karachi: International Islamic Publishers, 1981.

Sharabi, Hisham. "Islam and Modernism in the Arab World." In *Modernization and the Arab World,* edited by J. H. Thompson and R. J. Reischauer, 26–36. Princeton, N.J.: Van Nostrand, 1966.

Sharaf al-Din, Rislan. "Al-Din wa al-Ahzab al-Siyasiyya al-Diniyya." In *Al-Din fi al-Mujtama' al-'Arabi,* 171–88. Beirut: Center for the Studies of Arab Unity, 1990.

Shari'ati, Ali. *Marxism and Other Western Fallacies.* Translated by R. Campbell. Berkeley, Calif.: Mizan Press, 1980.

———. *On the Sociology of Islam.* Translated by Hamid Algar. Berkeley, Calif.: Mizan Press, 1979.

Shu'un al-Awsat no. 16 (February 1993): 59–60, 65–67.

Sidahamed, A. S., and A. Ehteshami, eds. *Islamic Fundamentalism.* Boulder, Colo.: Westview Press, 1996.

Sid-Ahmed, Mohamed. "Cybernetic Colonialism and the Moral Search." *New Perspectives Quarterly* 11 (1994): 15–19.

Siddiq, Ali. *Al-Ikhwan al-Muslimun Bayna Irhab Faruq wa 'Abd al-Nasir.* Cairo: Dar al-I'tisam, 1987.

Sihbudi, Riza. "Islamic 'Fundamentalism' and Democratization in the Middle East." *Iranian Journal of International Affairs* 6 (1994): 119–28.

Silverburg, Sanford R. *Middle East Bibliography.* Metuchen, N.J.: Scarecrow Press, 1992.

Sirriyya, Salih. "Risalat al-Iman." In *Al-Nabiy al-Musallah: Al-Rafudun,* edited by Rif'at Sayyid Ahmad, 31–52. London: Riad el-Rayyes Books, 1990.

Sisi, Abbas. *Hasan al-Banna: Mawqif fi al-Da'wa wa al-Tarbiyya.* Alexandria, Egypt: Dar al-Da'wa, 1981.

Sisk, Timothy. *Islam and Democracy.* Washington, D.C.: United States Peace Institute Press, 1992.

Sivan, Emmanuel. *Interpretations of Islam: Past and Present.* Princeton, N.J.: Darwin Press, 1985.

———. *Islamic Fundamentalism and Anti-Semitism.* Jerusalem: Shazar Library, Institute of Contemporary Jewry, Hebrew University of Jerusalem, 1985.

———. *Radical Islam: Medieval Theology and Modern Politics.* New Haven: Yale University Press, 1990.

Sivan, Emmanuel, and Menachem Friedman, eds. *Religious Radicalism and Politics in the Middle East.* Albany: State University of New York Press, 1990.

Smith, Wilfred C. *Islam in Modern History.* Princeton, N.J.: Princeton University Press, 1957.

Solh, Ragid. "Islamist Attitudes towards Democracy: A Review of the Ideas of Al-Ghazali, Al-Turabi and 'Amara." *British Journal of Middle Eastern Studies* 20 (1993): 57–63.

Spencer, William. *Islamic Fundamentalism in the Modern World.* N.p.: Millbrook Press, 1995.

Stowasser, Barbara. "Women's Issues in Modern Islamic Thought." In *Arab Women: Old Boundaries, New Frontiers,* edited by J. E. Tucker, 3–28. Bloomington: Indiana University Press, 1993.

———, ed. *The Islamic Impulse.* Washington, D.C.: Georgetown University Center for Contemporary Arab Studies, 1987.

Tachau, Frank, ed. *Political Parties of the Middle East and North Africa.* Westport, Conn.: Greenwood Press, 1994.

Taheri, Amir. *The Holy Terror: The Inside Story of Islamic Terrorism.* Johannesburg: Hutchinson, 1987.

Taji-Farouki, Suha. "A Case-Study in Contemporary Political Islam and the Palestine Question: The Perspective of Hizb al-Tahrir." *Studies in Muslim-Jewish Relations* 2 (1995): 35–58.

———. "From Madrid to Washington: Palestinian Islamist Response to Israeli-Palestinian Peace Settlement." *World Faiths Encounter* 9 (1994): 49–58.

———. *A Fundamental Quest: Hizb al-Tahrir and the Search for the Islamic Caliphate.* London: Grey Seal, 1996.

———. "Hizb al-Tahrir." In *Encyclopedia of the Modern Islamic World,* 125–27. New York: Oxford University Press, 1995.

———. "Islamic Discourse and Modern Political Methods: An Analysis of al-Nabahani's Reading of the Canonical Text Sources of Islam." *American Journal of Islamic Social Sciences* 11, no. 3 (1994): 365–93.

―――. "Islamic State-Theories and Contemporary Realities." In *Islamic Fundamentalism*, edited by A. S. Sidahamed and A. Ehteshemi, 35–50. Boulder, Colo.: Westview Press, 1995.

―――. "Nazariyyat al-Dawla al-Islamiyya wa al-Waqi' al-Mu'asir: Hala Dirasiyya." *Qira'at Siyasiyya* 5 (1995): 83–99.

Tamadonfar, Mehran. *The Islamic Polity and Political Leadership: Fundamentalism, Sectariansim, and Pragmatism.* Boulder, Colo.: Westview Press, 1989.

Tamimi, Azzam, ed. *Power-Sharing Islam?* London: Liberty for Muslim World Publications, 1993.

Taylor, Alan R. *The Islamic Question in Middle East Politics.* Boulder, Colo.: Westview Press, 1988.

Taylor, P. *States of Terror: Democracy and Political Violence.* London: Penguin and BBC Books, 1993.

Taymiyya, Ibn. *Al-Siyasa al-Shar'iyya.* Beirut: Dar al Fikr al-Hadith, n.d.

Tessler, Mark, and J. Jesse. "Gender and Support for Islamist Movements: Evidence from Egypt, Kuwait and Palestine." *Muslim World* 86, no. 2 (1996): 200–28.

Tetreault, Mary Ann. "Gulf Winds: Inclement Political Weather in the Arabian Peninsula." *Current History* 95 (1996): 23–27.

Tibi, Bassam. *The Crisis of Modern Islam in a Pre-Industrial Culture in the Scientific-Technological Age.* Salt Lake City: University of Utah Press, 1988.

―――. *Religious Fundamentalism and Ethnicity in the Crisis of the Nation-State in the Middle East: Subordinate Islamic and Pan-Arab Identities and Subordinate Islamic and Sectarian Identities.* Berkeley, Calif.: Center for German and European Studies, 1992.

―――. "The Renewed Role of Islam in the Political and Social Development of the Middle East." *Middle East Journal* 37, no. 1 (1983): 3–13.

Al-Turabi, Hasan. "Awlawiyyat al-Haraka al-Islamiyya." *Minbar al-Sharq* 1 (1992).

―――. *Al-Haraka al-Islamiyah fi al-Sudan.* Kuwait: Dar al-Qalam, 1988.

―――. *Al-Haraka al-Islamiyya fi al-Sudan: Al-Tatawwur wa al-Kasb wa al-Manhaj.* Khartoum: n.p., 1989.

―――. *Al-Iman wa Atharuhu fi Hayat al-Insan.* Jidda: Al-Dar al-Su'udiyya li al-Nashr wa al-Tawzi', 1984.

―――. *Al-Islam, Hiwarat fi al-Dimucratiyya, al-Dawla, al-Gharb.* Beirut: Dar al-Jadid, 1995.

―――. "The Islamic Awakening's New Wave." *New Perspectives Quarterly* 10 (1993): 42–45.

―――. *Al-Itijah al-Islami Yuqadim al-Mar'a bayna Ta'alim al-Din wa Taqalid al-Mujtama'.* Jidda: Al-Dar al-Su'udiyya li al-Nashr wa al-Tawzi', 1984.

―――. *Qadaya al-Hurriyya wa al-Wahda, al-Shura wa al-Dimuqratiyya, al-Din wa al-Fan.* Jidda: Al-Dar al-Su'udiyya li al-Nashr wa al-Tawzi', 1987.

―――. *Al-Salat 'Imad al-Din.* Beirut: Dar al-Qalam, 1971.

―――. "Al-Shura wa al-Dimuqratiyya: Ishkalat al-Mustala wa al-Mafhum." *Al-Mustaqbal al-'Arabi* 75 (1985): 4–22.

———. *Tajdid al-Fikr al-Islami.* 2d ed. Jidda: Al-Dar al-Su'udiyya li al-Nashr wa al-Tawzi', 1987.

———. *Tajdid Usul al-Fiqh.* Jidda: Al-Dar al-Su'udiyya li al-Nashr wa al-Tawzi', 1984.

———. "Utruhat al-Haraka al-Islamiyya fi Majal Al-Hiwar Ma'a al-Gharb." *Shu'un al-Awsat* 36 (1994): 21–26.

Turner, Bryan. *Orientalism, Postmodernism, and Globalism.* London: Routledge, 1994.

Al-'Unf al-Usuli: Al-Ibda' min Nawafiz Jahannam. London: Riad el-Rayyes Books, 1995.

Al-'Unf al-Usuli: Muwajahat al-Sayf wa al-Qalam. London: Riad el-Rayyes Books, 1995.

Al-'Unf al-Usuli: Nuwwab al-Ard wa al-Sama'. London: Riad el-Rayyes Books, 1995.

U.S. House Committee on Foreign Affairs, Africa Subcommittee. *Hearing on the Implication for U.S. Policy of Islamic Fundamentalism in Africa.* May 1992, Washington, D.C.

U.S. House Committee on Foreign Affairs, Subcommittee on Europe and the Middle East. *Hearing on Islamic Fundamentalism and Islamic Radicalism.* 24 June, 15 July, and 30 September 1985, Washington, D.C.

Uthman, Fathi. *Al-Salafiyyah fi al-Mujtama'at al-Mu'asira.* Cairo: Dar Afaq al-Ghad, 1982.

Vatikiotis, P. J. *The Modern History of Egypt.* New York: Praeger, 1969.

Voll, John. *The Contemporary Islamic Revival: A Critical Survey and Bibliography.* Westport, Conn.: Greenwood Press, 1991.

———. *Islam: Continuity and Change in the Modern World.* 2d ed. Syracuse: Syracuse University Press, 1994.

Voll, John, and John L. Esposito. "Islam's Democratic Essence." *Middle East Quarterly* 1, no. 3 (1994): 3–11.

Voll, John O., and Sarah Potts Voll, *The Sudan: Unity and Diversity in a Multicultural State.* Boulder, Colo.: Westview Press, 1985.

Von Grunebaun, Gustave. *Modern Islam: The Search for Cultural Identity.* Westport, Conn.: Greenwood Press, 1983.

Waal, A., ed. "Rethinking Ethiopia." In *Conflict and Peace in the Horn of Africa: Federalism and Its Alternative,* edited by P. Woodward and M. Forsyth. Dartmouth, England: Aldershot, 1994.

Warburg, Gabriel R., and Uri M. Kumpferschmidt, eds. *Islam, Nationalism, and Radicalism in Egypt and the Sudan.* New York: Praeger, 1983.

Al-Wasat. 11 November 1993–25 July 1994.

Waterbury, John. "Corruption, Political Stability, and Development: Comparative Evidence from Egypt and Morocco." *Government and Opposition* 11, no. 4 (1976).

———. "Democracy without Democrats? The Potential for Political Liberalization in the Middle East." In *Democracy without Democrats? The Renewal of Politics in the Muslim World*, edited by Ghassan Salame, 23–47. London: I. B. Tauris, 1994.

———. *Exposed to Innumerable Delusions: Public Enterprise and State Power in Egypt, India, Mexico, and Turkey.* Cambridge: Cambridge University Press, 1993.

"Wathiqat Muhakamat al-Nizam al-Musri." *Al-Nabiy al-Musallah: Al-Tha'irun*, edited by Rif'at Sayyid Ahmad, 273–83. London: Riad el-Rayyes Books, 1991.

Watt, W. Montgomery. "Islamic Fundamentalism." *Studia Missionalia* 41 (1992): 241–52.

———. *Islamic Fundamentalism and Modernity.* London: Routledge, 1988.

Weiner, M., and Ali Banuazizi, eds. *The Politics of Social Transformation in Afghanistan, Iran and Pakistan.* New York: Syracuse University Press, 1994.

"Will Democracy Survive in Egypt?" *Reader's Digest* (Canadian ed.) 131, no. 788 (1987): 149.

"Will Islamic Fundamentalists Spread?" *The Nation* 251, no. 2 (1990): 57.

Wright, Robin. "Islam's New Political Face." *Current History* 90 (1991): 25–30.

———. *Sacred Rage: The Crusade of Modern Islam.* New York: Simon and Schuster, 1985.

Yakan, Fathi. *Abjadiyyat al-Tasawwur al-Haraki li al-'Amal al-Islami.* 11th ed. Beirut: Mu'assasat al-Risala, 1993.

———. *Harakat wa Madhahib fi Mizan al-Islam.* 10th ed. Beirut: Mu'assasat al-Risala, 1992.

———. *Al-Mawsu'a Al-Harakiyya.* Amman: Dar al-Bashir, 1983.

———. *Nahwa Haraka Islamiyya 'Alamiyya.* 10th ed. Beirut: Mu'assasat al-Risala, 1993.

Yasin, Muhammad. *Muqaddima fi Fiqh al-Jahiliyya al-Mu'asira.* Cairo: Dar al-Zahra' li al-'Ilam al-'Arabi, 1986.

Yousef, Michael. *Revolt against Modernity: Muslim Zealots and the West.* Leiden: E. J. Brill, 1985.

Yusuf, Ali Abdallah. *The Glorious Qur'an.* Cairo: Dar al-Kitab al-Masri, 1934.

Zafarul, Islam Khan. "Hukumat-e Islami: Imam Khumayni's Contribution to Islamic Political Thought." *Al-Tawhid* 10, nos. 2–3 (1992–1993): 237–47.

Zahmul, Ibrahim. *Al-Ikhwan al-Muslimin: Awraq Tarikhiyya.* France: n.p., 1985.

Zartman, I. William. "Democracy and Islam: The Cultural Dialectic." *Annals of the American Academy of Political and Social Sciences* 524 (1992): 191.

Zartman, I. William, and William Mark Habeeb, eds. *Polity and Society in Contemporary North Africa.* Boulder, Colo.: Westview Press, 1993.

Zebiri, Kate. *Mahmud Shaltut and Islamic Modernism.* Oxford: Oxford University Press, 1995.

Zubaida, Sami. *Islam, the People and the State: Essays on Political Ideas and Movements in the Middle East.* 2d ed. London: I. B. Tauris, 1993.

Al-Zugal, ʿAbd al-Qadir. "Al-Istratijia al-Jadida li Haratat al-Itijah al-Islami." In *Al-Din fi al-Mujtamaʿ al-Arabi,* vol. 3, 339–50.

Al-Zumar, ʿAbbud. "Minhaj Jamaʿat al-Jihad al-Islami." *Al-Nabiy al-Musallah: Al-Rafidun,* edited by Rifʿat Sayyid Ahmad, 110–26. London: Riad el-Rayyes Books, 1990.

Index

Ahmad S. Moussalli is professor of political science at the American University of Beirut. He is the author of *Radical Islamic Fundamentalism: The Ideological and Political Discourse of Sayyid Quth*, which was selected an Outstanding Academic Book by Choice in 1994.